HUDSON COUNTY

THE LEFT BANK

Lewis Street, Now 38th Street in Union City: The Hudson Theater and a Hudson Dispatch *building on Lewis Street about 1915. The* Dispatch *was a daily newspaper serving Hudson County. It ended publication in April 1991. Courtesy, Jersey City Public Library*

Picture Research by Joseph C. Brooks

American Historical Press
Sun Valley, California

HUDSON COUNTY

THE LEFT BANK

Dear Helen,
    My best wishes to my
dear old friend from
St. Al's
        Love
        Joan

Joan Doherty Lovero

Photograph Credit Corrections:

From:	To:
Jersey City Division of	
Urban Research and Design	Jersey City Planning Division
Jersey City Library (JCL), K. Snell,	
Stevens Institute of Technology	Jersey City Public Library (JCPL)

Library of Congress Catalogue Card Number: 99-073518

ISBN: 1-892724-01-4

Bibliography: p. 182
Includes Index

Contents

I

The First Frontier

There were long faces on the members of the Dutch East Company in the spring of 1610. The report of Henry Hudson's transatlantic voyage had arrived at Amsterdam with the vexing news that he had failed to discover a new water route to the Orient. They had all been confident that a way could be found to sail west beyond the American landmass and on to the profitable markets of the East. Now their hopes were dashed.

Despite this keen disappointment, investors in Holland studied the accounts of the 1609 voyage closely to see if it offered any grounds for optimism. As described in the journal of Robert Juet, an officer on the ship, Hudson and his crew on the *Half Moon* had traveled along the coast of North America and visited land that was "as pleasant with Grasse and Flowers, and goodly Trees, as ever they had seene."

Moreover, this land was situated on a great bay fed by tidal straits and rivers, one particularly deep and wide, which formed a splendid natural harbor. The natives they met were a question mark. Too primitive to be valued as trading partners, they could not be characterized as either friendly or hostile. The Manhattans, who occupied a large island on the eastern bank of the great river, had attacked Hudson's crew and shot a fatal arrow into the throat of John Colman, but

the Hackensack tribe on the western shore had greeted the sailors with smiles and curiosity and supplied them with food in exchange for tools.

The Dutch merchants were not particularly interested in the reports of the agreeable climate, or the grass and flowers, or the good harbor. These they had at home. What did intrigue them were the accounts of a profusion of beaver and other furbearers. Here was a commercial commodity in great demand among the European elite, and the prospects of considerable profits cheered the Dutchmen immensely. It was also a well-known fact that the British, their competitors, had set up a colony on the coast in a place identified as Virginia. If North America had both the British and fur, it was worth further investment. They decided to claim the land visited by Hudson on behalf of their nation, and they began to send shiploads of trappers to this territory that they called New Netherland.

The Dutch made a wise decision. In time the harbor would be known as the Port of New York, the busiest in the world, and the great river would bear Hudson's name—as would the pleasant land on the western bank, which eventually became Hudson County, New Jersey.

The Dutch fur traders dispatched to New Netherland roamed widely to secure their pelts, but they made their head-

This 1854 print of Henry Hudson is based on a seventeenth-century painting by Van der Helst. Although Verrazano had been in the bays of New York, Newport, and Boston in the 1520s, it was Hudson's trip of 1609 that stayed in Europe's imagination. According to the log kept by Robert Juet, the Half Moon *sailed through the Narrows on September 11, 1609, and then proceeded up the the river that would be called, first, the North and then the Hudson. Hudson believed that he was enroute to Cathay. JCL*

quarters at the southern tip of the island occupied by the Manhattan Indians. Here they found deep water for docking, firm bedrock, and a superbly defensible position. On the western riverbank the water was shallow, much of the land was marshy, and defense was difficult. It was these geographical characteristics that originally set the course of the region that the world has come to know as the New York metropolitan area.

In 1624 the Dutch West India Company, a trading firm, followed the colonizing lead of the British and sent its first permanent residents to Manhattan Island, which they named New Amsterdam. To encourage development the company sold large tracts to patroons who guaranteed to supply the residents needed to populate their plantations. Michael Pauw, a burgomeister of Amsterdam, took advantage of the land offer and bought two shoreline properties on the mainland

across the river from New Amsterdam. The first tract, called Hobocan Hackingh by the Indians (and so recorded in Pauw's deed), covered approximately the current boundaries of Hoboken. The second consisted of two parts, Harsimus and Aressick, and extended southward from the present Jersey City-Hoboken border through the Bayonne peninsula. Pauw called this land Pavonia, basing his choice upon the Latin spelling of his own name, *pavo,* which means "peacock." In the same year he also purchased Staten Island from the Indians.

Michael Pauw never crossed the Atlantic and in four or five years he was forced to return his holdings to the Dutch West India Company. Before this resale took place, he had hired Cornelius Van Vorst to conduct the fur trade and to arrange for the farmers who were expected to move to Pavonia. Van Vorst, who spoke French and Dutch and was probably a

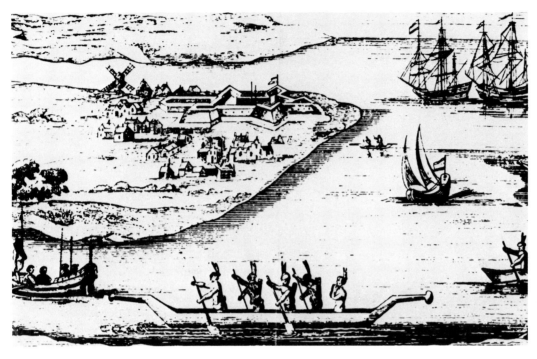

Walloon, as were many of the early colonists, built his family home on Harsimus Cove and, though hot-tempered and fond of French wine, he became a man of considerable importance in New Netherland. To secure its interests, the Dutch West India Company hired its own agent, known variously as Michael Paulaz or Michael Paulusen, whose name became attached to Aressick, a sandy hillock that jutted out into the river. Today that part of Jersey City is still known as Paulus Hook.

It requires an imaginative effort to picture the land as it was when the Dutch arrived, but it is possible to have a glimpse of the past by looking at the undeveloped portion of the Hackensack meadowlands. The low-lying Hudson River shore had a similar marshy quality except for a few land formations. In the Jersey City area, Paulus Hook rose several feet above water level and was separated from the land at its west by a creek that was navigable at high tide. There was a second rise near today's Van Vorst Park and a third on Harsimus in the vicinity of Hamilton Park. In Hoboken the low land rose dramatically to the cliff that became known as Castle Point. The

shoreline differed markedly from modern times. Harsimus Cove north of Paulus Hook and Communipaw Cove on its south both covered shallow mud flats and pushed the shore westward for up to half a mile, leaving the exposed hook as the closest point of land to New Amsterdam and the ideal location for ferry traffic.

West of this low-lying land rose a dominant rocky ridge, a relic of volcanic activity. Visible as no more than a slight incline on the southern peninsula, now Bayonne, it gained in height to the north until it culminated in the Palisades of the Hudson. On the western side of this basalt hill were more marshes. Several creeks marked the boundaries of the fertile Secaucus tract, with its southern rise known as Snake Hill. Then west of the Hackensack River lay the peninsula that was first known as New Barbadoes Neck and is today East Newark, Harrison, and Kearny.

This virgin terrain was the home ground of a few thousand natives of the Algonquin nation. They belonged to the Hackensack branch of the Lenni Lenape and were later known to the English as the Delawares. These Indians taught the Dutch how to grow maize, beans, and

This circa 1635 print is based on a drawing by a Dutch officer. The Jersey shore is at the right. On New Amsterdam (Manhattan) are a few stepped-gable, stone houses of the Dutch and their new fort. The Indians of the area felt they should have access to the orchard and bouweries of New Amsterdam, and this caused skirmishes and sometimes death on both sides. (This print has been reproduced many times in the last two centuries, and sometimes it is seen in the reverse.) JCL

In the Year of Our Lord 1660
By permission of
PETRVS STVYVESANT
Director General and
Consul of New Netherlands

Sculptor J. Massey Rhind completed this bronze statue of Peter Stuyvesant in 1913 for Bergen Square. While serving as the Dutch West India Company's director of the Island of Curacao, he lost a leg attacking the Portuguese. From 1647 until 1664 he served as the director-general of New Netherland. In 1660, from his headquarters in Manhattan, he gave a charter for Bergen Township, thus authorizing the first municipal government in the area that would become New Jersey. Photo by Joseph C. Brooks

squash; showed them their trails; and instructed them in using nature's products for survival. They provided the pelts that made the fur trade possible, and their homes of bent saplings and bark were the models for the first temporary shelters of the Europeans.

The Dutch West India Company did try to deal fairly with the natives and required the patroons and governors to purchase their tracts from the Indians, but the Indians' concept of land ownership differed from that of the white men. They believed that the sale of land did not deprive them of its use, and they were angered when the Dutch tried to restrict access to their new farms. Adding to the problems were slick and unscrupulous traders who cheated the Lenni Lenape in fur and food transactions and sold them bad whisky. In contradiction to the orders of the company, some traders exchanged firearms and gunpowder for better pelts. Indian resentment simmered

and occasionally boiled over in attacks upon Dutch cattle and property, while efforts to punish the Indians fueled animosity and new assaults.

It is tempting to believe that the settlements at Pavonia and Hoboken would have been permanent if William Kieft had not been appointed director-general of New Netherland in 1638. Kieft was energetic, self-confident, and an aggressive administrator. He approached the Indians as if they were his own subjects and tried to collect taxes of furs, maize, and wampum by threatening to use force to insure that his orders were obeyed. His directives were ignored, however, and several murders on both sides aggravated the tense relations between the white and red men.

Kieft looked for an opportunity to bring the Indians to heel, and he found it in 1643 when the Lenni Lenape of the Hudson River valley fled south to escape the marauding Mohawks. The refugees applied at New Amsterdam for protection and then encamped at Communipaw. Kieft saw his chance to punish the natives for their defiance and dispatched a contingent of soldiers with instructions to drive them away or destroy them. What followed was a cold-blooded massacre. Eighty Indians—men, women, and children—were surprised as they slept, and many were slaughtered by the soldiers who lost not one man. Indian retaliation was swift. Dirck Straatmaker from Caven Point ventured out to see what had happened and was struck by a poisoned arrow. Aert Teunissen Van Putten was killed and all of his Hoboken bouwerie destroyed, except for the brewery. The Van Vorst home at Harsimus was set ablaze and a child, Ide Van Vorst, taken as captive. The less unfortunate Dutch escaped to New Amsterdam, where they watched the fires that ravaged their homes and their crops. Pavonia was desolate.

The Pavonia landholders were indignant. Supported by men like Captain David Pieterz De Vries of Staten Island, who maintained friendship with the Indians and who ransomed the young Van Vorst boy, they charged Kieft with misgovernment. Settlers from Long Island, to which Kieft's war had spread, joined the attack upon the director-general. He was summoned to Holland to defend his administration, but his ship was wrecked off the coast of England. Both he and all his documents were lost. It was not until August 30, 1646, that a peace agreement between the Dutch and Indians was concluded, and the surviving Pavonia settlers slowly returned to their land to rebuild their homes.

On May 11, 1647, Kieft's successor arrived to assume leadership of New Netherland. He was Peter Stuyvesant, "Peg Leg Pete," who wore a wooden leg with silver trimming to replace the limb lost in Dutch military service. The new director found a distressing situation with low morale and a spirit of anarchy among the population. The Indians were claiming that the terms of the peace treaty were being flouted, and once more they were becoming hostile. Stuyvesant responded diplomatically by appointing an advisory board of representatives from Manhattan, Brooklyn, and Pavonia, who adopted a successful conciliatory approach. No serious disturbances marred the peace, and the settlements at Pavonia recovered and expanded.

In the first move north of Hoboken, Maryn Andriaensen acquired the Weehawken grant in 1647, but further growth in this area was hindered by the rising palisade nearing the shoreline. Instead newcomers headed south. In 1646 the Dutch West India Company granted Jacob Roy, its chief gunner or constable, the land in present-day Bayonne that retains the name Constable Hook. This grant was not cultivated, however, and the first settlement in Bayonne occurred in the Pamrapo section in 1654. In the same year the tract known as Minkakwa and later as Greenville was conveyed, and the first white residents moved in. Unfortunately just as Pavonia seemed on the brink of prosperity, a new outbreak of war erupted. The cause was forbidden

fruit.

On an evening in the autumn of 1655, an Indian girl slipped into an orchard in Manhattan to pick some of its ripe peaches. The orchard owner, Henry Van Dyck, saw her, fired his shotgun, and the girl fell dead. At that time Stuyvesant and a party of 600 men were away routing Swedes from settlements on the Delaware. The Indians believed that New Amsterdam was virtually unprotected, and hundreds of warriors boarded their canoes to exact vengeance. Van Dyck was wounded and his neighbor slain, but the remaining Dutch guard on Manhattan was able to drive off the attackers, who then crossed the river to Pavonia. There they continued to seek revenge by burning the homes and killing or capturing all the white settlers who were not able to flee to New Amsterdam for safety.

When Director-General Stuyvesant returned from the Delaware, he entered prolonged negotiations with the Indians to ransom the captives. The exchange was made at Paulus Hook, where the Indians had camped with their prisoners. Stuyvesant then attempted further conciliation by offering to repurchase the western shore. The Indians agreed and on January 30, 1658, nine Hackensack chiefs crossed the river to Fort Amsterdam and entered the council room where they

Engraved by J.W. Casilear and based on a work by New Jersey painter Asher B. Durand, this 1836 print is called the Wrath of Peter Stuyvesant. *Peg Leg Pete and the folksy Dutch became subjects of popular literature and art in the early nineteenth century. Stuyvesant probably visited the Dutch of Bergen—he certainly had governmental relations with them. He was described by his biographer, Bayard Tuckerman, as "headstrong and violent in his temper . . . but animated by good motives." JCL*

Above
A group of dancers dressed as the seventeenth-century Dutch of Bergen are pictured in this 1930 photograph of a celebration of the 300th anniversary of the settlement of Pavonia. JCL

Right
Pictured circa 1926, this house was built in Bergen Square in 1664, probably by Nicholas Varlett, to whom Stuyvesant had deeded this property. It was sold twice before Jan Adriaensen Sip bought it in 1699, when it became known as the Sip Manor. In 1926 it was sold to Arthur Rule. For three years it was measured by architect Bernard Miller and disassembled by the Goldberg Wrecking Company, and then rebuilt in Westfield. JCL

made their marks on the document that relinquished to the white men all the lands between the Hackensack and North (Hudson) rivers from Weehawken and Secaucus to the Kill van Kull. The price was eighty fathoms of wampum, twenty fathoms of cloth, twelve brass kettles, guns, blankets, and a half barrel of strong beer. This deed is preserved in the New York State archives in Albany.

Peter Stuyvesant was an intelligent and exacting governor who realized that the dispersal of colonists along the Pavonia shore made each separate farm vulnerable to renewed Indian attacks. Even though the residents themselves were unhappy with his proposal, he persuaded the ruling Council of New Amsterdam to issue edicts requiring the settlers to congregate in a defensible area. The search began for a suitable location. In 1660 the director-general and the council found acceptable a site on the hilltop near the Indian maize fields.

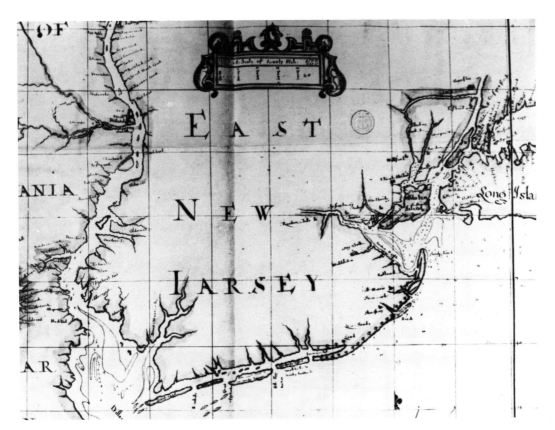

This early map is probably from circa 1700 when New Jersey was divided into two parts, East and West. "Communipaw" and "Barghan" are the only settlements shown in Hudson County's area. The shape of New Jersey is seriously distorted. Courtesy, Library of Congress

Jacques Cortelyou surveyed the land and marked out the lines of the central square and the four surrounding blocks that would be palisaded. Today the outline of Cortelyou's work is visible at Bergen Square in Jersey City where Academy Street and Bergen Avenue intersect. This was the first example on American soil of the town design that became known as the Philadelphia Square.

The new residents selected their strips of land by lot and promised to erect their homes within six weeks. By the late summer of 1660 the new town called Bergen was a reality, and it has the distinction of being the first permanent nucleated settlement in New Jersey. Later in 1660 the original Communipaw farmers created a small village on the shoreline and enclosed their own homes with a palisade of logs. A wagon road following Indian trails connected the two fortified areas. Communipaw was subordinate to Bergen, which became the headquarters for public activities, government, and the school. From this beginning Bergen Township

grew north and south until it encompassed all the land east of the Hackensack River that is now part of Hudson County.

In 1661 the Bergen townsmen petitioned the council at New Amsterdam to set up a court at the new town because it was too inconvenient to cross the river to resolve disputes. The council granted this request, which had the effect of slackening the ties binding the two banks of the river. The council also required the Bergen residents to establish a church. Peter Stuyvesant had imposed this condition upon all Dutch settlements in an effort to curb the frontier atmosphere prevalent in New Netherland. The Dutch Reformed Church at Bergen, the first religious congregation in New Jersey, was organized in 1662 and continues today as the Old Bergen Church at the corner of Bergen and Highland avenues in Jersey City. Across the street the stones of its cemetery still stand to remind the passerby of the Newkirks and Vreelands and Van Winkles and of the other pioneers who once farmed this land.

Farmers
and
Fighters

It took the Dutch thirty years to create a permanent town west of the Hudson, and only four years later they lost it. The British, who had been distracted by domestic turmoil during the Cromwellian Protectorate, were back in the game of colonizing. Peter Stuyvesant's domain, midway between Massachusetts and Virginia, looked particularly attractive. Spurred on by his advisers and by the New England merchants who coveted the commercial prospects of the mid-Atlantic region, the Stuart king Charles II dispatched troops and four frigates with orders to take New Netherland. The vessels anchored off Gravesend and the soldiers marched across Brooklyn to a point just opposite Manhattan. When the frigates sailed into the bay and aimed their guns at the fort, the Dutch leaders reluctantly conceded the hopelessness of their position. On September 8, 1664, New Amsterdam surrendered both its allegiance and its name and became New York. Soon after the residents of Bergen made their pledges to their new rulers.

British sovereignty marked a significant legal step in the separation of the settlements on opposite sides of the Hudson River. King Charles awarded all of New Netherland to his brother James, Duke of York, and the Duke then granted that portion lying between the Hudson and Delaware rivers to two friends, John

Lord Berkeley and Sir George Carteret. These two royal cronies thereby became the first proprietors of a new province that the duke named New Jersey to honor Carteret, a native of the Channel Island of Jersey and a defender of the royal cause during the Protectorate. They appointed Philip Carteret to be their representative and provided him with a document titled the "Concessions and Agreements of the Lord Proprietors of New Jersey." Its reasonable and democratic terms attracted settlers from England and other colonies, and within a short time towns were established at Elizabeth-Town, Middletown, Newark, Piscataway, Shrewsbury, and Woodbridge.

In 1668 William Sandford left his home on the West Indian island of Barbados to act as agent for his uncle, Major Nathaniel Kingsland, who had obtained a grant of land from the proprietors. Sandford purchased the territory from the Indians and negotiated an arrangement with his uncle that gave him title to the southern portion of the grant. Sandford's land became known as New Barbadoes Neck, a variant of the name of his island homeland. It covered the area that today includes the west Hudson communities of East Newark, Harrison, and Kearny and their immediate northern neighbors in Bergen County. It is the only property within

present-day Hudson County that was never part of Bergen Township.

To the northeast of New Barbadoes Neck, the tract known today as Secaucus was acquired by Nicholas Bayard and Nicholas Varlett, a brother-in-law of Peter Stuyvesant. They sold it to Edward Earle, Jr., in 1676, and then three years later he sold half of it to William Pinhorne. Varlett also bought Van Putten's deserted brewery in Hoboken, and in 1678 Bayard took possession of Weehawken, where he built saw and corn mills. Elsewhere in Bergen new families occupied land increasingly distant from the town center. By 1680 the Van Buskirk plantation in present-day Bayonne was thriving, and smaller villages were developing along the Hudson River shoreline. The hardiest among the hardy moved into the densely wooded highland north of Bergen Square. David Demarest, a Huguenot, purchased the land that became Hackensack Township and moved there with a group of his followers.

As the white settlers advanced, the Lenni Lenape retreated. Unlike the bellicose tribes, they chose to yield rather than to fight. Afflicted by disease and bereft of their traditional land, the Indians in New Jersey dwindled to a few hundred by the mid-1700s. Of these, most lived in western New Jersey under the protection of the Quakers.

The amity among the colonists in New Jersey at this time was in distinct contrast to the hostilities among the mother countries. In Europe changing alliances and war moves prompted the government of the Netherlands to dispatch a formidable fleet across the North Atlantic to harass British shipping. In 1673 these vessels entered New York Bay and exchanged a few volleys with the English defenders. The Dutch troops landed on Manhattan, north of the city, and quickly captured it. For over a year they occupied the region, but the direction of European politics turned against them, and a treaty signed at Westminster in 1674 reestablished British dominion over the territory that had been the resurrected New Netherland.

After British repossession of the province came changes in the governmental structure of New Jersey. The two original proprietors, Berkeley and Carteret, sold shares to investors and divided the province into the two Jerseys, East and West. This division lasted from 1676 until 1702 when proprietary rule, but not land ownership, ended and New Jersey became a unified royal colony. For the next thirty-six years, the two colonies of New Jersey and New York were administered by the same royal governors. Not until 1738, after much public agitation, did New Jersey finally welcome its own governor, Lewis Morris.

Other changes in government directly affected the local areas. In 1675 Bergen County was organized with its territory being loosely described as Bergen Township and the adjacent plantations. In 1693 the county was enlarged and divided into two townships, Bergen and Hackensack. Then in 1709, in response to the rapid population growth in the northwestern section of the county, the court was moved from Bergen to Hackensack. The next year New Barbadoes Neck was separated from Essex and added to Bergen County.

Except for the removal of the court to Hackensack, the changes had little impact upon the daily lives of the people of Bergen Township. The Dutch retained their own traditions and their own language in their private lives, although they mastered English for commercial transactions. They were an industrious people who seemed to enjoy work, but they did not rely solely upon their own efforts to construct their homes and barns and cultivate and transport their crops. Chronically short of labor in their colonies, the Dutch as well as the English were slaveholders. A 1726 head count revealed that 18.4 percent of the Bergen County population was Negro. The English also practiced indenture in which white men contracted for years of labor in exchange for basic support. The alternative for those without resources was to wear the large blue letter "P," for pauper, and to depend upon the uncertain charity of their neighbors.

It was a black slave whom legend makes responsible for discovering copper in New Barbadoes Neck on the property of Arendt Schuyler, a native of Albany who purchased land on New Barbadoes Neck in 1710 to build a three-story mansion overlooking the Passaic River. Within a few years of his arrival his copper was being mined, sold, and exported to Europe. By 1738 the Schuyler mine had produced over 13,000 tons of ore. It continued in operation despite mechanical breakdowns until 1773 and then was revived in 1793 and worked off and on throughout the nineteenth century. The Schuyler copper mine, along with iron mines in the Ringwood Tract and in Morris County, provided the earliest heavy industrial activity in New Jersey.

With the exception of the mines, the entire province was essentially agrarian, with the Dutch particularly devoted to the farming life and to the quiet, homely ways known as "Plain Dutch." Efforts to establish foreign ports at Perth Amboy and Salem ultimately failed in the face of overwhelming competition from the shippers of New York and Philadelphia. In addition, no significant city developed within the province. Even after it became a unified royal colony in 1702, New Jersey maintained two alternating capitals, one at Perth Amboy and the other at Burlington, an outcome of the psychological cleavage between East and West Jersey that persists to the present. Then, as now, Philadelphia and New York were the magnets that drew New Jersey apart and then, as now, a sophisticated transportation system evolved to handle the demands imposed by geography.

Fortunately, New Jersey was blessed with a number of navigable rivers that aided the shipment of ores and farm goods. Augmented by ferries and roads, these waterways formed the freight transportation network of the province but, for the growing movement of passengers, land routes were preferred. One of the

most important began in Bergen. In 1765 the provincial legislature passed an act to lay out a major road between Newark and Paulus Hook, and the next year John Mercereau started a stage service between these two points.

Demonstrating marketing flair, Mercereau called his vehicles the Flying Machines, but they were really farm wagons to which he added springs to cushion the ride on the "corduroy" roads. Ferries provided the crossings over the Hackensack and Passaic rivers. From Five Corners, a short distance from the center of Bergen, another road went north to Hackensack. From Paulus Hook a third major thoroughfare ran south to Bergen Point where it connected with the ferry to Staten Island. Hudson River ferries ran from Communipaw, Pavonia, Hoboken, Weehawken, and most importantly and reliably from Paulus Hook, where travelers could rest at an inn.

Within a few generations Bergen County, as well as the province as a whole, had accomplished much. In his book *New Jersey from Colony to State*, Richard McCormick cites the royal governor, Jonathan Belcher, who observed in 1748, "Take this province in the Lump, it is the best country I have seen for men of middling fortunes, and for people who

An old slave cabin at the Kearny entrance to Arendt Schuyler's estate is depicted in this 1903 photograph. Schuyler came from Albany to this area, then called New Barbadoes Neck, in 1710. He bought a plantation and built a mansion. According to legend one of his black slaves discovered copper on his land and made him even richer. In 1800 Bergen County, including what is now Hudson County, had 2,800 slaves out of a total of 16,000 people, but in 1804 legislation for gradual emancipation was passed in New Jersey. JCL

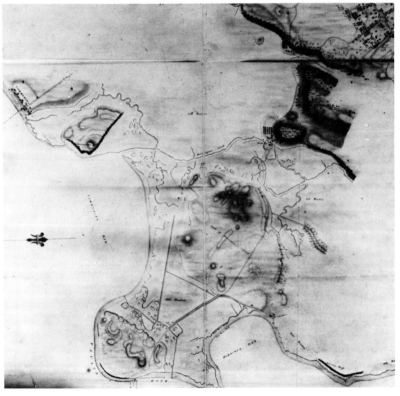

Left
Engineer J. Hills produced this map in 1781. It depicts part of what is now Jersey City, from the square arrangement of Bergen (upper right) near the bluff of the palisade hill, down to the Hudson River and the settlement of Communipaw (the line of houses and their road in the upper left). The peninsula is Paulus Hook, named for Michael Paulusen, an agent in this area in 1633, and the Dutch word hoeck, *meaning "point of land." The "V" of roads from the hook forms basically what are now Grand Street and Newark Avenue. JCL*

Above
Between 1902 and 1906 the New Jersey Title Guarantee and Trust Company reissued a series of nineteenth-century prints of historical views, of which this is one. This easterly view is of Paulus Hook, with New York beyond, during the American Revolution when the hook was held by the British. The ditch contained sharpened stakes. The approach-bridge marks the eastern terminus of Newark Avenue. Paulus Hook and Fort Delancey in Bayonne were the main British strongholds on the west bank of the Hudson River. JCL

have to live by the sweat of their brows."

During their years as a colonial power, the English had been relatively lax overseers who allowed their subjects in the New World a significant measure of independence, but this changed when European rivalries eventually intruded upon the North American continent, and France became the foremost threat to British dominance. Starting in 1689 when William of Orange and his wife Mary accepted the English throne and continuing until 1815 with the final defeat of Napoleon, these two nations were repeatedly at war with one another. In America hostilities between the two broke out sporadically from 1689 until the signing of the Treaty of Paris in 1763. Fighting centered upon the Canadian borders and the western lands of the Mississippi Valley.

In 1755 the government of New Jersey asked its men to enlist in the service of the king in the fight against the French and their Indian allies. One particularly patriotic son of Bergen County, Peter Schuyler of New Barbadoes Neck, the fourth son of Arendt, volunteered to raise 400 men at his own expense. In 1756 Schulyer and his regiment of Jersey

Blues were captured at the battle of Oswego. His later release elicited great joy, with a bonfire greeting him in Manhattan and a cannonade welcoming him at his home plantation of Petersborough. He returned to battle several times and ransomed some 114 prisoners of the French with his own money. For his gallantry, courage, and generosity Peter Schuyler was universally praised. His death several years later was greatly lamented, but it spared him the necessity of choosing sides in the greater conflict to come.

Following the victory over the French, London introduced measures to increase its control over North American affairs and to raise funds to pay for the war and for the costs of colonial administration. His Majesty's oldest American colonies, Virginia and Massachusetts, which had the most to lose from the new policies, led the opposition to the Crown. By 1775 when blood was shed at the battles of Lexington and Concord, it was clear that war, not negotiation, would settle the conflict. For six years the outcome was uncertain until the British defeat at Yorktown. At the signing of the Treaty of

This nineteenth-century print shows Prior's Mill on Mill Creek and the road running from Paulus Hook to Bergen. This site is where Columbus Drive and Fremont Street would meet in modern Jersey City. Mill Creek ran from Communipaw on the Hudson River shore almost to Hoboken, and small boats could carry the farmers' produce inland. The steeple in the upper right is that of the Old Bergen Church. JCL

R.W. Welsh's undated print shows the Old Bergen Church as it looked when newly built in 1773. A petition to the governor general of New Netherland in 1662 marked the beginning of this Dutch Reformed congregation. A small, octagonal church was built about 1680 just outside the stockade on Bergen Avenue at Vroom Street. This 1773 church replaced the first. JCL

Paris of 1783, the thirteen colonies were recognized as independent.

From 1776 until the end of the war, the British occupied New York and forts in New Jersey at Paulus Hook and Bergen Neck. The Dutch in Bergen accepted the British occupation with equanimity. Perhaps they were predisposed to continued European hegemony as a result of a split which had developed among the Reformed Churches in New Jersey. In opposition to the Raritan Valley Dutch, who favored American direction of their ecclesiastical affairs, the people of Bergen looked to Holland for the training of the clergy and for ultimate religious authority. During the Revolution this inclination toward the Old World was reinforced by

military necessity and by the expanding market for produce provided by the thousands of British troops nearby. Furthermore, many of the people of Bergen were still Dutch enough to look upon the war as a quarrel among Englishmen.

Nonetheless, some pro-Patriot sentiment existed such as that displayed by Jennie Tuers, who alerted General George Washington to the impending defection of Benedict Arnold when she passed on news overheard in a New York tavern by her slave. The minister or dominie of the church, William Jackson, who was related by marriage to the Raritan Valley church officials, was the most prominent and outspoken rebel. A renowned preacher, he gave a sermon to the Tories of Bergen

Neck, but he was driven back to New York. Both sides foraged for supplies and timber, sometimes paying for them and sometimes not. The high ground on the Bergen hill was used as a vantage point by American officers spying on the British on the low ground near the river. After several reconnoitering expeditions, Major Henry Lee realized that the British position at Paulus Hook was carelessly guarded, and he persuaded Washington to authorize a raid upon the fort. On August 18, 1779, the troops set out. Slowed by the dense woods of the Bergen hill and then by the marshes of the lowland, Lee and his men did not reach their goal until three o'clock in the morning of the nineteenth. They succeeded in surprising the defenders and in taking over 150 prisoners, but they lacked the time to destroy the fortifications before daylight would threaten their retreat. Militarily inconclusive, this enterprise against Paulus Hook nonetheless renewed the spirit of the American force. As a reward Congress bestowed upon Lee one of only eight medals awarded during the entire war.

Paulus Hook remained the last place in New Jersey at which the British retained a position. When the news of the completion of the preliminary peace treaty reached America in January 1783, the evacuation of the Loyalists began. Responsibility for this delicate task fell to Sir Guy Carlton, the new British commander, who also supervised the maintenance of civil order in the area occupied by his army. During the summer of 1783, he consulted with General Washington and advised him of his intent to remove his troops from northern Manhattan and Long Island on November 21, from Paulus Hook on November 22, and from lower Manhattan and Brooklyn on November 24. When this was accomplished on schedule, Washington led his victorious forces into New York. On December 4 he said farewell to his officers at Fraunces Tavern. Then he sailed west over the Hudson and traveled south to his Virginia home, leaving thirteen independent states in awe of their own achievement.

Neck on the theme of treachery and the thirty pieces of silver, implying that the worshippers were all Judases. For this he was arrested and brought to New York, but Lord Howe, who knew and liked him, dismissed him with a reprimand. Undeterred by the British and by their sympathizers in his own congregation, Dominie Jackson continued his battle from the pulpit for the duration of the war and won some converts to the American cause.

Although New Jersey was the scene of several major battles, only minor raids and skirmishes took place in southern Bergen County. In September 1776 the British commander briefly occupied the Schuyler mansion in New Barbadoes

A Great City
on the
West Hudson Shore

Still speaking Dutch in their private dealings and remaining rather insulated by both geography and custom from the concerns of their neighbors, the farmers and artisans of Bergen Township resumed their prewar pursuits, but their agrarian, provincial ways could not endure. Around them there was too much energy, too much talent, too much initiative eager to test new ideas to allow life to remain unchanged. Among those who would alter the traditional patterns, no one was more keen to greet the future nor more influential in shaping it than the man who had been the treasurer of New Jersey during the Revolution: John Stevens.

Secure in his family's fortune and proud of his King's College degree, Colonel Stevens was the highest bidder at the 1784 auction of the confiscated estates of the Bayard family, Loyalists from Hoboken. The next year Stevens added to his Hudson River waterfront holdings by buying lower Weehawken. He built a magnificent home on the high ground at Castle Point, filled it with fine European furniture, and surrounded it with orchards and extensive landscaping. A shrewd and practical businessman, Stevens launched a vigorous campaign to promote his property and began by taking over the ferry and by leading the efforts to build the Bergen Turnpike,

which connected Hoboken to Hackensack.

After recurring outbreaks of yellow fever devastated crowded Manhattan in the late 1790s, Stevens surmised that the Hoboken waterfront would appeal to people seeking a healthy environment not too far from New York, and, as a result, in 1804 he had some of his acres surveyed and advertised for sale. Simultaneously a few well-to-do New Yorkers saw exciting prospects for the west shore of the Hudson. John B. Coles, a flour merchant and occasional New York alderman, purchased the Duke's Farm at Harsimus in old Pavonia, located near Nathanial Budd's ferry to Cortlandt Street that had been running since 1802. Coles never lived on his land, but he had sufficient confidence in the area to join a third plan to develop the river front.

Early in 1804 Anthony Dey of New York approached Cornelius Van Vorst, the owner of Paulus Hook, with an acceptable offer to buy the land between the Hudson River and present-day Warren Street in Jersey City. Joining Dey were two other principals, Richard Varick and Jacob Radcliffe, men who are numbered among the mayors of New York, and backing them were an additional thirty-two investors including John B. Coles and the governor of New Jersey, Joseph Bloomfield. They were incorpo-

Aaron Burr (left) and Alexander Hamilton are pictured in these nineteenth-century prints. Burr had been the vice-president of the United States under Thomas Jefferson. Hamilton had been in the cabinet of President George Washington. In the early morning of July 1, 1804, in two row boats, they went from New York to a shelf of rock at Weehawken's shoreline. They stepped a few paces, turned, and at the word "present" they shot point-blank, with Burr giving Hamilton a mortal wound. The nation mourned, and the archaic practice of dueling was made illegal. JCL

*Opposite page
Thomas Kitchin produced this map of New York and its environs for the* London Magazine *of 1778. About two-thirds of Hudson County's Hudson River shoreline is seen along the left side. In this year the only road indicated is that from the Paulus Hook ferry to Bergen Square. In 1804 the Paulus Hook peninsula was sold by the Van Vorst family to three New York entrepreneurs—Dey, Varick, and Radcliff. The estate of Archibald Kennedy is noted, and in 1804 that land was bought by John B. Coles, a New York flour merchant and speculator. JCL*

rated as the Associates of the Jersey Company, according to the terms of a bill that had been drawn up by Alexander Hamilton, their counsel, shortly before his death from wounds suffered in a duel with Aaron Burr at Weehawken. Advertising their development as "The Town of Jersey Commonly Known as Powles Hook," the Associates secured some sales of lots suitable for homes or businesses. The urbanization of the future Hudson County was underway.

As a real estate venture, Paulus Hook, or Powles Hook as it was known at that time, had the advantage of name recognition. Certainly men of a sporting nature were familiar with the place, for in 1769 Van Vorst had laid out a racecourse on his property that attracted lovers of the turf during peacetime for the weekly runnings. Yet those who knew the new town best were travelers. The 1765 road from the Hook to Newark carried more passengers than any other route in the state with twenty stages a day, and the ferry service at that point was the shortest, most frequent, and most reliable across the Hudson.

Within a year the Associates con-

structed the Hudson Hotel and hired Andre Michaux to plant hundreds of poplar trees. A public building went up and several churches were organized, but despite these efforts, the Town of Jersey was not an immediate and dazzling success. From a total of fifteen inhabitants at the time of the purchase by Dey in 1804, the population grew to 1,025 in 1829, an increase of only 1,010 persons in twenty-five years, and there were fewer sales of property in Hoboken and Harsimus. Many held New York responsible for this slow growth, and indeed they had cause to resent the clout of their big neighbor.

Citing the royal grant of the former New Netherland to the Duke of York and his grant in turn of the land between the Hudson and Delaware rivers to Berkeley and Carteret, New York State had long maintained that it owned all the water between the two states up to the low watermark on the western shore. As a corollary New York City declared its jurisdiction over the piers and wharves on both sides of the river. The early British governors, Richard Nicolls, Edmund Andros, and Thomas Dongan, who held office during the proprietary period, believed that New Jersey was part of New York and thought that the duke had acted illegally, as well as foolishly, when he bestowed this "dependency" upon Berkeley and Carteret. Governor Andros even charged Philip Carteret with usurping the rights of government and had him arrested, but a jury acquitted him and allowed him to return to New Jersey. During these years Staten Island, part of the 1630 purchase by Michael Pauw, slipped into the control of New York despite repeated but futile protests by the proprietors. The feeling was not one-sided. When the province became a royal colony in 1702, there were some Jerseymen who sought to incorporate East New Jersey into New York.

In the years before 1804 New York's claim to the waters between the states affected the people of Bergen only indirectly. By impeding the rise of an international port at Perth Amboy, New York had insured that New Jersey would remain as Thomas Jefferson's ideal—an agrarian society—for a longer period than its natural situation would suggest. During that time New York was able to consolidate its own assets and to develop the intricate web of financial institutions necessary for foreign trade. When the land sales of 1804 raised the threat of competitive cities emerging on the shores of Bergen Township directly across the Hudson River, however, New York asserted its old claim. The New York City Council issued the following warning on June 4, 1804:

The Board having been informed that sundry persons have lately undertaken to construct wharves within the bounds of the City between high and low water mark on the west side of Hudson's River, without any authority for so doing from the people of the State of New York, or from this Board, Do hereby give Public Notice, that such encroachments being made without their permission or consent must be at the peril of the persons concerned.

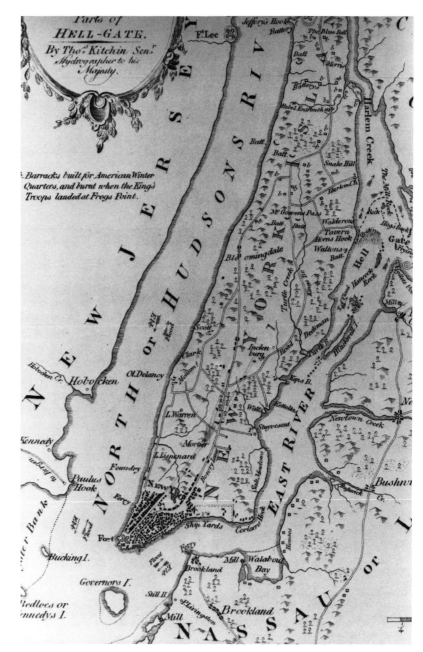

Above
Copyrighted by T. Gubelman in 1901 and executed by F.L. Henry, this print shows the steam-ferry boat Jersey, *built by Robert Fulton in 1812, landing at Paulus Hook. JCL*

Top
The Holland-American Line established its large docks and piers at the foot of Fifth Street in Hoboken. JCL

Naturally the Associates of the Jersey Company referred the matter to their attorneys who, in opposing the New York stand, based their argument upon the law of nations and upon the English common-law understanding that the boundary between two states should be the middle of the intervening body of water. The State of New Jersey, still smarting from a 1774 decision that awarded many disputed miles on its northern land border to New York, backed the Associates and in 1806 appointed commissioners to deal with the issue. The New York representatives, however, refused to yield and the commission broke up. To a new overture made by New Jersey in 1818, New York responded with silence. In the 1820s raids

by New Yorkers upon New Jersey oyster beds and the service of New York writs upon persons standing on wharves in New Jersey intensified the animosity and renewed efforts to find a solution.

Finally a suit was initiated and directed to the Supreme Court on behalf of New Jersey's position. This move led to an out-of-court settlement in which a bistate commission produced a treaty ratified in 1834. Under its terms the boundary was set as the middle of the Hudson River and New York Bay. To secure the agreement New Jersey conceded New York's jurisdiction over Staten, Ellis, and Bedloe's (now Liberty) islands. The treaty contained provisions on fisheries, quarantine, and criminal process and acknowledged New Jersey's right to Raritan Bay.

The main issue was decided in New Jersey's favor, but differing interpretations of the treaty have produced occasional disagreement. A joint commission, meeting between 1887 and 1889, defined the Raritan Bay boundary and then dealt anew with the boundary in Arthur Kill, Kill van Kull, New York Bay, and the Hudson River. When the Holland Tunnel opened in 1927, New York temporarily claimed police power and the right to the patronage of police appointments throughout the tunnel's length. Even in the 1980s the two states are contending over the status of the twenty-four-and-a-half acres of landfill that have augmented the original three acres of Ellis Island and are disputing the ramifications of the terms "sovereignty" and "jurisdiction."

The boundary conflict of the early 1800s created legal uncertainty over the use of shorefront property, and this hindered the sale of lots in the Town of Jersey. In a related matter the attempts of New York to control the navigable waters between the states hampered Hoboken and gave rise to the "Steamboat Controversy" and a landmark decision by the United States Supreme Court.

The early ferries that crossed the Hudson River and all other inland waterways were powered by sail or by oar. They were slow, dangerous, and subject to the

vagaries of weather and tide. After James Watt produced a workable steam engine in 1769, many mechanics and entrepreneurs on both sides of the Atlantic tried to adapt steam power to water transportation. John Fitch, operating on the Delaware River, achieved some success and applied to a number of states for monopolistic privileges. By 1787 he had obtained such rights from New York State for a fourteen-year period. Fitch was never able to launch a practical steamboat, but others were working toward the same goal. Among them was Hoboken's John Stevens.

In 1798 Stevens joined in partnership with Robert Livingston, his brother-in-law and an important New York political figure. Livingston used his considerable influence to secure passage of a law transferring to himself all the monopoly rights that had been granted to Fitch and, to take advantage of this law, a steamboat designed by Stevens was set afloat. To their dismay it failed the speed test, and the Livingston-Stevens partner-

ship faded before Livingston left America to serve as ambassador to France.

In Paris Livingston met Robert Fulton, an artist and engineer who shared the ambassador's interest in steam-powered vessels. In 1802 they signed a partnership agreement. Five years later, in the vessel that came to be known as the *Clermont,* Fulton and Livingston completed the journey between Manhattan and Albany and thereby acquired the monopoly granted by New York. By its terms no one could run a steamboat in New York waters without a license from the partners, and the police powers of New York could impound unlicensed craft. In anticipation of an enormous demand for steamboats from all sections of the country, Fulton bought land at Paulus Hook and began construction of a shipyard.

Meanwhile Stevens had continued his experiments, and in 1808, just a few months after the *Clermont* voyage, he completed work on the *Phoenix,* which used his invention of the twin-screw propeller. He put it on a ferry run between

This view southeast from Weehawken down the Hudson River to New York Bay is a photograph of an aquatint done in 1834 by Sigmund Himely, based on a slightly earlier painting by French artist Louis Garnay. The people strolling and picnicking on the grass are relaxing on the palisade at Weehawken. The road is probably the Bergen/ Hackensack Turnpike, while at the left are the buildings of Chelsea in New York City. At the right is a jut of land which was part of Elysian Fields. Another jut of land with buildings in the distance (right) is Paulus Hook. JCL

Bergen Square, the center of Bergen Township, is pictured as it appeared in 1852. In 1660 Bergen became the first permanent community in New Jersey. This view—east down Academy Street looking from Bergen Avenue—shows the Columbia Academy (the large pitched-roof building) built in 1790, and demolished in 1857. JCL

New York City and New Brunswick, but competition and threats of impoundment made Stevens back off, despite his contention that the New York monopoly violated the United States constitutional provision for free commerce between the states.

In 1811 Stevens tried again, this time using a steamboat on the Hoboken to New York ferry run, and once more he yielded to Livingston and Fulton pressure. He continued the ferry but substituted horsepower for steam, using a curious vessel called a teamboat. This was propelled by horses working a treadmill connected to a paddle wheel, and it was slow and uncertain. Travelers attributed movement to the wind and tide more than to the sad animals slowly walking their way across the river. Finally in 1822, with the monopoly under se-

vere legal assault, Stevens felt free to challenge it anew, and he resumed steampowered ferry service between Hoboken and Barclay Street. In 1812 Fulton started his own trans-Hudson ferry service with a vessel called the *Jersey,* which took fifteen minutes—under good conditions—for the crossing between New York and Paulus Hook. To Stevens' great annoyance this boosted the prospects of the young Town of Jersey at the expense of Hoboken.

The New Jersey legislature, angered by New York's claims to all the waters between the two states, passed its own law in 1811 granting steamboat monopoly privileges. These were sought by Stevens but were awarded instead to Aaron Ogden, who had operated a sail ferry on the run between New York and Elizabeth. Ogden's efforts to put a steam vessel on this route were vigorously challenged by Fulton and Livingston. Unlike Stevens, Ogden eventually made his peace and paid the license fee to the monopoly. However, Thomas Gibbons, a former partner, started a competitive and unlicensed ferry captained by the young Cornelius Vanderbilt. Ogden, as a licensee, now found himself representing the monopoly's interest in a civil suit. The case, known as *Ogden* v. *Gibbons*, reached the Supreme Court in 1824 when Chief Justice Marshall delivered a lengthy opinion favoring Gibbons. The court declared the New York monopoly void on the grounds that it interfered with the right of Congress to regulate trade between the states.

This decision did not address the question of one state's claim to the entire body of water shared by two, but it did weaken states' rights as it strengthened the powers of Congress. It created a legal atmosphere that was receptive to the position of New Jersey on the boundary issue.

The stand of New York undoubtedly retarded the west Hudson waterfront development, but it would be unfair to place the blame for the slow growth solely upon the Empire State. The fledgling New Jersey towns had their own handicaps. A location on the banks of the river was their chief asset, but it was also a problem; the land in Hoboken, Harsimus, and Paulus Hook was perhaps too close to the water. At high tide each area was an island separated from the higher land by creeks and salt marshes. A prospective home owner of 1804 would have to be farsighted indeed to see the ungraded, unlighted, isolated streets, surrounded by water and marsh, as appealing places to settle.

An added difficulty was the uncertainty over the conduct of government. Legally belonging to Bergen Township, the three developments were under the jurisdiction of the court at Hackensack and were part of the Bergen County legislative district. But for the daily management of civic business the waterfront communities were on their own. In 1820

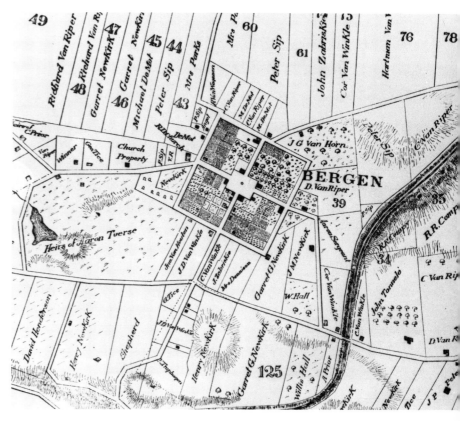

the first act of incorporation of the City of Jersey City passed the state legislature. Under its terms five selectmen were elected who could levy taxes up to a total of $100 for the entire city. So desperate were they for working funds that the selectmen paid from their own pockets one dollar each for the costs of each meeting and fined themselves additional sums for tardiness (twenty-five cents) and absence (fifty cents). Such arrangements were more suited to a Junior Town Meeting than to serious municipal government.

Jersey City had to present repeated petitions to the legislature for more liberal charters. An act of 1829 expanded the responsibilities of the selectmen, but it was not until 1838 that the city had a workable governing structure with a common council and a mayor empowered to regulate public affairs. The charter of 1838 also legally separated Jersey City from Bergen Township, thereby starting an independence movement that would make the name of Bergen only a memory within a generation.

A detail of L.F. Douglass' 1841 map of part of Hudson County shows Bergen Square, laid out in 1660 by Jacques Cortelyou, and several roads, as well as the names of the property owners. In the square the road going left-right is Bergen Avenue, and that crossing it is Academy Street. The lowest left-right street is Summit Avenue, and the left-right road which meets Academy at the top of the square is Tonnele Avenue. The junction at the lower right is Five Corners, where Newark and Hoboken avenues meet Summit Avenue. These roads were all fully developed by 1800. JCL

IV

Business Begins

The mood among the 20,000 spectators was tense and expectant as Charles Ferson Durant distributed his poetical address. Yet the excited throng gathered at Castle Garden at the tip of Manhattan had not paid fifty cents apiece to hear oratory. Instead they were on hand to witness a manned balloon flight across New York Bay. At five o'clock on this afternoon of September 9, 1830, Durant waved from his gondola, released the restraining ropes, and took off on his aerial voyage. At 6:46 he landed safely near South Amboy, New Jersey, and was escorted in an impromptu parade of farmers to Perth Amboy. At twenty-five years of age, this young man from Jersey City had become the first native-born American to fly.

Durant learned his skill in Paris in 1828 where he studied with the pioneering French balloonists. Following his first Castle Garden flight, he made repeated ascensions from New York, Boston, and Baltimore. Only marriage brought him down to earth, for his wife favored less perilous pursuits. He then spent his leisure time growing silkworms and writing treatises on subjects such as astronomy and the algae of New York harbor. Throughout his life Durant took a keen interest in the public affairs of Jersey City, where he built an arcaded market and named it in honor of his scientific hero, Johann Kepler.

The graceful worldly style of life represented by Charles Durant flourished only briefly in Bergen. In the early 1830s the area was poised between the old agrarian ways and a new order of tough-minded industrial enterprise. In these years Washington Irving was still poking fun at the farmers of Communipaw. He chided them for keeping their sleepy manners and their old-fashioned dress and for believing that Holland, of which they had heard so much, was located somewhere east, perhaps on Long Island.

In fact, the energetic Dutch continued to make good livings supplying their urban neighbors with fish, cabbages, and clover. They held onto their farms tenaciously, dividing them among their sons and passing them down through families for generations. A prime reason that Bergen, the first town in New Jersey, did not attain the population growth of other early settlements is that the Dutch took title to most of the tillable land very quickly and, instead of accepting subdivision, sons of large families left Bergen for more spacious tracts in other counties. Rarely did lots on the hill become available for newcomers.

By the early decades of the nineteenth century, this pattern was breaking down and Bergen was acquiring some of the amenities of modern life. Columbia Academy, a private school, started classes in

Right
Flying through the air carried by balloons made of silk and filled with hydrogen gas was a prophetic sport. Charles Ferson Durant, who lived in Jersey City, became internationally known as America's first native aeronaut. Between 1830 and 1834 he made twelve successful ascensions, most of them from Castle Point, New York City. This poster of 1830 advertises his first flight on September 9, soon after his return from Paris, where he learned the art. JCL

1790 near the intersection of Bergen Avenue and Academy Street. Nearby the first physician of Bergen County, Josiah Hornblower, opened his medical office with a practice which extended north as far as Fort Lee and Hackensack. Then new religious congregations began to form, a few at Paulus Hook and others south at Bergen Neck and north near the English Neighborhood. They reflected changes in the ethnic and social composition of the area as Methodists, Episcopalians, Presbyterians, and Catholics arrived and sought their own houses of worship. The Associates of the Jersey Company encouraged this religious interest by providing free lots for church structures. Elsewhere itinerant clergymen visited clusters of worshippers scattered among the hamlets within Bergen Township.

During the War of 1812 the federal government built an arsenal on the hilltop site where Dickinson High School now stands in Jersey City, and the New Jersey militia set up a training camp at Paulus Hook. In this period, as turnpikes began to cross the state, frequent stagecoaches left Paulus Hook heading south to Philadelphia and north to Rockaway and Hackettstown. Enroute they stopped at roadside taverns where travelers brought news to the local residents of the world beyond their home territory. From the southern tip of Bergen at Bergen Point to the northern border with Hackensack Township and the English Neighborhood a more knowing, cosmopolitan spirit was taking hold.

To the west of Bergen Township, New Barbadoes Neck on the Passaic River, once dominated by the Schuyler family, was emerging as a suburb of Newark. On the eastern point of the Neck, two wooden toll bridges crossing the Hackensack and Passaic rivers had been erected in 1795 to supplant the ferries. Separated by the Hackensack River and by extensive marshes from Bergen Township, the New Barbadoes Neck area shared only the common court and the road jurisdiction of Bergen County with its neighbor to the east.

In 1815 the residents of New Barbadoes chose a new name for their large town which stretched northward from the Neck to the border of Hackensack Township. Displaying a surprising worldliness they selected Lodi in homage to Napoleon's 1796 victory over Austrian forces at a northern Italian town. The southern portion of Lodi officially became Harrison Township in 1840 and was so named in honor of the hero of Tippecanoe, President William Henry Harrison.

In New York City, Brooklyn, and Newark enterprising businessmen were setting up small factories, and the trend was soon taken up in Bergen. On the tip of Constable Hook the Hazzard family built a gunpowder factory on land they purchased from the Van Buskirks in 1798. On this isolated spot, surrounded by water and farms, they made the ammunition for the harbor's warships and forts during the War of 1812. Coincidentally, the chief competition of the Hazzard firm, the E.I. Dupont Company of Delaware, was founded by French émigrés who spent their first years in America, from 1799 to 1802, living close by at Bergen Point.

Among the pioneers in the Town of Jersey were the Edges. The head of the family was a baker, Isaac Edge, who erected a giant windmill for grinding wheat on the waterfront at the foot of Montgomery Street. His landmark stood from 1815 to 1839 when its position was usurped by the railroad, and then it was removed to Long Island where it continued to give good service until a fire destroyed it in 1870. Edge's son, also named Isaac, had served in the New Jersey militia where he gained experience with military fireworks. In 1828 young Edge opened his own pyrotechnical laboratory on Steuben Street. This was probably the first commercial fireworks factory in America, and there he originated movable pieces, the first being a representation of the Battle of Vera Cruz that he displayed over Boston Common. His advertisement in the 1856 Jersey City directory boasts

that he was the pyrotechnist of Niblo's and Castle Garden in New York, and adds that he had provided the material for over 3,000 exhibitions in the previous twenty-eight years. Edge lost some accounts in 1858 when his exploding fireworks inflicted extensive damage upon New York's City Hall after a gala spectacle in honor of the laying of an Atlantic cable. Nonetheless, his business was so lucrative that his son and his brother started a rival establishment on Bay Street that they called the United States Laboratory.

In later decades competitors, including Gustavus Lilliendahl, Detwiller and Street, and International Fireworks, set up shop in the area so that by 1900 Hudson County held a dominant position in the manufacture of fireworks. Yet it was a hazardous occupation and, after making powder for use in World War I, the industry moved to more suitable rural locations.

These early businesses were small operations staffed mainly by family members because other workers were unavailable. The persistent shortage of labor, which had induced the first settlers to rely upon slaves and indentured servants, continued to retard the economy. Another difficulty hampering industrial development was the poor and uncertain

Left
The P. Lorillard Tobacco Company in Jersey City employed some 4,000 people in 1884, including several hundred women and girls who stripped stems off tobacco leaves to produce 120,000 pounds of tobacco plugs a day. The factory employed 350 children under the age of fifteen. Leonard S. Gordon, Lorillard's physician and chemist, set up a night school for children and adults in 1884. This print of a women's class is taken from Frank Leslie's Illustrated Newspaper *of 1885. JCL*

Opposite page, bottom
An engraving by John Andrew from Ballou's Pictorial Drawing Room Companion *of 1856 is partially "modern" and, in the lower half, nostalgic. The cider mill in the upper left and the apple harvest at the upper right are indications of the agrarian nature of New Jersey. The settlement of Communipaw in Bergen Township was still living off its farms and orchards. The locomotive in the upper right is an indication of 1850s "progress." The State Arms shows Liberty and Ceres (the latter holds the cornucopia), three ploughs, and a horse head. JCL*

Hook and Ladder Company No. 2 in West New York is pictured in this 1924 photograph. The police and fire departments were slow to organize in North Hudson County. By 1876 the whole area which is now Union City and West New York had only three fire houses. This particular fire station was built circa 1923, and today is H&L No. 6 at 22nd and Jackson streets. JCL

quality of tools. The best, like the engineers needed to design and use them, were British imports. These two obstacles bedeviled both John Stevens and Robert Fulton as they constructed their steamboats. Indeed after Fulton opened his drydock at Paulus Hook, accusations of theft of workmen intensified the rivalry between the two men. Fulton's shipyard in the Town of Jersey, which held much promise as a business catalyst, lasted only until his death in 1815. After that James Allaire purchased the equipment and moved the works to Cherry Street in New York.

The first firm in Bergen to employ numbers of workers unrelated to the owners was incorporated in 1825 to manufacture glass and porcelain. The Jersey City Porcelain and Earthenware Company used French and Irish artisans to make porcelain so fine that in its second year the company was awarded a silver medal at the exhibition of the Franklin Institute in Philadelphia. In 1829 David Henderson bought the plant and changed the product to a superior flint stoneware. Four years later in 1833 Henderson opened the American Pottery Manufacturing Company nearby. In a similar venture the Dummer brothers, Phineas and George, started the Jersey City Flint Glass Works which used the sandy soil of Paulus Hook to good advantage. Not only did these factories turn out quality merchandise, they also served as practical vocational schools where some of the best potters and glassblowers in America learned their craft.

The owners of these porcelain and glass factories also provide the earliest local example of corporate philanthropy. Many of their employees were Roman Catholics whose nearest church was in Manhattan. Perhaps these businessmen pitied the infants being borne across the river for baptism. Perhaps they realized that workers who did not travel to New York on Sunday would be more likely to appear promptly for work on Monday. Whatever their motives the Dummer brothers and David Henderson secured the part-time use of a public hall and then of St. Matthew's Episcopal Church for the Catholic congregation. They then obtained a lot on Grand Street and contributed building funds. In an example of interstate cooperation, the Catholics of New York volunteered to assist their New Jersey sisters and brothers, and the ferry company gave free transportation to these hundreds of helpers with their wagons and horses. After a construction setback, attributed to the marshy soil, they completed St. Peter's Church in 1837, the first Catholic church in Bergen.

An extraordinary effort produced the First Presbyterian Church of Jersey City. When a stone-steepled meetinghouse on Wall Street in New York was put up for sale, the Presbyterians bought it, carefully dismantled it, transported its numbered stones across the river, and meticulously re-erected it on Sussex Street. It served as their house of worship from 1845 until 1888.

Incrementally the society of Bergen Township was maturing, with Jersey City at Paulus Hook as the leader of change. New enterprises included distilleries, hotels, a jewelry workshop, a ropewalk where ship rigging was produced, and starch and sugar factories. After the failure of several commercial financial institutions, the Provident Savings Institution, the first savings bank in the state, was incorporated in 1839. To deal with the growing population and with the numbers of transients, four members of the earliest police force, called the Jersey City Watch, were appointed in 1837.

Firefighting was accomplished initially by bucket brigades using river water, but, as the city expanded, it became necessary to use more effective methods. In 1829 the first volunteer fire company was organized and, with great fanfare, a hose and engine were put into service. All the water, for firefighting and for every other purpose, was drawn from wells. The superior quality of the drinking water from the Bergen hill gave rise to a thriving business in which kegs of water from hill wells were delivered to the homes on the lowland in Jersey City.

Until 1828 Bergen citizens had to depend upon New York newspapers and upon the *Sentinel of Freedom,* published in Newark, but in that year a weekly began publication in Jersey City. Called the *Bergen County Gazette and Advertiser,* it was the first commercial response to the public's desire for news of the local community.

Although each village within the township made some provisions, often rude, for the schooling of their children, no formal structure existed for the intellectual needs of adults until the Jersey City Lyceum was organized in 1837. Its constitution specified that it was established by men who

. . . having in view the improvement of our minds, and the pleasant employment of a portion of our time, and believing that those objects can in few ways be more fully attained than by exercising the mind in literary composition, and in discussions of general subjects, have formed ourselves into an association for the accomplishment of these objects.

The Lyceum also lobbied, prematurely, for a public library.

The flights of Charles Durant and the success of the Edge fireworks business were only two examples of a new trend in society, the quest for organized recre-

ation, and ready to satisfy that quest were several enterprises. On Essex Street at Communipaw Cove in Jersey City, the Thatched Cottage Garden drew local people and New Yorkers for picnics, dancing, and sports. In June 1835 an enormous crowd gathered there to watch the rowboat race between two New York amateur boat clubs for a truly grand prize of $1,000. The course led from the Thatched Cottage around Bedloe's (now Liberty) Island and back to the starting point where the owner of the cottage added fifty dollars to the jackpot. Up on Bergen hill, near the present site of Christ Hospital, the Beacon racecourse attracted those who enjoyed gambling and horse racing. The finest local playground for adults, however, was designed by the always resourceful Stevens family.

Above
This nineteenth-century print is probably a scene of circa 1855, just after Castle Stevens was completed on top of Castle Point, Hoboken. JCL

Left
During the eighteenth century the Bayard family had a plantation in Hoboken and a chateau atop Castle Point. In 1780 the American patriots burned it, and in 1784 Colonel John Stevens bought the land from the new government of New Jersey. He built a mansion in 1835, three years before his death. The Stevens "Castle," seen in this 1955 photograph, replaced that building after a fire of circa 1851. From the Indicator (January 1955). Courtesy, Stevens Institute of Technology

John Stevens never tired in his efforts to promote Hoboken. When the steamboat monopoly thwarted his plan to provide swift and dependable transportation to and from New York, he proposed a bridge over the Hudson River and then a tunnel, large enough to accommodate carriages, to rest on the riverbed. He could find financing for neither, and he had to admit that his hopes for a flourishing city around Castle Point would not soon be fulfilled. Yet Stevens was clever enough to turn adversity to advantage, and he was blessed with talented sons who shared his dreams and advanced his projects. If Hoboken would not be the premier city on the west bank of the Hudson, it could be the leading pleasure

resort in the New York area.

Soon after 1821 when the Hoboken Steamboat Ferry was incorporated, the Hoboken shorefront and the hills leading to the Weehawken heights became a thriving amusement park and recreation area for the residents of crowded Manhattan. For the northern section, which they called the Elysian Fields, the Stevens family designed gardens and pathways. They laid out athletic fields and erected pavilions and colonnaded restaurants in the style of Greek temples. In southern Hoboken, near the ferry, they installed a circular railway track and a forerunner of the Ferris wheel. On the fields of Hoboken cricket teams competed, and there the first organized baseball game was played on June 19, 1846, when the Knickerbocker Club defeated the New York Club by a score of twenty-three to one.

In this sporting atmosphere John Cox Stevens, the oldest son of the colonel, was celebrated. Known as the leading yachtsman of his day, he organized the New York Yacht Club and in 1845 donated a clubhouse near the Elysian Fields which served the group for twenty years. In 1850 Stevens accepted a British challenge and, aided by his brother Edwin and by other sailing men including Colonel James Hamilton, the son of Alexander Hamilton, he contracted for a state-of-the-art yacht, the *America*. The next year this vessel, under the command of John Cox Stevens, defeated the entry of the prestigious Royal Yacht Squadron in a race around the Isle of Wight. The victors welcomed Queen Victoria and Prince Albert on board and then returned home, bringing with them their nation's first international trophy, the America's Cup.

In 1838, the year of Colonel Steven's death at the age of eighty-nine, the Hoboken Land and Improvement Company was organized to develop the amalgamated landholdings of the Stevens family. Hoboken's fame as a resort town continued until about 1850 when the encroaching population growth and industrial development made the land too valuable to remain a bucolic haven.

If thoughts of public sanitation, health care, education, and slavery are suppressed, these days of yore seem indeed to have been halcyon. There were beneficient employers, a decent level of prosperity, and public-spirited camaraderie. Yet the slow and steady pace of growth that produced these conditions would not endure. European political upheavals and natural catastrophes combined with American technological advances in transportation to make drastic changes in the size of the population, the types of work people did, and the very contour of the land. The industrial revolution was at hand, and it would quickly engulf Bergen.

Above
In 1838 the Stevens family formed the Hoboken Land and Improvement Company to develop their properties. This 1893 photograph shows the company at Newark and River streets. From Art Work of Hoboken *(1893)*

Top
The first yacht club house built in America is pictured in this circa 1900 photograph. The structure was built in 1845 to house John Cox Stevens' New York Yacht Club, which he organized in 1844 aboard his schooner Jimcrack. *JCL*

The Pace Accelerates

On April 26, 1825, a herd of Wall Street bulls stampeded off the ferry at Jersey City and raced west to an office building on Grand Street. There they succumbed to the latest speculative craze by buying up all the shares of the Morris Canal and Banking Company. The state of New Jersey, previously niggardly in its award of bank charters, had added banking privileges to the powers of the new firm as an inducement to investors. The ploy worked so well that the initial public offering of one million dollars was oversubscribed sevenfold. The capital was on hand to start work on a waterway that would cross the state from the Delaware River to the Hudson.

In the 1820s the United States was caught up in a mania for canals. The longest, the most exciting, and eventually the most profitable was the Erie Canal, which joined Lake Erie at Buffalo to the Hudson River at Albany. From the time construction began in 1817 until its successful completion in 1825, the Erie captured the imagination of the public as accounts of its progress encouraged similar schemes in other states. Sharing the enthusiasm were a number of men who proposed two canals across New Jersey. One would cut across the waist of the state and join the Delaware and Raritan rivers, from Bordentown to New Brunswick. The other, the Morris, would take a northern route. Ultimately both canals were built, and ultimately both failed, although the shorter and simpler Delaware and Raritan would outlast the longer and more complex Morris.

The specific idea for the Morris Canal is credited to George P. Macculloch, the president of the Morris County Agricultural Society. After more than a century of intense cultivation, the soil of Morris County was being depleted and no feasible way existed to ship fertilizers to the farms. Macculloch became convinced that a canal could alleviate the farmers' troubles and, of even greater importance, could rescue the dying iron mines of Morris and Sussex counties. These businesses consumed huge amounts of charcoal obtained from felled trees, but timber in the required quantity was becoming scarce. Deep in the fields of neighboring Pennsylvania was an abundant supply of coal which was being recognized as a suitable fuel for industrial purposes. The problem was finding a way to transport it.

The state's rivers could not help because they ran in the wrong direction. Pack horses were too slow and too unproductive for so heavy a product as Pennsylvania anthracite. A cross-state canal, however, could bring limitless quantities of coal to the mines and then carry away the finished iron products and the agricultural goods from farms along the

route. Fruits and vegetables, which per-
ished on an overland journey, would arrive fresh at market after a canal trip
and fertilizers could be shipped back. Finally, it was apparent that little manufacturing could develop until fuel became
available to power the factories. The canal, therefore, would be a catalyst for
new economic development as well as an
indispensable aid to existing businesses.

The route of the Morris Canal wound
northeast from Phillipsburg on the Delaware through Lake Hopatcong and Morris County to Paterson where it turned
and headed south to Newark. This hilly
region, which reached a peak of 914 feet
above sea level, posed a monumental
challenge to the canal engineers. Because
they deemed the traditional locks to be
inadequate, they opted for the innovative
use of inclined planes as a supplementary
way to surmount heights. For motive
power to pull the boats across the state,
the canal's planners stayed with the traditional sturdy mules walking on a towpath adjacent to the water.

The technical difficulties of building
the locks and the inclined planes were
compounded by the scarcity of workers
for digging. Irish peat bog cutters had
been recruited from their native land to
work on the Erie Canal and many shifted
to New Jersey when the New York project was finished, but even this foreign
supply of labor was insufficient for expe-
ditious construction. Furthermore, work
slowed in the summers as deadly Asiatic
cholera claimed many victims. Not until
April 1832 was water let in to allow traffic between the Delaware and Passaic
rivers, but even then the canal was not
complete because in 1827 a decision had
been made to extend it to Jersey City. The
fact that a great deal of waterfront property in Jersey City was owned by Cadwal-
lader Colden, the company's president,
may have encouraged the directors to
vote for the additional mileage. However,
the public and plausible reason was that
the small canal boats could not withstand
the stress of the long tow from Newark
Bay to New York. A terminal on the

Hudson was more suitable. It took until
1836 for the canal to arrive at its final
destination, a basin on the southern edge
of Paulus Hook.

The Morris Canal must be considered a
financial failure. Not until 1849 did it
make its first fair profit and only during
the 1860s was it truly prosperous. In 1871
the Lehigh Valley Railroad, a coal carrier, leased it for ninety-nine years. Unable
to run it profitably, the Lehigh concluded
that the canal's main asset was its Jersey
City waterfront property. The last year of
any appreciable use was 1902. A legislative committee made a trip on the canal
in 1912 and concluded that "from Jersey
City to Paterson it was little more than
an open sewer." In 1922 the state acquired the water rights and most of the
property and in 1925 a legislative act
provided for the canal's drainage.

The canal, though a financial disappointment, turned out to be a develop-
mental success. Towns along its path
were revived and the manufacturing ca-
pacities of both Newark and Jersey City
were stimulated by the ready access to
coal and iron which the canal provided.
This 104-mile waterway assured the commanding manufacturing position of
northeast New Jersey and particularly of
Hudson County.

The Morris Canal was limited by winter weather, by its leisurely pace, and
above all by its intrinsically local nature.
What was needed was a transportation
system flexible enough to serve small
towns and vast enough to open up the
heartland of the expanding American nation. Even before the canal reached the
Hudson River in 1836, men were cutting
through the Bergen hill to bring a railroad to the Jersey City waterfront. The
iron rail would replace the towpath and
would remain supreme for well over a
century.

With this new mode of travel and
transport, John Stevens and his family
once again demonstrated their acumen.
On February 6, 1815, he received the first
American charter to operate a railroad as
a common carrier. During the years of ca-

nal fever, Stevens proclaimed the anticipated superiority of rail travel, but he
was ridiculed as harebrained and, finding
no financial backing, let his charter lapse.
His vision was indeed in advance of the
manufacturing capabilities of his countrymen. No one in the United States was able
to build a locomotive until Stevens imported English mechanics and set them
up in a workshop. On May 13, 1826, his
efforts were rewarded when the first
steam locomotive in America circled a
track on his Hoboken property. This
demonstration and reports of success in
Great Britain quickly changed investors'
minds while the puffing engine appealed
to the public's fancy.

In 1830 a new state charter was granted
for a railroad called the Camden and
Amboy. Two of Stevens' sons, Robert
Livingston and Edwin Augustus, became
president and treasurer of the company
and over half of the stock was purchased
by the Stevens family. In 1831 the Camden and Amboy was "married" by legislative act to the Delaware and Raritan
Canal and the two potential rivals, now
known as the Joint Companies, were giv-
en a state monopoly to provide rail and
canal service between New York and
Philadelphia. In 1833 the rail line opened
with its British locomotive, the *John
Bull,* pulling its coaches between South
Amboy and Bordentown. By the end of
1838 new trackage connected Trenton to
New Brunswick.

The railroad bug was contagious and
new charters were swiftly granted by the
legislature. In 1831 the Paterson and
Hudson River Rail Road was organized
to cover a route from Paterson to Jersey
City. After bridging the Hackensack and
Passaic rivers and crossing the saturated
meadows of Secaucus, it lost its zeal
when confronted with the need to cut
through the Bergen hill. The young line
decided to deposit its passengers on the
west side of the hill where they could
board stagecoaches for the remainder of
the journey to the river front.

As they heard about the plans of the
first railroad companies, the people of

Newark, Jersey City, and Elizabeth pressed for their own rail link, and on March 7, 1832, with backing from New York financiers and the Associates of the Jersey Company, the New Jersey Railroad and Transportation Company was incorporated to connect Jersey City to New Brunswick. The company concluded an agreement with the Paterson and Hudson River Rail Road to share the costs of slicing through the Bergen hill at the Shanley Cut where the Journal Square Port Authority Trans-Hudson (PATH) station is now located. In order to provide through service to New York, the New Jersey Railroad obtained a lease of ferry rights from the Associates of the Jersey Company.

By the fall of 1834 a temporary track had been laid over the hill and horse-drawn trains were able to run from the Hudson River north to Paterson and west to Newark. Several more years were needed to complete the cut and to extend the line's southern route. Finally on New Year's Day, 1839, a steam-powered locomotive left Jersey City and connected with the Camden and Amboy at New Brunswick. Continuous rail service between the Hudson and Delaware rivers had officially begun, and the area that would soon become Hudson County would no longer be a small rural outpost.

In other parts of New Jersey and throughout the Northeast, numerous railroad companies were being organized, and industrial Darwinism prevailed as the weaker lines yielded to the stronger. The major trunk lines of the region vied with one another to lock into the traffic of the Port of New York. This was the railroads' idea of heaven, the largest market in America, and to achieve this paradise they had to enter through the pearly gates of the Hudson County waterfront.

In 1852 the New York and Erie Railroad leased the tracks of the Paterson and Hudson Rail Road and four years later bought more than 200 acres at Pavonia Avenue where it erected a new terminal on landfill. Because this site was more than a mile north of the old depot,

the Erie decided to blast a tunnel through the Bergen hill and so avoid a circuitous route through the cut. The heavy expense of this difficult excavation, followed by the Panic of 1857, brought the Erie to bankruptcy. It was rescued by an infusion of cash from a small New Jersey line, the Morris and Essex, controlled at the time by the Stevens family. Work resumed and in November 1860 a locomotive steamed through the first tunnel through the Bergen hill.

The Morris and Essex had been struggling along as a small passenger railroad until Edwin Stevens bought a majority interest in the line as a flanking effort to protect the Camden and Amboy. Stevens' influence with the legislature was immense, and he easily won authorization for a projected extension of the Morris and Essex to Hoboken. After it bailed out the Erie, this small line's assets included the use of the new Bergen tunnel and the right to build its own waterfront depot. Then the Delaware, Lackawanna, and Western, a rich coal carrier, made an overture to discuss leasing arrangements, and the Morris and Essex was receptive. In 1868 an agreement between the two lines gave the DL & W control of the M & E and thus access to Hoboken. Another major railway had arrived at the Hudson River. Within a few years the Lackawanna would excavate its own Bergen hill tunnel and expand its terminal facilities southward from Hoboken into neighboring Jersey City.

"The Big Little Railroad," the Jersey Central, grew from a local mid-state line officially renamed The Central Rail Road Company of New Jersey in 1849. By 1852 the Central ran from Phillipsburg to Elizabeth where its passengers transferred to the New Jersey Railroad for the trip to Jersey City. Throughout the 1850s the Jersey Central petitioned the state in vain for an extension to the Hudson River, but this was opposed successfully by the New Jersey Railroad, which wanted to keep the lucrative transfer business. Then in 1860 the Central's president, John T. Johnston, approached the Camden and Amboy and made a deal on splitting western business. Within three weeks the state legislature responded with the required authorization to construct a drawbridge over Newark Bay. The Central purchased extensive acreage at Communipaw and more land at Bergen Point; its properties on the shore covered two and one-half miles. The first locomotive chugged over the bridge on August 1, 1864, and the Central's Communipaw ferry to Liberty Street in New York started shortly afterward.

The influence of the Camden and Amboy has only been suggested by the part it played in bringing the Jersey Central to the Hudson River. Awarded a monopoly on traffic between New York and Philadelphia in 1831, it dominated the state legislature for nearly forty years. Its taxes, known as transit duties paid by through passengers, and its dividends on the 2,000 shares it had given to the state filled the treasury of New Jersey. The legislators had every motive for maintaining the monopoly. For many years the state obtained all its general revenues from railroads and had no need for other forms of taxation. Local shippers, who did not pay transit duties, shared the lawmakers' delight.

This cozy arrangement was bitterly criticized by New York and Philadelphia business interests, which resented the transit duties and the high rates charged by the Camden and Amboy. Within New Jersey also there were many vocal anti-monopolists, but their numbers dwindled when out-of-state assaults were made upon the Camden and Amboy. Remembering the obstacles that had been placed in New Jersey's way by its more powerful neighbors, even New Jerseyans who disliked the monopoly tended to support it when outsiders attacked it.

The protection of the monopoly did not produce superior service on the Camden and Amboy. Not until the Civil War did it install double tracks, and its accident record was not admirable. In contrast the New Jersey Railroad between Jersey City and New Brunswick was

Top
This print of 1866 shows the great slaughterhouses at Philip Street near Bramhall Avenue on the Communipaw, or South, Cove in Jersey City. This "abbatoir" of the New Jersey Stock Yard & Market Company was opened in this year, but with the landfilling development by the Central Rail Road of New Jersey, the cove was filled and these slaughterhouses were nonexistent by 1887. From Frank Leslie's Illustrated Newspaper (November 17, 1866)

Bottom
In urban areas trains presented serious dangers to pedestrians and traffic on the streets crossing the tracks. To eliminate grade crossings elevated tracks were constructed. This circa 1890 print depicts Railroad Avenue as it crosses Newark Avenue in Jersey City. These tracks were built by the Pennsylvania Railroad about 1890 and were 3,000 feet long. The inhabitants of the tenements, into whose windows the coal smoke blew, were not comfortable. A station of the PATH tubes is now at this intersection, but the elevated tracks were demolished in the mid-1960s. JCL

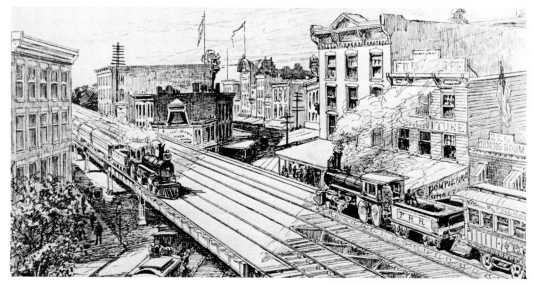

highly regarded for its passenger service, safety, and lower fares. In 1853 the New Jersey floated bonds worth $485,000 and with the proceeds purchased the property as well as the water and ferry privileges of the Associates of the Jersey Company. It then embarked upon a major expansion program at Jersey City. To accommodate a new depot and ferry slips, the New Jersey built out into the river on landfill and created the area known as Exchange Place. By 1858 its ferries to New York ran at ten-minute intervals during the day and fifteen minutes apart after 10 p.m.

Although the New Jersey and the Camden and Amboy shared traffic, the managements grew increasingly unfriendly

and both lines hatched plans to invade the other's territory. In 1860 and 1861 these two rivals engaged in legal battles. After the New Jersey Railroad lost, the Camden and Amboy altered its mood and decided to conciliate. Its monopoly would expire in 1869, and prudence dictated that it husband its resources to fight the anticipated entry into its market by the mighty Pennsylvania Railroad Company. Accordingly, starting in 1863 the New Jersey Railroad and the Camden and Amboy suppressed their hostility and embarked upon a process which ended in the consolidation of the two lines. An agreement approved by the legislature on February 27, 1867, produced a merger. The new entity would be known as the

Artist J. Lauber's print was published in 1880 and shows Christmas Day at a longshoreman's church, Jersey City. Over the door are the words "Free Union," which indicates that this is probably a Protestant boat-chapel. There is a model of a ship hanging inside the chapel. Actual churches—especially wood-frame, Gothic Revival-style churches—were often built with exposed-beam ceilings, like the interior of a ship. In this print, one sees the many masts of the Hudson River docks. JCL

United Railroads and Canal Companies of New Jersey.

During the Civil War the New Jersey Railroad obtained a sizable amount of freight traffic, and it began to eye the Harsimus Cove area north of its terminal as a likely site for the expansion of its freight capacity. The merger with the Camden and Amboy made possible the purchase in 1867 and 1868 of 1,300 feet of waterfront south of the Erie, a total of about seventy acres of land, most of it underwater. Of the total cost of $1,500,000 $500,000 went to the state for riparian rights. Yet the business of the United Companies did not increase at a sufficient pace to pay for the development of this new acquisition. Moreover, the monopoly was about to expire and the

Pennsylvania Railroad had been exerting pressure to lease the Jersey City terminal and the tracks across New Jersey. The Pennsylvania, which by now ran to the Midwest, had the funds to transform the Harsimus Cove area into a major freight facility, but it did not own the property. The United Companies owned the property but lacked the capital. The inevitable agreement was reached. In 1871 the Pennsylvania leased the United Companies and immediately undertook a lengthy and expensive upgrading of the Jersey City plant. The fourth major trunk line had gobbled up a big chunk of the Hudson River waterfront. As the mayor of Jersey City lamented, "We might as well be an inland city."

VI

Civil War
and
Civic Maneuvers

Even though New Jersey was the only northern state to vote against Lincoln, ultimately about one in eight of its residents entered the Civil War. Hudson County's terminals were the embarkation points for many Union soldiers going to the fronts. This print shows the Sixth Regiment of Massachusetts Volunteers leaving the New Jersey Railroad and Transportation depot in Jersey City. Many Union flags are waving. From Frank Leslie's Illustrated Newspaper (April 18,1861)

The people of southern Bergen County had legitimate complaints. Every property owner who wished to record a deed, every businessman involved in a civil suit, and every summoned juror had to trudge north to Hackensack, the county seat. To accommodate them the legislature, on February 22, 1840, organized Bergen Township, southern Lodi Township, and Jersey City into a new county to be called Hudson. At the same time the lawmakers at Trenton sanctioned the creation of Harrison Township from the New Barbadoes Neck section of Lodi. As the site of their new court the voters selected a central point in Bergen Township near Five Corners. Covering forty-six square miles of land, Hudson is the smallest county in size and the most densely populated in New Jersey.

The explosive growth which followed the canal and railroads to Hudson County also produced demands for the subdivision of Bergen Township into smaller and more manageable local units. The first break had occurred in 1838 when Jersey City became independent. Three years later the contiguous settlement of Harsimus obtained its own charter and became Van Vorst Township; in 1851 it merged with Jersey City. The biggest amputation from Bergen occurred in 1843 when the area between the New Jersey Railroad cut and the border with Bergen

County broke away to become North Bergen. In 1849 Hoboken Township severed its ties to North Bergen and in 1855 acquired a city charter.

North Bergen was further reduced when Hudson Town, just north of the railroad, was formed in 1852 and in three years became Hudson City. In 1859 a real estate development called Guttenberg was settled within North Bergen and, in the same year, Weehawken became independent. Two years later West Hoboken Township and Union Township broke away.

By the time the Civil War began in 1861, the shape of present-day north Hudson was apparent but not complete. In the succeeding decades additional changes altered municipal charters and brought new communities into legal existence. Hoboken, Weehawken, and West Hoboken swapped land. Guttenberg, which became part of Union Township in 1861, became independent in 1878. Union Town was set off in 1864 from Union Township, which, in turn, was replaced by West New York in 1898. Secaucus broke away from North Bergen in 1900. Finally the last municipal boundary change within Hudson County occurred on June 1, 1925, when Union Town, usually known as Union Hill, merged with West Hoboken to become Union City. Despite all these losses of territory,

46

Above
This 1959 photograph shows the parade on Bergenline Avenue, celebrating the founding of Guttenberg. Barrels of beer from Guttenberg breweries were delivered by wagons such as this one. JCL

Top, far right Weehawken's bluffs on the Hudson were the site for the large Palisades Amusement and Exhibition Company's El Dorado Park during the 1890s. Like other cities in Hudson County, Weehawken also had a period of being New York's playground. From Art Work of Hoboken (1893)

North Bergen remains as a sizable independent township.

The separation process continued in the south. As one writer said, "Bergen was like a fine Dutch cheese exposed to busy mice. It was nibbled at from all sides." In 1861 Bayonne Township, the peninsula south of the Morris Canal, was removed from Bergen and in 1869 became Bayonne City. It acquired a sliver of its northern neighbor about 1890. In 1863 Greenville, the area north of Bayonne, became an independent township. Finally Bergen Town was formed in 1855 and absorbed what remained of the original Bergen Township in 1862.

In west Hudson, Harrison lost the area north of the Paterson Plank Road to Bergen County in 1852. Then Kearny became independent of Harrison in 1867 and in turn lost East Newark when this new borough was organized in 1895.

All these changes were practical responses to natural and man-made land formations and to ethnic divisions. Yet just as the process of splitting into smaller units reached its climax, the idea of municipal consolidation gained currency.

In the 1860s the native-born residents of Jersey City felt overwhelmed by the rapidly increasing number of immigrants. To escape, many moved to the Bergen hill where they built spacious homes on lots carved from the farms of the Dutch. This land went on the market when the old farms lost their competitive edge once the railroads began to carry produce from other counties and states into the metropolitan area. The old-time residents who remained in Jersey City realized that the newcomers were gaining political power, and they tried to fight this trend with a plan to expand the municipal borders to include more native-born Americans. The prospect of increased efficiency was also put forth as a compelling reason to consolidate independent towns and cities. Accordingly a vote was taken in April 1869 to decide if all the municipalities east of the Hackensack River should be unified into one great city. Bergen, Hudson City, and Jersey City voted in favor, and a merger of the three was completed in 1870. Union Town and the Township of Union also voted affirmatively, but because West Hoboken, which lay between Union Town and Hudson City, rejected the proposal, these north Hudson communities remained independent. In 1873 Greenville joined Jersey City which thereby acquired its present borders.

The 1870 consolidation did not work out as its proponents had hoped. Because the immigrants continued to win at the polls, the native-born state legislators from Hudson County tried a different tactic. In 1871 their colleagues in the state capital voted a new charter for Jersey City which transferred many of the powers of local government from the aldermen to commissioners appointed in Trenton. The police force, for example, came under the jurisdiction of such commissioners. The elected local officials also lost the right to let contracts for public works. The aldermanic districts were revamped and the immigrants gerrymandered into the U-shaped Horseshoe section. Executive powers were not restored to elected commissioners until 1877.

The touted advantages of efficiency were also lost in the consolidation as a result of financial scheming compounded by the depressive effects of the Panic of 1873. Bergen and Hudson City had lagged behind Jersey City in initiating public improvements and, when merger became likely, these two municipalities embarked upon extensive building and bonding programs in the expectation that the costs would be distributed among all the citizens of the enlarged city. Contributing to the disarray was the excessive spending of the commissioners led by William Bumstead. As a result, the consolidation started inauspiciously with the need for sharp tax increases. Then the municipal treasurer, Alexander D. Hamilton, skipped town for Mexico with all the city's cash and bonds. Jersey City was in practical default. City employees went unpaid, and schoolteachers were laid off. Financial recovery took many years.

The immigrants who so alarmed the native-born Americans were principally the Irish who began to come to the United States in significant numbers about 1820. The early arrivals included some artisans, farmers, and many strong men who dug the canals and built the first railroads. But in the mid-1840s tens of thousands of refugees from the failed potato crop emigrated, many sent on their way by English landlords who found it cheaper to buy ocean passage for their

tenants than to feed them. These men crowded into a job market diminished by the lingering effects of the Panic of 1837 and threatened to lower the pay rates of the native workers. In addition to these economic consequences the Irish were Roman Catholic, a religion alien to the dominant Protestants. The natives were dismayed and frightened by these foreigners in their midst.

The fear was widespread throughout the United States and expressed itself in the Know-Nothing party and in numerous nativist organizations. Most of the Hudson County newspapers adopted this anti-immigrant position. Nonetheless

Above
This plate from Art Work of Hoboken *shows Bergenline Avenue in Union Hill. JCL*

Top
In 1883 this house passed into the hands of James Flemming, a prominent criminal lawyer. Flemming's parlor, pictured, had antique bronzes and paintings. JCL

Right
From the 1840s Irish and German immigrants began to populate Hudson County. This 1904 photograph shows a group of musicians at Adolf Daniel's Music Conservatory, just behind Saint Matthew's German Lutheran church in Hoboken. Music playing was a major source of entertainment before the radio and phonograph, and Daniel's pupils—of several ages and both sexes—seem proud to have learned their various instruments. Photo by W. Manewal. JCL

Right
From the 1840s Irish and German immigrants began to populate Hudson County. This 1904 photograph shows a group of musicians at Adolf Daniel's Music Conservatory, just behind Saint Matthew's German Lutheran church in Hoboken. Music playing was a major source of entertainment before the radio and phonograph, and Daniel's pupils—of several ages and both sexes—seem proud to have learned their various instruments. Photo by W. Manewal. JCL

Opposite page
The sturdy-looking Romanesque style in architecture was made nationally popular circa 1870 to 1886 by the eminent H.H. Richardson. This Richardsonian-Romanesque style structure is Public School Number 6 in Hoboken. It was designed by the architects Beyer and McCann in 1891 and was built that year at Willow Avenue and 11th Street on land obtained from the Hoboken Land and Improvement Company. The red brick schoolhouse was renamed the Wallace School after three World War II heroes, and in 1972 it was demolished to make way for a modern Wallace School.
Art Work of Hoboken (1893)

there were many more miles of railroad track to be laid, and millions more pieces of coal to be carted, and a myriad of other menial jobs to be performed; the newcomers were needed. The Irish displayed a knack for gaining political power which, once attained, they held as tenaciously as any Dutch farmer had ever kept his land.

Late in the 1840s the Germans began their immigration to the United States. For some America was a refuge from the European year of revolution, 1848. But most saw their new home as the proverbial land of opportunity where their energies and talents would be richly rewarded. The Germans arrived as skilled apprentices with commercial and entrepreneurial ambitions. From small shops they advanced to the ownership of large breweries and other manufacturing enterprises. Split along religious lines they banded together ethnically in a multitude of clubs for gymnastics, for music, and for mutual benefit. They transformed north Hudson and Hoboken by creating cities where there had been only hamlets.

The Germans opened hotels, restaurants, and butcher shops and entered the building trades. The Hoboken waterfront

became the East Coast home of several German steamship lines. Schools in Hoboken instructed their pupils in the German language. Culturally the Teutonic influence was felt also in German-language churches and newspapers and in places like Schuetzen Park in North Bergen, which grew from a shooting club to become a major recreational center.

It would be an exaggeration to claim that the Germans were welcomed enthusiastically by the American natives; their beer gardens, particularly those open on Sunday, and the number of freethinkers in their midst were a constant scandal to those natives who were rigorously religious. Despite these difficulties the Germans were readily assimilated, and they prospered. Though not such avid politicians as the Irish, they did participate in local government, and they produced a number of civic leaders.

The newcomers to Hudson County who achieved the most rapid acceptance were the thousands of New Yorkers who moved to Jersey City and Hoboken starting in the 1840s. For the most part these were businessmen who found overland commuting in expanding Manhattan too tiresome. Travel by ferry had more appeal than a long haul northward from their stores and offices in the commercial district. Possessing moderate wealth they built the brick and brownstone homes which are the focus of current historic preservation efforts. They also entered the political fray, and from their numbers came many of the mayors elected between 1838 and 1869. They were the forerunners of the tens of thousands of commuters who continue to make the daily trip between New York and New Jersey.

As all these changes were generating their own steam in Hudson County, the issue of slavery was firing the nation at large. Toward this pernicious institution the people of New Jersey historically had demonstrated mixed reactions. In the northern and eastern sections of the state, especially in the farm communities where the Dutch had settled, slavery had been commonplace. In the 1800 census Bergen County recorded 18.97 percent blacks among its population. In western New Jersey, however, the Society of Friends exerted strong moral pressure in favor of abolition. As early as 1696 the Quakers voted to recommend that their fellows cease further importation of slaves.

The Quaker influence grew in strength and, after the Revolution, legal restrictions were placed upon slave owners, which included their obligation to teach black children to read and write. In 1804 the state's abolitionists obtained new legislation that provided for the gradual elimination of slavery. It was not until 1846, however, that it was abolished by statute in New Jersey, and even this law substituted apprenticeship for slavery. This change of status continued many of the practical arrangements which had existed, but it gave the new apprentices some rights. They could not be sold without their written consent; their children were to be absolutely free; and they acquired the same legal remedies against their masters as did white apprentices and servants.

Legally the slaves had few rights, but the courts of New Jersey had dealt liber-

ally with the issue of manumission; when the evidence was inconclusive, the presumption of freedom was made. Some freedmen even voted. The state constitution of 1776 granted the franchise to "all inhabitants of this Colony" who met fixed property and residency requirements, and both women and freed slaves cast ballots in early state elections. This unwitting loophole was eliminated by statute in 1807, and the constitution of 1844 limited the vote to white men.

Slaves in New Jersey performed a wide variety of jobs as laborers, stablemen, stage drivers, boatmen, miners, bakers, cooks, and personal servants. Female slaves became spinners, barbers, and nurses and performed general household tasks. At the time of the Civil War, the native blacks of New Jersey possessed employment skills suitable for an urban situation. The last slaves recorded in Hudson County were shown in the federal census of 1850 when one was reported in Harrison and two in North Bergen. In 1860 "colored" persons numbered 648 in a total Hudson County population of 62,717.

In 1850 Congress passed the Fugitive Slave Law, and slave hunting in the North became profitable. Responding to

Cities in Hudson County were assigned quotas for Civil War recruits in 1864. This 1901 photograph is of a Union veterans' group in front of a beer garden in West New York. The sign at left reads "Union Brewery, Lager Bier." JCL

this challenge were the abolition societies that helped the runaway slaves flee to freedom. For many blacks the goal was free Canada. By covered wagons, stages, and sometimes by train they traveled northward hoping to board a night train to Albany or a Hudson River boat heading for the Erie Canal. Because of its position as a transportation hub, Jersey City became an important station on this Underground Railway. The principal local agents of the abolitionists were John Everett and Peter James Phillips. Some blacks were hidden at the home of Dr. Henry Holt on Washington Street, others

at the Holden Observatory on Clifton Place. When the coast was clear, they were slipped onto the ferry or hidden in the cargo bays of the coal boats leaving the Morris Canal basin for upstate New York. The boat owners, glad for the free labor, cooperated willingly or else were paid off by the abolitionists. Although this movement was necessarily conducted in great secrecy with no records maintained, it is estimated that up to 60,000 slaves went through Jersey City.

When the Civil War erupted in 1861, the immediate response of the people of Hudson County was to rally patriotically around the Union flag, even though New Jersey had been the only northern state to vote against Lincoln. Anticipating that the war would be swiftly concluded, men volunteered for three-month terms as members of the Second Regiment of New Jersey. Yet as the hostilities wore on, the original enthusiasm for military service dissipated, and Congress had to resort to a draft. This was resisted by the poor and circumvented by the wealthy. The calls of 1864 which assigned quotas to each city aroused great anxieties, and the individual municipalities had to pay bounties nearing $700 per man to supply the numbers required. By this time the war had taken so great a toll that only the most desperate would exchange their service for the proffered sum. Neighboring cities competed among themselves to raise troops by topping each other's offers. Some Hudson County men who were willing to enlist enrolled in Newark or Elizabeth, which paid higher amounts of cash than did their hometowns. To raise these bounties the cities issued bonds which had to be paid off when the war ended.

Among the many Hudson men who fought valiantly on their nation's battlefields, one stood out as a model of gallantry, skill, and courage. He was Phillip Kearny of Harrison, a natural soldier who gloried in war and excelled at it. "You must never be afraid of anything," he told his junior officers. The French Legion of Honor had been his reward for voluntary service in Algeria and in Italy. He had leaped at the chance to fight in the Mexican War, where he earned many honors at the price of losing his left arm. At the start of the Civil War Lincoln selected Kearny to be Brigadier General in charge of New Jersey troops. On September 1, 1862, he died at the Battle of Chantilly in Virginia. When the Republican residents of north Harrison successfully obtained their independence from Democratic south Harrison in 1867, they named their new community Kearny to honor their fallen neighbor.

When the conflict ended another war

hero moved to Hudson County. Sergeant Decatur Dorsey, a former Maryland slave, had enlisted in the 39th Regiment of the United States Colored Troops and, for his bravery during the Battle of Petersburg in 1864, was awarded the Congressional Medal of Honor. After the war, Dorsey and his wife settled in Hoboken where they lived until their deaths in the 1890s. Both are buried in North Bergen's Flower Hill Cemetery.

Despite the human anguish and the financial drain which the war inflicted, it also produced some beneficial side effects for Hudson County. As troops from New York and New England waited in Jersey City to board trains to take them to battle, they were greeted by women from local churches who manned canteens and served food and hot beverages to the young soldiers. When the wounded returned in hospital trains, they were tended by volunteers who did what they could to make them comfortable. Other volunteers made bandages and organized fairs to raise funds for medical care. This large scale altruistic activity was the first of numerous philanthropic endeavors carried out by Hudson County women in the decades to come.

The war effort was obvious throughout the county. The federal government set up a camp in West Hoboken. Local business gained as it supplied the Union army with uniforms, food, weapons, ammunition, and transportation. Charles Knapp of Harrison amassed a fortune manufacturing guns. To accommodate war traffic the long overdue double tracks were laid on the Camden and Amboy Railroad. The Joseph Dixon Crucible Company in Jersey City began the manufacture of lead writing sticks for use by soldiers in the field, a product which quickly developed into the profitable line of Ticonderoga pencils. Steel makers and shipbuilders flourished, among them the Secors Company, which constructed six iron clad monitor ships in its Jersey City drydock. The Irrepressible Conflict accelerated the pace of the industrialization of Hudson County.

VII

Different Accents

Although a few Italian immigrants had arrived earlier, a great many came in the 1880s. To serve them Italian Catholic churches were established. This is the 1923 wedding picture of Ralph and Mary Piciullo, who were married in Holy Rosary Church, founded in Jersey City in 1885. Courtesy, Church of the Holy Rosary

The figures rate a second look. In 1840 only 9,483 people were sparsely dispersed throughout Hudson County. Thirty years later the population numbered 129,067. By 1910 the total was 537,231. The pace continued until the peak of 690,730 reached in 1930.

Tens of thousands of the "wretched refuse" of the teeming shores of Europe were crowding into Hudson County. They found work, usually menial, and housing, mostly shabby, and added their own ingredients to the melting pot. Italians, Poles, Slovaks, Russians, and Ukrainians joined the Irish and the Germans as the major ethnic forces fighting for a share of the American promise. Immigrants came from Hungary, Greece, and Holland, from Great Britain and from Scandinavia, and from all the European lands—Hudson County was truly a home for all nations. The newcomers from Europe brought only their energy and raw strength to America, but they found employers willing to hire them. A synergistic blend of transportation, manufacturing, and labor made Hudson County an industrial powerhouse.

It would have been delightful to report that all these different people cooperated with one another and that the more established ethnic groups assisted the newcomers. Of course this did not happen. Uninspired human nature prevailed as

differences were scorned and exploited. The Irish lorded it over the Italians; the Poles congratulated themselves for not being Russian; the natives maintained their sense of social, if not numerical, superiority. Reinforcing this separateness was the tendency of nationalities to congregate in their own neighborhoods, to shop in their own stores, and to prefer their own company. These attitudes formed in the late nineteenth century would persist and would shape county politics decades later.

In addition to these local effects, the preponderance of the foreign born among the population placed Hudson County across a psychological divide from rural New Jersey, while ties to New York were strengthened by the similarity of the population on both sides of the Hudson River. The people of Hudson County continued to be more attuned to Manhattan than to Trenton, even though the legislators in the state capitol had the power to affect their tax rates, riparian rights, and corporate prerogatives.

As the number of people increased, the farms dwindled and eventually disappeared everywhere but in Secaucus, which retained an agricultural character until the mid-twentieth century. The first community to become urbanized was Jersey City, the home of so many factories that it justified its welcoming slogan

Above
In 1845 David La Tourette bought Bon Sejours, *the former mansion of Victor Du Pont. La Tourette had a dock built and reconstructed and expanded the wood-frame building into this large Gothic-Revival style hotel. From the* Bayonne Centennial Historical Revue *(1961) by W.F. Robinson*

Top
Some boys and a priest in front of Hoboken's city hall on Washington and Newark streets are pictured in this circa 1900 photograph. The city was incorporated in 1855, and this block was the market square owned by the Hoboken Land & Improvement Company until 1880, when it was conveyed to the city. JCL

"Everything for Industry." Hoboken with its railroads and busy piers followed. As Hoboken declined as a resort town, Bayonne briefly took its place. Its southern waterfront attracted a clientele more wealthy than the day-trippers who had boarded the ferry for an outing at the Elysian Fields. At the 200-room LaTourette Hotel at Bergen Point, fashionable people from New York, Pennsylvania, and Washington, D.C., spent relaxing summer weeks escaping the heat of the cities. General Ulysses S. Grant and the Emperor of Brazil were among the guests who sunned on the broad veranda and gazed at the Staten Island hills. Yet gracious Bayonne, the home of oystermen, yielded to the Industrial Revolution in the late 1870s when the Tide Water Oil Company and the Standard Oil Company built refineries and pipeline terminals at Constable Hook. In the next decades major chemical plants, foundries, and a multitude of other factories located in the Peninsula City.

The west Hudson communities, so close to bustling Newark, were also favored by manufacturers. In the early 1840s a japanning factory in Harrison provided modest employment. Following this lead came box makers, stove works, tanners, and wire, trunk, and shade roller factories. Peter Hauck ran a large brewery in Harrison, and in 1880 Thomas Edison rented space and employed over 200 workers to turn out his new electric lamps in a factory which was the forerunner of the General Electric plant. In the 1870s a spinning and spool mill mushroomed into the works of the Clark Thread Mills situated in the section that would become East Newark. The smokestack of the Clark O.N.T. (Our New Thread) mills was for many years the tallest in America.

To man the thread and linoleum firms, workers from Scotland were recruited and their descendants became the dominant group in Kearny. Swedes and Belgians were attracted to the northern section known as Arlington. In Harrison the Irish and later the Italians and the

Poles formed the major groups.

In north Hudson the earliest commercial enterprise, aside from scattered mills and taverns, had been the venture known as the Frenchman's Garden located at the site of the present-day Machpelah Cemetery in North Bergen. Here, shortly after the close of the American Revolution, Andre Michaux, who boasted that he was an agent of the king of France, acquired about thirty acres for horticultural experiments. Michaux and his associates claimed credit for introducing several foreign plants to America, among them the Lombardy poplars with which he landscaped the new Town of Jersey. Another local business rose from the processing of cattails and other plants growing wild in the Hackensack meadows. These weeds, converted into thatch for roofs and rush for chairs, gave winter employment to the nearby farmers.

On the northern Bergen hill the flourishing oak trees were eagerly sought by the shipbuilders of New York. Weehawken heights with a commanding view of the Hudson became a suburban retreat dotted with the substantial summer homes of the wealthy from neighboring cities. In 1852 the ferry at lower Weehawken was incorporated and the old ferry service was revived.

Heavy industry never dominated north Hudson and Secaucus. Instead a melange of small businesses catering to regional needs developed, among them wholesale florists, breweries, and silk mills. Italians worked in the dye shops of West Hoboken, and German Jews labored in cigar factories. From the rock of the Palisades stone was quarried to supply the Belgian blocks which paved the streets of New York. Starting in the 1880s the north Hudson communities became home to the largest Swiss colony in the eastern United States. These immigrants created the Schiffli industry, which remains the major source of embroidery in America.

In the decades following the Civil War the tremendous industrial expansion of the United States, so apparent in Hudson County, was cheered by those who cor-

rectly saw this growth as the source of America's wealth. But others discerned the human cost of the nation's riches. For the factory workers, for the railroad crews, for the laborers who dug the ditches, life was often a bleak succession of days of unremitting toil and of nights in pestilential "living" quarters. The constantly replenished supply of unskilled immigrants kept wages low and working conditions harsh.

A good case may be made that among all who tried to help the working man his best friend was his neighborhood saloon. When he was out of work, the bartender

Above
The former Clark's ONT Thread Works in East Newark, built about 1881, are depicted in 1985. The Clark Thread Mills were the wonder of residents and visitors because of their "huge proportions." Photo by Joseph C. Brooks

Right
Dr. George Epps Cannon, seen in a photograph from circa 1910, received his medical degree from the New York Homeopathic Medical College and Flower Hospital in 1900. From that year he practiced medicine in Jersey City and was very active in advocating the political rights of black people. His sister Etta P. Cannon became the first black to be principal of a public school in Jersey City. Courtesy, Lafayette Presbyterian Church, Jersey City

In 1861 West Hoboken separated from North Bergen. In 1889 businessman and builder Otto Schultz began developing Bergenline Avenue in West Hoboken, and in 1890 this colorful, brick, French-chateau style bank, the Hudson Trust and Savings Institute, was built on the northeast corner of the avenue and the Hackensack Plank Road (32nd Street). This photograph was taken circa 1893. The building was demolished in 1921 when a granite, Classical-Roman style bank was built. West Hoboken merged with Union to form Union City in 1925. From Art Work of Hoboken *(1893)*

gave him that supposedly nonexistent commodity, a free lunch. When he was a bachelor living in a rooming house, his tavern cronies became his family. When he had neither time nor money for picnics or sports, he went to the corner bar for recreation. The saloon was more than a solace at the end of a hard day; it was a meeting place where the politically ambitious could win votes and where the labor activist could find recruits. One of Hudson County's towns was born figuratively in a tavern or Wein-stube in Manhattan where German employees of the Hoe Company were griping about their crowded surroundings. For a change of scene they planned an outing in New Jersey. When they climbed the Bergen hill, they were so enchanted by the clean air and the sweeping vista that they determined to move there as a group. Thus was Union Hill settled in 1851.

The saloon, of course, had its enemies who triumphed during the Prohibition era, but it filled a basic need. It was not, however, a social agency. To get at the roots of urban ills and to remedy them, new institutions arose. Among them were labor unions; hospitals; homes for the care of children, the aged, and the handicapped; schools and colleges; and philanthropic endeavors. Although they did not

create an Eden, they had considerable impact and produced significant and long-range changes.

The labor movement's earliest activities in Hudson County took place before the Civil War. In the 1870s and 1880s attempts to organize workers on an industry-wide basis failed in the face of determined resistance by business abetted by government. The Knights of Labor, which experienced a meteoric rise in the 1880s only to fade in the 1890s, sponsored several strikes in the area. In 1887, when the port of New York was shut down, rioting occurred in Hoboken and Weehawken as strike-breakers were brought in under Pinkerton protection. At the same time the Knights backed another unsuccessful action, this time at the large Lorillard tobacco plant in Jersey City. Not until the 1930s, with the formation of the CIO and the protection of federal laws, did industry-wide labor organization become successful.

In the meantime others made brief appearances upon the labor stage. Friedrich Sorg, a longtime resident of Hoboken and a friend of Karl Marx, became general secretary of the International Working-Man's Association and in 1878 organized the silk workers of Paterson. The Industrial Workers of the World, known as the Wobblies, opened a local unit in Jersey City in 1905 and, in 1915, when the coopers and the still cleaners refused to work at the Bayonne plant of the Standard Oil Company, the IWW provided leadership. This strike and another one in 1916 convinced Standard Oil to give benefits to its employees and to encourage unionism, but the price was high. At least ten lives were lost, strike leaders were fired, and ethnic resentments intensified between the Italian, Polish, and Slovak workers and their second generation Irish foremen.

Only the trade unions which organized along craft lines were genuinely effective. Representing skilled workers such as masons, printers, and telegraphers, they protected their members from the enormous pool of unskilled labor as well as from

Left
This senior class pho-
tograph must be from
the early part of the
twentieth century,
judging from the girls'
Mary Pickford-like
curls. The school is
Saint Michael's Catho-
lic High School in
West Hoboken (Union
City), and the school
building still stands.
This Catholic school at
New York (formerly
Clinton) Avenue and
15th (formerly High)
Street was erected in
1896 by the Passionist
Fathers, whose former
monastery church
dominates Union City
architecturally. JCL

their employers. Affiliated with the American Federation of Labor, they and the railroad unions carried the torch for the labor movement for several generations.

Slowly and reluctantly government on different levels began to consider the human needs of its citizens. In 1826 Bergen Township had located its first almshouse on a farm in Secaucus. In the same area Hudson County erected a penitentiary in 1869, where it was anticipated that the prisoners could break up the marketable traprock of Snake Hill. Then in 1873 a county insane asylum was added, making Secaucus the principal home of Hudson County's welfare institutions. The state established a home for disabled soldiers in Newark in 1866 and moved it to Kearny in 1888. In 1915 the state opened a parental home in Bayonne. As its contribution to the commonweal, the federal government yielded to the complaints of New York State, which had maintained an immigration reception office at Castle Garden, and assumed responsibility for the multitudes arriving in America. In 1892 it opened the federal immigrant sta-

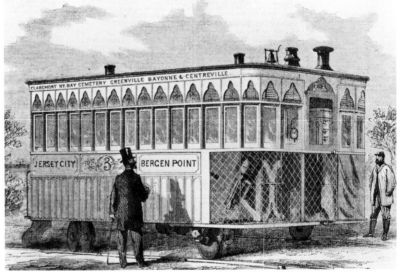

tion on Ellis Island, just off the Jersey City shore. This symbol of simultaneous hope and fear processed as many as 5,000 arrivals per day. Once they cleared the scrutiny of the inspectors, many took the boats to Hudson County where they settled down for their great adventure.

This modest level of care provided by governmental units was augmented by private and religious efforts to help those

Above
In 1863 the Jersey
City and Bergen Rail-
road finished these
trolley tracks from
"The Junction" in
Bergen (now Jersey
City) to Bergen Point
(Bayonne). From The
New York Illustrated
News *(March 28, 1863)*

in need. The Roman Catholic order of the Sisters of the Poor of Saint Francis started two hospitals, Saint Mary in Hoboken in 1863 and Saint Francis in Jersey City in 1864. These sister institutions were the first private hospitals in New Jersey. They began with an emphasis upon nursing services in the home and lodged children including orphans of the Civil War. The Episcopal Church opened the Hudson County Church Hospital and Home (later Christ Hospital) in Jersey City several years later. With its Daisy Ward it too provided specialized care for children in need of a home and medical attention. These three facilities matured to become major health care providers and employers in Hudson County.

The first municipal hospital in the county was in Jersey City. Opened in 1867 on Essex Street, it moved and expanded through different stages until it developed into the Jersey City Medical Center. The Bayonne Hospital and Dispensary accepted its first patients in 1890. After the turn of the century North Hudson and West Hudson hospitals opened to serve their surrounding communities. The German Hospital was founded in south Jersey City in 1912. Then, during the frantic years of World War I, its directors felt obliged to change its name to Greenville Hospital.

Ethnic and religious groups also found-

ed homes to care for the aged, the blind, working women, and children. In 1898 the Plattdeutsch Volkfestverein opened the beautiful Fritz Reuter Altenheim which stands today in North Bergen overlooking both the Hackensack meadowlands and New York. The Sisters of Saint Joseph of Peace started their home for working girls in 1885 and their Institute for the Blind several years later. Saint Ann's Home for the Aged and the Home for Aged Women both serve as witnesses to the vision and hard work of their founders. The Salvation Army waged its battles on several fronts with workshops for needy men and care for unwed mothers. When the Army cut the ribbon for its new building on Erie Street in Jersey City in 1911, it celebrated the occasion with a sumptuous banquet. Its honored guests were the poor.

In the days when early death was not uncommon and when only meager amounts of insurance were available through mutual benefit associations, many children were left homeless and orphanages were opened to accommodate them. Only one remains today, New Jersey's Boystown, founded in 1872 as The Catholic Protectory. Ten years later it purchased the Kearny estate of munitions maker Charles Knapp and soon moved its young charges to this renovated mansion.

Jews began to settle in Hudson County just before the Civil War, and the first of many Hudson synagogues was organized in Jersey City in 1864. Like the Christians, the Jewish people sponsored institutions to aid their members. The Hebrew Home for Orphans and the Aged in Jersey City, first opened in 1915, developed into the Jewish Hospital which now emphasizes long-term care and rehabilitation services for all people.

Other efforts were directed toward education. Private academies and religious schools were organized and the first public high school in the county opened in Jersey City in 1872. When Edwin Stevens, the president of the Camden and Amboy Railroad, died in 1868, he left a bequest

Top
The view of the Hudson River pictured is northeast from Fifth and River streets, Hoboken. This photograph was reproduced by F. Gutekunst circa 1889, using the phototype process from negatives by William H. Bristol, professor of mathematics at the Stevens Institute of Technology. From The Stevens Institute of Technology, Hoboken; Views *(circa 1889). JCL*

Opposite page
In 1901, the approximate date of this photograph, the citizens of the North Hudson communities established the North Hudson Hospital in this house, at the southwest side of Palisade Avenue and 40th Street in Union City. From the Business Directory of North Hudson *(Town of Union, 1905)*

Bottom
Hoboken's Stevens Institute football team is pictured in 1904. Their highly padded trousers, high-lace boots (with no spikes) and easy, gentlemanly manner indicate their turn-of-the century era. Photo by W. Manewal. JCL

W. Manewal's 1902 photograph shows a rough-and-tumble gym class at the Stevens Institute of Technology. In 1846 Hoboken was the site of the first baseball game played in America, and sports have figured strongly in Hoboken's history. There have been clubs—both high and low—dedicated to cricket, riding, football, racing, tennis, and yachting. JCL

of $500,000 for an institution of learning. From this foundation the Stevens Institute of Technology in Hoboken grew to earn national recognition for its graduate and undergraduate programs.

The Jesuits contributed to the educational advance of the immigrants by opening Saint Peter's College in 1878 with a roster of 107 students. This institution gave middle-class Catholics the background which propelled them into careers in law, business, medicine, and education. Saint Peter's today can justly claim credit for the education of many of the leaders of the New York metropolitan area.

Hudson County never had a Jacob Riis whose photographs of the lower East Side in New York provided such vivid depictions of the lives of the immigrants. But

although no pictorial account exists, there is a verbal record compiled by a remarkable institution led by a singular woman. In 1893, after apprenticeships in East London and at Hull House in Chicago, Cornelia Bradford arrived in Jersey City to open the first settlement house in New Jersey. From her Grand Street headquarters named in honor of her friend, the poet John Greenleaf Whittier, Miss Bradford tapped a reservoir of humanitarian concern. With support from the financially fortunate, Whittier House set out to help families in distress by teaching homemaking skills and by giving youngsters a safe and clean place to play. It also launched other movements and organizations, among them the Legal Aid Society, the New Jersey State Consumers' League, the Hudson County Tuberculosis League, and the Jersey City Negro Welfare Association. Over the years Whittier House evolved to become the Boys Club of Jersey City.

In a series of reports published by Whittier House Associates between 1904 and 1912, this institution made its greatest contribution by documenting the plight of the people it served. Some of their studies depict tenement life with buildings so dark that a resident depended upon his hearing rather than his sight when he stepped in a hallway. They noted the prevalence of vermin, of foul smells, of nearly unbelievable overcrowding, and of primitive sanitary facilities. Other reports describe the working conditions imposed upon the young women and girls who sold and wrapped merchandise in the local stores. Their lengthy workdays, nine hours on Monday to Friday and thirteen hours on Saturday, were made more onerous by the requirement that they stand at all times. There were no chairs and no breaks except for a brief lunch period. The Christmas season with its extended sales day was anticipated with particular dread by the "shop girls," even by the youngest who were still at the age when this holiday should have held special delights. These studies and the lobbying efforts of Whittier House were partially responsible for the passage of state laws regulating tenement houses and restricting working hours for women and children.

Given these hardships it is remarkable that the flow of immigrants continued. What they found here must have been better than what they left behind. What they contributed improved what they found. In 1886 on an island just off the Jersey City shore, the New World enshrined its welcome to the Old when it dedicated the gift of the people of France to the people of the United States. "Give me your tired, your poor," wrote Emma Lazarus, and so Bartholdi's statue, which "twin cities frame," became the symbol of liberty for Yankee and immigrant alike and the promise of a solid berth upon America's teeming shore.

Cornelia Foster Bradford, pictured circa 1900, came from the family of Governor William Bradford of Plymouth Colony. She graduated from Olivet College in Michigan, and in 1892 she visited a settlement house in London and Jane Addams' Hull House in Chicago. In 1893 she chose downtown Jersey City as a location for a charity house because of the great number of poor immigrants. At Whittier House, named for her friend, the poet, John Greenleaf Whittier, Bradford established many useful services, including a free kindergarten, a sewing club, and a free milk dispensary. JCL

VIII

The Teeming Shore

This circa 1918 photograph depicts the lucky returning doughboys in the "yard" in Hoboken. Between May of 1917 and November of 1918 two million men sailed for France from Hoboken's docks. An appalling number came back in wooden coffins. A doughboy is a flour dumpling cooked in soup and is what cavalrymen called infantrymen because of the shape of the infantry's coat buttons. Major-General Shanks preferred this name for the soldiers of World War I, rather than what the French were calling them, namely "Sammy" (Uncle) and "Teddy" (Roosevelt). From With the Army in Hoboken *(1919) by K. Snell*

"Manhattan Transfer!" It was the call that roused millions of commuters from their local trains and sent them out to a platform in Harrison to await the mighty steam locomotives of the Pennsylvania main line. It was the call that thrilled midwesterners when they neared New York and paused while an electric engine replaced the steam behemoth that had pulled them eastward. To New Yorkers it was a station "out in the wilds of Jersey." To the people of Hudson County it was just one of many railroad installations in their midst.

Opened in 1910 for the mundane purpose of switching between electric and steam-powered trains, Manhattan Transfer was a train station in the meadows with no entrance or exit to a street. But its name, its isolation, and its panorama of men and their monster machines at work evoked a special response. At twilight, with New York's skyscrapers shining in the distance and with the barges of the Passaic River floating below, thousands of travelers would stand on sentry duty as the advancing army of locomotives emerged from the Kearny yards, headlights ablaze, building up heads of steam for their westward hauls. Here, as the promise of technology was fulfilled, the romance of the railroads exerted its most powerful allure.

Thanks to the railroads a similar sense of energetic purpose permeated all of Hudson County. Until 1871 the rail lines consisted of ribbons of track fanning out only at the water's edge in Hoboken, Jersey City, and Bayonne, but this configuration altered rapidly when the volume of traffic multiplied. New lines entered the market and older ones expanded their facilities dramatically. Ferries, barges, lighters, and carfloats crowded the river. The activity was palpable; it could be seen, heard, smelled, and even tasted.

As the major American center for international trade, Manhattan Island was a geographic anomaly. Although it possessed a good natural harbor, its shoreline was insufficient to accommodate all the shipping being generated. Furthermore, it lacked the back-up space needed to supply the ships, and it was separated from the rest of the United States by rivers. To adapt to these physical constraints a pattern of usage evolved which, though inefficient, worked well enough to keep New York far ahead of any rival ports. In 1870 its municipal government created a department to acquire and manage its docks. This expensive strategy eventually gave the city control of its waterfront. By way of contrast, the New Jersey waterfront remained in private hands. Manhattan became the center for passenger ships. Brooklyn, an independent city until its consolidation with New

Pictured circa 1955, this ferry shows the landing at Weehawken in the foreground and New York City in the distance. The line is the New York Central/ West Shore Rail Road, and although the last ferry to leave Hudson County was in 1967, ferry service may soon be re-established between Hudson County and the metropolis. Photo by Van News Photo, JCL

York in 1898, attracted most of the freight shipping, and New Jersey drew the railroads. Hudson County, therefore, served as a conduit to New York.

Once this pattern was in place, the railroads displayed an increasingly voracious appetite for Hudson County property. With most of the Jersey City and Hoboken shore occupied, two new lines, the New York, West Shore, and Buffalo and the New York, Ontario, and Western, joined forces in 1881 to build a terminal in Weehawken and to tunnel through the Bergen hill. Because the shore ledge narrows as it moves north, the two lines had to spend a fortune to adapt their structures to the awkward terrain. Waiting in the wings to provide funds to the joint venture was the New York Central, which was eager for its own piece of the Hudson County waterfront. After executing a 475-year lease for the West Shore line effective in 1886, the New York Central also took over ferry service from Weehawken to Manhattan. Within a few years the West Shore expanded north into West New York, and the Erie added tracks and a freight terminal in Weehawken.

Although the individual railroad companies were fierce competitors, they made numerous deals which enabled them to share facilities and to lease

tracks and equipment. By means of such agreements, the Lehigh Valley, the Philadelphia and Reading, the Susquehanna, and the Baltimore and Ohio all gained access to the waterfront terminals. In addition to these major carriers, a number of small, specialized junction lines were organized to connect the freight movements of the larger companies. They supplied the vital links which made the system work.

The expansion of the railroads within Hudson County continued in other ways. In North Bergen, Secaucus, and Kearny vast classification yards were laid out where freight cars were sorted and stored. Near the Hudson waterfront huge warehouses and grain elevators were built and, because it was easier to ship beef on the hoof, stockyards were enclosed. Occasionally the animals escaped from their pens, and nearby residents were treated to a touch of the Wild West as they cheered the renegades while railroad employees attempted a roundup. As the volume of traffic continued its phenomenal growth, the rail lines replaced their terminals with larger and better structures built out into the river on landfill. The most ambitious undertaking was the Jersey Central's transformation of the Communipaw mudflats into its mammoth and innovative terminal and coal-dumping facility.

The waters touching Hudson County were as congested as the land. Passenger ferries from each terminal crossed the Hudson every few minutes while Erie Canal boats and ocean liners traveled north and south. From the rail yards tugs maneuvered countless barges and lighters between New Jersey and Brooklyn and moved carfloats, which carried entire freight cars, east and west. Though visually exciting this busyness was time-consuming and potentially dangerous. In the pre-automobile age it was marine traffic that was threatened with gridlock.

To avoid the diagonal river crossing from its yards at Harsimus Cove and to position itself directly across the Upper Bay from Brooklyn, the Pennsylvania purchased in 1899 one of the last available properties on the Jersey City waterfront. There it constructed on landfill the port's largest and most complete marine freight terminal known as the Greenville Yards. The Lehigh Valley, the Black Diamond line, also extended its operations in the southern part of Hudson County with its Tidal Basin terminal, its Claremont yards, and its operations at Black Tom and at Constable Hook.

With all this high-powered activity, with the many industrial plants and with the presence of fuel and other inflammable material, the port had its share of disasters. In 1900 a fire at the Constable Hook refineries in Bayonne burned for an entire week. On June 30, 1900, a blaze igniting four transatlantic liners tied up at the Hoboken piers destroyed an additional twenty-seven work vessels and claimed between two and four hundred lives. Then on July 30, 1916, the combustion of ammunition illegally stored on board Lehigh Valley cars at Black Tom in Jersey City created an explosion of enormous force blamed on wartime saboteurs. In less spectacular ways rail traffic contributed to dangerous congestion in the streets until some, but not all, lines eliminated grade crossings by elevating or depressing their tracks.

The entire port of New York with its dispersed operations in Manhattan, Brooklyn, and Hudson County was far from a textbook model of efficiency, but it worked because labor was cheap and plentiful. The system gave Hudson County an abundance of jobs and even increased its size as landfill augmented the shoreline. These were the facts which the railroads produced whenever they were criticized. And they were criticized bitterly for a variety of reasons, for poor local safety practices, for low taxes set by state assessors, and for their sponge-like absorption of prime real estate. The relationship between the rail lines and Hudson County was a complex blend of love and hate.

There can be no doubt that the railroads made Hudson County an industrial

star. They also made it easy for many of the county's wealthier citizens to move to the residential areas of Essex, Morris, and Bergen counties. Alone among Hudson County communities to profit from this railroad suburb trend was Kearny, where the Arlington station was the catalyst for the construction of many attractive, substantial homes.

In contrast to these railroad suburbs, the northern and southern parts of Hudson County could be described as trolley suburbs. Electric trolleys were introduced in 1892 and generally replaced the horse-cars, run on tracks, which had made their first appearance in 1859. The horsecar operators and their successors were noteworthy for the engineering ingenuity, which they brought to the problem of the looming Bergen hill. In north Hudson where the hill's grade was the steepest, the local transit companies erected an inclined plane and later towering elevators, which bore the horsecars or the trolleys upwards to trestles in less than a minute. Despite their heart-stopping appearance, the elevated lines had a notable safety record.

As helpful as the trolleys were in extending the residential frontiers of the county, each line was designed to transport people to the Hudson River crossings. Travel within the county was decidedly subordinate to the goal of

This photograph of circa 1880 shows the incline of the wagon elevator which went from the Hoboken side of the base of the Palisades up to Palisade Avenue and Ravine Street in Jersey City. The elevator itself, on which this horse-drawn trolley sits, is a right angle triangle, a wooden platform on wheels, and it is pulled by steam engines up to the station (seen at the right). From there the trolley continued to Central Avenue in Jersey City. As one elevator came down, another went up the tracks. In 1886 service began on the elevated trolley from Hoboken's Lackawanna Station and ferry to Central Avenue, so after that year this elevator hauled wagons, not trolleys. This apparatus was built in 1874 and was used until 1928. JCL

As seen in this photograph of 1909, certain cars on the Hudson Manhattan lines were reserved exclusively for women. The Pennsylvania Railroad helped finance the tunnels and permitted the Hudson & Manhattan's electric cars to share the Penn trackage through the Bergen cut in Jersey City. JCL

bringing commuters to and from New York. Even in the present, as bus lines trace the old trolley routes, it remains easier to travel from Bayonne to New York than to West New York, Kearny, and Secaucus.

With New York the ultimate goal of both the railroads and the local commuter lines, the pressure was on to improve the passage across the Hudson River. As technology advanced, the old bridge and tunnel dreams of John Stevens were rejuvenated in the practical minds of numerous engineers. The first effort to tunnel under the river, the Dewitt Haskin plan, was struck by disaster in 1880 when twenty trapped sandhogs met their deaths. In 1888 a firm backed by British investors resumed work and introduced the Greathead shield which improved the boring method, but financial difficulties called this attempt to a halt in 1892. In 1901 William McAdoo revived the Haskin plan and in 1908 his electrically powered commuter rail line ran under the Hudson River between Hoboken and New York. Named the Hudson and Manhattan Railway and referred to locally as the Tubes, this road became the Port Authority Trans-Hudson System or PATH line in 1962.

The Hudson and Manhattan was a splendid success. By 1909 two underwater tunnels were in operation, the huge Hudson Terminal on Church Street in New York was occupied, and new stations had been opened in Jersey City and New York. By 1911 the line extended from Thirty-Second Street and Sixth Avenue in New York to Harrison and Newark in New Jersey. McAdoo, who insisted upon the novel policy of paying women employees the same salary as men for the same job, turned William Henry Vanderbilt's infamous dictum on its ear and chose for the company's motto, "The Public Be Pleased." Any trainman hectoring his passengers with orders to "Step lively!" would be fired.

While work was in progress on the Hudson and Manhattan, the Pennsylvania Railroad was completing plans for its own passenger service tunnel and its massive terminal at Thirty-Third Street in New York. Because it was essential that the Penn use electricity to power its trains through the tunnel and then change to steam for its overland long-distance service, a switching station was required. This was the celebrated Manhattan Transfer which served until 1938, three years after Pennsylvania Station in Newark opened. With the completion of the tunnel project in 1910, Hudson County lost its role as the line's eastern terminus.

Despite these technical innovations the growth of business threatened to exceed the capacity of the area's rail and marine operations. During World War I the threat became a reality when the port was virtually clogged. The demand for material by both domestic and European markets exceeded the shipping capacity. The situation was aggravated by Atlantic naval operations which made shipowners cautious in dispatching their vessels. With too few ships to receive their cargo and with overflowing warehouses, the freight cars could not be unloaded, and they lay full and idle in the Hudson County yards. This decreased the nation's supply of rolling stock to such a degree that coal could not be shipped, and many Americans endured freezing winters. To combat this crisis and to coordinate the work of the competitive rail-

*Left
Man and two of his
best friends—his dog
and his horse—seem to
be posing as dignitaries just before a winter's drive in 1906.
The man is Mr. Harry
Blessing, a salesman,
who lived at 644 Jersey Avenue, Jersey
City. The place is
Greenville (Jersey
City) at Schuetzen
Park, which was established by Charles Armbuster in 1881 and was
in operation until
1926. Besides famous
shooting matches,
these parks also hosted
equestrian displays
and competitions, as
well as picnics and
dancing. JCL*

*Bottom
William Gibbs McAdoo, seen in a circa
1906 photograph, was
responsible for the
completion of the
Hudson and Manhattan tubes under the
Hudson River. The
project, conceived by
engineer D.C. Haskins,
had begun in 1874 but
was suspended several
times. Under the entrepreneurial genius of
McAdoo, a wealthy
lawyer, the necessary
terminals and franchises were acquired
by 1903. In 1908 the
service from Hoboken
to mid-town New York
began and in 1909 that
from Jersey City to
Cortlandt Street in
lower Manhattan
opened. JCL*

the sacrifices of its young soldiers and in the activities which arose in response to the war effort. In south Kearny on the Hackensack River workers at the shipyards labored mightily to produce the vessels needed to carry men and supplies across the Atlantic. Hoboken became the nation's port of embarkation when the federal government confiscated the waterfront property of the German steamship lines and converted the ships and piers to military uses. This city suffered a grievous blow as a result of the war. Not only did it lose the taxes paid by the steamship lines, its shipping activity never again approached the pre-1914 levels. The German community, which gave Hoboken and north Hudson its style and its tone, retreated into itself. Old clubs disappeared and venerable institutions changed their names. The army closed the beer gardens and taverns, and the loss of tax revenues resulting from this move and from Prohibition added to Hoboken's financial woes, although it was known in the 1920s as a wet and wild town.

road lines, President Woodrow Wilson appointed William McAdoo to be a national railroad czar. From December 1917 until March 1920 the operations of the railroads were directed by Washington.

The war was felt in Hudson County in

Movie actress Pearl White and cameraman Arthur Miller are pictured in 1918 filming The House of Hate *on the cliffs of the Palisades. Ms. White worked for Pathe studios, Jersey City and starred in a very popular series of twenty movies called* The Perils of Pauline. *Between 1903, when Kearny's Passaic River banks were the scene for chases in the landmark movie* The Great Train Robbery, *and 1919, when Universal, Pathe, and the Biograph studios had left for Hollywood, Hudson County was home for silent movies. Courtesy, Library of Congress*

Despite these setbacks most of Hudson County continued to advance economically. Blue collar pride was evident among Italian stonemasons, among Ukrainian butchers, among black Pullman car porters, and among all those who manipulated their machinery and performed their jobs with skill and precision.

Gradually women assumed more public roles, as nuns and other female administrators ran hospitals, schools, and orphanages. Whittier House was a focal point for a number of talented women, including Mary Philbrook whose struggle to become New Jersey's first female attorney succeeded in 1895. Caroline Bayard Wittpenn of Hoboken's Stevens family, the "best loved woman in New Jersey," served as county probation officer and as head of the State Board of Children's Guardians. Hetty Green, Hoboken's "Witch of Wall Street" who packed a pistol to protect herself from lawyers, displayed such uncanny financial acumen that she was deemed the richest woman in America at the time of her death in 1916. Other women banded together in clubs where they exerted pressure, used their influence, and contributed their funds to a myriad of civic

improvement activities.

For a short time Hudson County, along with its neighbor Fort Lee, was the home of the movies. The proximity of the Black Maria studio of Thomas Edison in West Orange gave this region a head start on moviemaking, particularly for outdoor scenes. Before the industry moved to Hollywood, movies were shot in Weehawken, Union Hill, and Hoboken. Pathé Frères opened its American studio at One Congress Street in Jersey City in 1912 and remained there until 1919. In these early years the Currie's Woods section of Bayonne was the background in many Westerns released under the Centaur and Nestor labels.

Though life remained difficult, advances in working conditions gave growing numbers the time and the money for recreation. The wealthier could drive about in their new automobiles or enjoy trips to New York theaters. Those with less pocket money could find entertainment close to home. Weehawken attracted visitors to its famous Eldorado, a Moorish extravaganza which staged elaborate spectacles in the 1890s. The area's reputation for horse racing was continued at the Gut, the Guttenberg racetrack, actu-

This charming photograph taken on February 22, 1907, by H.C. Lederer shows a group of gypsy children, with their tents behind them, encamped in the stables of the North Hudson Driving Park, which had been the rowdy Guttenberg racetrack. The horse-racing track was opened in 1885 and expanded in 1888, but legislated out of existence in 1893. It was actually in the town of North Bergen on the Bull's Ferry Road, not in Guttenberg. The track was standing until 1919, and in the summers of the turn-of-the-century gypsy caravans stayed there. Hudson County was, and is, the residence of people of virtually every culture on earth. JCL

ally situated in North Bergen, which drew a raffish crowd of wagerers and vagabonds from 1885 to 1893. Then Hudson became part of the theatrical and vaudeville circuit as entertainers like Eddie Cantor and Burns and Allen took their acts across the river. The Hudson Theater in Union Hill, later a burlesque house, was particularly popular on Sunday nights when New York's vaudeville was shut tight. In the late 1920s Christopher Morley brought legitimate theater to Hoboken which he described as the "Last Sea Coast of Bohemia." Perhaps the children enjoyed life in Hudson County most of all. They could sneak onto ferries and ride to New York. They could prowl around the outskirts of the rail yards behind the backs of the railroad bulls and observe tugboats easing their vessels into berths. They could watch horses being shod and see movies being made. Innocent of environmental worries they could even swim in the Morris Canal. It must have been terrific fun.

Planning with a Regional Perspective

In the midst of decades of hurly-burly production of taller smokestacks, longer trackage, and bigger factories, the nation paused in 1893 and celebrated the Columbian Exposition, also known as the Chicago World's Fair. In a setting designed by Frederick Olmstead, leading architects created spectacular temporary structures resembling marble which comprised a model for the city of the future and gave hope for a better urban life. Tied in with the Progressive movement which sought to improve living standards, this interest in the appearance of cities was a significant change in the way Americans viewed their culture.

Unlike Europe which possessed the architectural legacy of monarchs and princely churchmen, America had grown up haphazardly with scant regard for design, style, and decoration. Amenities such as parks, monuments, and beautiful public spaces and buildings were not the concerns of the democratically elected aldermen struggling to provide basic services to a population unwilling to accept constraints upon individual liberty. Indeed plainness had its philosophical advocates among many of the early American settlers, although it may be assumed that they did not foresee squalor as the alternative to ostentation. Hudson County shared this no-nonsense view and paid the price with a drab visual landscape.

Despite some attractive residential sections, not even Hudson's fondest partisans could describe this robust and interesting area as charming or pretty.

Inspired by the Columbian Exposition and by the writers who celebrated its vision, the nation's premier cities strove to give substance to the ideal of the "City Beautiful" by producing elaborate and imposing civic designs. Less affluent Hudson County adopted more modest measures. The completion of Hudson Boulevard in 1894 was the county's first effort to provide a major facility that was both visually attractive and functional. It was intended to be a pleasure road running north-south on the apex of the Bergen hill from Bergen Point in Bayonne to Nungesser's hotel and transfer station in North Bergen. Its later northern branch, Boulevard East, winding high along the edge of the Palisades, took advantage of the stunning view of the Hudson River and Manhattan.

In 1903 Hudson County accepted the legislative challenge of the state and formed a commission to acquire land for parks. After securing the services of landscape architects, the new commission went to work in Bayonne, Hoboken, Harrison, Kearny, Jersey City, North Bergen, and Union City. Where possible the parks were located on the Boulevard and with their lakes, fountains, and sports

Mobility between communities depended on the horse and buggy. The Samuel Tompkins family of Jersey City (pictured in 1903) bought a one-cylinder Cadillac circa 1909. Eventually the fume and noise of automobiles replaced the manure and clop of horses. In this mid-nineteenth century neighborhood, near the Junction in Jersey City, there is a mixture of brick, urban row houses and wood-frame suburban houses, like that of Nicholas Vreeland seen in the background. The suburbs were to move further and further away as industry grew and transportation improved. JCL

In North Bergen at Hudson (now Kennedy) Boulevard and the Hackensack Plank Road (32nd Street) is this "Second-Empire" style structure erected in 1898 by the Plattdeutsche Volksfestverein to house their senior citizens. It is named the Fritz Reuter Altenhiem (home for the elderly). Reuter was a German poet and writer on topics concerning housing problems. This institution is adjacent to Schuetzen Park. Photo by Joseph C. Brooks

fields became immensely popular. In the same decade the county commissioned a new courthouse, designed in the Beaux-Arts style by Hugh Roberts, which opened in 1910. An attempt to raze this building in the 1960s was averted by popular outcry, and in 1970 it became Hudson's first entry into the National Register of Historic Places.

The individual municipalities entered into the spirit of the times by holding architectural competitions and erecting impressive public buildings. Commercial firms and churches also contributed attractive structures, and some private organizations commissioned commemorative monuments. These efforts had their impact, but it must be admitted that they were too little and too late. Design by doing had already set the visual pattern just as it had determined the economic pattern. A crowded, predominantly working class and immigrant population lacked both the resources and the desire to demand significant aesthetic improvements. Hudson instead concentrated its resources upon a struggle for efficiency, a struggle which had some modest successes offset by a number of setbacks.

One response to the interest in civic betterment was the repeated call for consolidation of the different municipalities within Hudson. But the majority resisted the idea for political reasons and from fear of total domination by Jersey City, and the only merger ever effected was that between Union Hill and West Hoboken which combined to produce Union City in 1925. As a result, the limited tax and bonding base of each community

precluded the development of large-scale projects. Bayonne, for example, considered the erection of a waterfront facility which would rival in size and function the Bush Terminal in Brooklyn. However, the voters rejected the idea several times because it would have been too costly. Not until the late 1930s did an attenuated version of Irving Bush's proposal rise from the waters off Bayonne's shore. During World War II this was taken over by the federal government in whose hands it has remained as the Military Ocean Terminal.

This was the beginning of the era of city planning, and in 1912 Jersey City followed the lead of major American cities and hired consultants to prepare a recommended procedure for civic improvement. If the city fathers paid for an honest appraisal, they got their money's worth. No sensibilities were spared in pointing out deficiencies and failures, although some kind words were found for the water supply and for the transit system. A waterfront park, the consultants advised, would be a tremendous asset; sixty-four years later Liberty State Park opened. They recommended a wholesale food distribution center; for decades that suggestion has been on New Jersey's agenda. They urged that factories be segregated; zoning was adopted in Jersey City in 1921. They also pointed out that intercity cooperation was essential as communities struggled with problems that originated or terminated beyond their legal borders. Dealing with complex issues that spanned multiple jurisdictions was to be the hallmark of the future.

Ultimately all matters of civic planning, all hopes for an improved visual prospect and a higher living standard depended upon a flourishing economy, and the future of the region's economy was threatened by the growing problem of freight congestion in the port, a problem evident to any casual observer of the railroad and marine operations jammed along Hudson's waterfront. The initial step in a lengthy process which revolutionized transportation and shipping in

The beautiful, classical courtyard and arcade pictured is part of the Bayonne Public Library at Avenue C and 31st Street. The arcade is part of an expansion in 1933, but the central section opened in 1904 was built in the Beaux-Arts style with money donated partially by Andrew Carnegie. In the nineteenth century some businesses set up private libraries, and in Bayonne the Humphreys family set up a "Workman's Library" circa 1880. That collection became a major part of the Public Library. New Jersey legislation in 1884 stimulated the building of the several "temples of knowledge," that is, libraries, in Hudson County. Photo by Joseph C. Brooks

the region took place in 1911 when both New Jersey and New York appointed commissioners to deal jointly with this issue. This solution did not work out. The two states remained apart with each emphasizing proposals peculiar to its own position. New York allowed its commission to lapse, but New Jersey persevered and in 1915 created a permanent Board of Commerce and Navigation. In its first report this board argued that the existing rail rates, which were uniform throughout the region, were unfair to New Jersey which did not require expensive marine lighterage and carfloat operations. It filed a formal rate complaint with the Interstate Commerce Commission which resulted in the famous *New York Harbor Case* of 1916 or, as it was popularly known, the *Lighterage Case*. New Jersey also charged that the railroads maintained circuitous routing and excessive local joint rates to deter interchange between terminals. The ICC was asked to compel the rail lines to operate a switching service which would be comparable to the water belt line available to New York's shippers.

The railroads registered a vigorous dissent. They wanted no change in the rate structure which was part of a system which governed the entire East Coast.

They also opposed any efforts to facilitate interline switching, maintaining that their competitive positions were dependent upon control of their terminals and approaches.

Eugenius Outerbridge, president of the New York State Chamber of Commerce, recognized the vital importance of the rate differential complaint and convinced New York State and New York City to intervene. The New York side argued that New Jersey's inability to reap all the potential benefits of the port's commerce stemmed from its failure to control its waterfront and provide public improvements. Instead of contention, New York maintained, let there be cooperation. The port was one unit, and both sides were economically knit together.

In 1917 the ICC sided with New York. ". . . historically, geographically, and commercially New York and the industrial district in the northern part of the state of New Jersey constituted a single community." Cooperation and initiative could bring about the desired improvements in the port's operations. In deciding against reciprocal switching by the railroads, the ICC stated that it was beyond its power to compel the railroads to provide such service. Defeated on both counts, New Jersey was chastened temporarily, but it

These are "sand hogs" digging McAdoo's Hudson and Manhattan tubes about 1905. The tunnels under the Hudson River were a triumph of technology, although the practical accomplishment of the claustrophobic burrowing took over twenty-five years, and the lives of many workers were expended. Irish immigrants and blacks formed a large percentage of that labor force. The tunnels went from the Lackawanna, Erie, and Pennsylvania stations on the Hudson to 33rd or Cortlandt streets in New York, and to the Manhattan Transfer in Harrison and eventually to Pennsylvania Station in Newark. JCL

revived the lighterage issue again in 1929 and in 1937. The ICC denied the second complaint in 1934 and rejected New Jersey's application in 1937.

On both sides of the river businessmen and state leaders viewed the outcome of the case as an opportunity for conciliation, and they set up two organizations to deal with the problems of freight movement. The New Jersey Interstate Bridge and Tunnel Commission was created to work with its New York counterpart to build a vehicular tunnel linking Canal Street in Manhattan and Twelfth Street in Jersey City. The tunnel opened on November 12, 1927, after seven years of construction marred by bureaucratic delays and quarrels over land condemnation. Excavation techniques adapted from the earlier railroad tunnels were used, but ventilating the exhaust fumes had posed a new challenge. Clifford Holland, the brilliant chief engineer, found the solution but pursued his work with such zeal that he died of exhaustion in 1924. His tunnel was named in his memory.

The New York, New Jersey Port and Harbor Development Commission recommended that a permanent bistate agency be formed to conduct and administer a comprehensive study of the region's transportation which would serve as a guide for fifty years. On April 30, 1921, a

compact was signed creating the Port of New York Authority with jurisdiction over an area roughly twenty-five miles in each direction from lower Manhattan and encompassing all of Hudson County. In 1972 this agency's name was changed to Port of New York and New Jersey Authority.

The Port Authority's early years were spent in futile efforts to coax the rail lines to join in a coordinated plan involving belt lines, a union terminal, and interline switching. The experience of the federal government, when it controlled the port during the war, was cited as evidence that cooperation as opposed to competition would work wonders of efficiency. But the railroads were not persuaded and legally they could not be coerced. They would not go along with the comprehensive plan.

Neither did Washington. The Port Authority saw the existing piers and rail links in Hoboken as a ready facility which would increase shipping activity in New Jersey. During the war the federal government took over the Hoboken Manufacturer's Railroad as well as the property of the German steamship lines. Although the piers were transferred to the United States Shipping Board, the War Department retained the railroad, popularly known as the Hoboken Shore Line. The Port Authority wanted to buy this rail line, but its attempts were stymied by the department's secretary and by a clique of powerful colonels who were ideologically opposed to public ownership of transportation facilities. The city of Hoboken also opposed the sale because it wanted the property back on its tax rolls. The Port Authority's offers were rejected. In 1927 Hoboken Terminal Properties, Inc., bought the Hoboken Shore Line and in 1931 it was acquired by Seatrain Lines, Inc., at auction.

Frustrated in its efforts to improve freight movement by rail, the Port Authority turned its attention to vehicular traffic. Spurred on by the declared wishes of both states, it embarked upon a program to build bridges linking Staten Island to Perth Amboy, Elizabeth, and Bayonne. In 1925 it was given the go-ahead to plan the George Washington Bridge over the Hudson between 178th Street in Manhattan and Fort Lee in Bergen County. In 1930 the Holland Tunnel came under the Port Authority's jurisdiction. During these years the Authority mastered many difficult feats of engineering and financing and of placating its still mutually suspicious components.

The Port Authority attempted two more projects in Hudson County before World War II. One succeeded: the Lincoln Tunnel joining Weehawken to midtown Manhattan. After the failure of the bond market, the federal Public Works Administration stepped in with a loan of $37,500,000 which financed work on the first tube which opened on December 22, 1937. Construction continued during the war, and traffic moved through the second tube on February 1, 1945.

The failed project was an effort, initiated in 1927, to develop a modern steamship terminal at the Little Basin, the Jersey City terminus of the abandoned Morris Canal. Both the municipality and the Port Authority worked out a joint program incorporating four piers with rail and vehicular access, and the city began negotiations with prospective clients. Before financing could be obtained, the money markets collapsed and the worldwide depression drastically reduced the demand for pier space. As a result Hudson County's first significant publicly owned transportation enterprise was lost in the planning stage. The city of Bayonne, which produced its own city plan in 1929, also met the implacable foe of depression, and its hopes for new waterfront development on both shores were frustrated.

Two other planning agencies came into being in the 1920s. In 1921 a group of influential citizens from New Jersey, New York, and Connecticut banded together to make a survey and plan for New York and its environs. The cost was met by the Russell Sage Foundation headed by Robert W. deForest, the president of the Hackensack Water Company, supplier of water to north Hudson since the 1880s. The scope of the survey included sanitation, recreation, and public design as well as industrial growth and traffic movement. In 1929 the study group which completed the survey became a permanent organization, the Regional Plan Association.

In 1922 the North Jersey Transit Commission was charged by the state with the task of upgrading area transit for passengers at the time when the Port Authority was immersed in freight problems. This commission did not accomplish physical changes, but it did heighten the perception that regional planning was imperative. Its final report delivered in 1929 presents a cogent case for the creation of a regional governing body vested with financial autonomy. "As long as the New Jersey section of the New York metropolitan area is broken up into an uncoordinated mass of counties and municipalities, it is, and must continue to be, at a disadvantage in dealing with New York City in matters of regional concern . . . . No amount of brilliant play can take the place of teamwork."

Nonetheless the tension between local autonomy and regional cooperation has persisted. In the 1970s New York City decentralized its own municipal planning process to meet political demands as well as to elicit the ideas of people most knowledgeable about a neighborhood and most affected by any change. In New Jersey the powers granted to the regional Hackensack Meadowlands Development Commission in 1968 have not been given to the Hudson River Waterfront Commission in the 1980s because the individual municipalities refuse to surrender control of their river front. When matters of local pride and prosperity are involved, mere exhortation to cooperate has not been compelling. When the call for any regional approach extends across state boundaries, the response is even more guarded than for intrastate planning. The process begun before World War I has not yet reached maturity.

X.

Politics Triumphant

Jersey City's famous mayor, Frank Hague, stands elegantly (front row, fifth from left), posing with these politically-active women in 1930. The occasion was the tercentenary of the establishment of "Pavonia," the land which became Hudson County. Many of the ladies are costumed as Dutch, English, and Huguenot settlers. Democrat Hague's mayorality was 1917 to 1947, and he was at his height in the 1930s, when his grand construction schemes helped Hudson County during the Depression. One of these was the Jersey City Medical Center, whose director, George O'Hanlon, M.D., stands at the far right. At Hague's right is Assemblywoman Mary M. Carty, and to his left is Freeholder Kathleen W. Brown. Photo by H.A. Schoenals. JCL

"If you want to know who's in charge, start something." In 1910 the wise visitor to the office of Jersey City Collector "Little Bob" Davis saw this sign on the wall and knew exactly what it meant. Davis was the kingpin of local politics, the boss who inherited the leadership of the Democratic political organization that had been gathering strength since the 1870s. Upstairs in City Hall Mayor Otto Wittpenn planned his civic improvement projects and plotted his own dead-end campaign for governor. Downstairs Davis awarded the jobs and distributed the favors and received in grateful return loyalty and votes.

The political machine run by Davis, who had risen to power with the backing of local tycoon E.F.C. Young, was well developed but not yet triumphant. In fact, it had recently experienced the unsettling years from 1901 to 1907 when Mark Fagan, a Republican mayor and a poor Irish Catholic one at that, had ruled the city for three consecutive terms. This young undertaker's assistant possessed his own Progressive vision of the role which government should play in alleviating the terrible burdens of poverty. He was a new face in 1901, a popular man with no ties to the existing machine, and he was backed by the uptown businessmen who wished to capture control of municipal government after nearly three

decades in the political wilderness.

Canonized in Lincoln Steffens' book *Upbuilders,* Fagan was an activist idealist. At his side as the city's corporation counsel was George L. Record, a disciple of Henry George, the Single Tax advocate. Fagan and Record launched a number of court attacks upon the preferential tax rates and assessments enjoyed by the railroads and utilities, and they won some legal battles. But their success insured the enmity of formidable opponents, and Fagan was defeated in 1907 by Democrat Otto Wittpenn.

Wittpenn had been handpicked by the organization, but he had his own ambitions and was not the complete pushover that Boss Davis had counted upon. For one thing, despite objections by Davis, Wittpenn selected the leader of the second ward for the patronage-rich post of City Hall custodian. When Davis died in 1911, this Wittpenn appointee emerged as the new man to reckon with and the likely heir to the title, Boss. The new man was Frank Hague, a son of the Horseshoe, who was born in 1876 when ward politicians were becoming brokers between the citizens and the city officials. During the last quarter of the nineteenth century, when the burgeoning population constantly required additional, expensive services and the municipal treasury was chronically short of funds, the politician

Top
Silas W. Kagan's meat market is pictured circa 1900 on Newark Avenue in Jersey City. Mr. Kagan is in the front center, and to his right are his adult workers, with the boy workers to his left. JCL

Bottom
Mark Fagan, seen in a photograph of circa 1910, was born into the poor, Irish Catholic working class, and as a young man worked as an undertaker's assistant in downtown Jersey City among the impoverished. He became fired by a social consciousness, and in 1901 became, at age thirty-two, the mayor of Jersey City. JCL

Opposite page
An Aerial View of the Jersey City Waterfront, 1999. This view shows the Avalon Cove apartments in the foreground. Avalon Cove began with two mid-rise buildings that rented so quickly that the 25-story tower seen in the lower right was built. North of Avalon Cove is Newport. On the center right side the ventilation tower for the Holland Tunnel is visible jutting out into the river. Courtesy, The Lefrak Organization

was the man to see to have a street paved or a sewer laid. From this background grew the pervasive belief that providing ordinary services was a favor to the politically connected, not a routine operation of government.

Like Mark Fagan, Frank Hague was poor and Irish and had little formal education. Expelled from the sixth grade for truancy, Hague turned to prizefighting, where he made a local reputation as a tough boxer and manager. He quickly distinguished himself from other young men by dressing nattily and formally and thereby caught the eye of ward leaders on the lookout for party recruits. Throughout his long career Hague was a model of sartorial correctness, and he demanded a spit and polish appearance from his appointed officials and uniformed employees. Clothes helped to make this man as did the physical toughness which he exhibited in the ring. But it was his shrewdness and his will for power which made Frank Hague mayor of Jersey City for three decades as well as the undisputed boss of Hudson County, the dominant figure in state government, and the richly

rewarded although disdained ally of Franklin Roosevelt.

Hague was elected to citywide office in 1913 when the new commission government replaced the old mayor-alderman arrangement. As commissioner of public safety he waged war upon inefficiency and corruption in the police force and

Above
In the right of this 1972 photograph is the deep "Bergen Cut" originally dug in the 1830s. It divided Bergen from North Bergen in the 1840s, was inherited by the Pennsylvania Railroad, and later shared by the Hudson and Manhattan tubes, now the PATH line. Courtesy, Jersey City Planning Division

Right
Liberty Landing Marina, 1999. Located in the Tidal Basin at the northern end of Liberty State Park, this is one of five new marinas on the Hudson River waterfront. Courtesy, Liberty Landing Marina

Left
One of the Slices of Heaven, American-ization Day, Jersey City, 1998. These young dancers are celebrating the amaz-ing diversity of the city. In the back-ground is part of a panoramic historical mural created by the Pro Arts organization to enliven the buildings on Columbus Drive between Grove and Barrow streets. Photo by Alton O'Neill

Above
101 Hudson and the Colgate Clock, Sep-tember 1994. The state's tallest build-ing and the world's biggest single-faced clock identify the Jersey City water-front for the many recreational boats and commercial vessels that sail the Hudson River. The smaller structures are the NOL Center on the right and the former First Jersey National Bank building, now a part of Fleet Bank. Photo by Robert H. Barth

Top
*Between circa 1905
and 1915 many tinted
postcards of Hudson
County sites were pro-
duced in Germany.
They were sold in the
railroad terminals as
souvenirs to the mil-
lions of people who
passed through Hud-
son County's stations.
The Pennsylvania
Railroad station at Ex-
change Place (Jersey
City) is seen in this
postcard of circa 1910.
Courtesy, Charles
Balcer*

Center
*This tinted postcard of
circa 1905 shows a
view looking north up
Central Avenue from
Hutton Street on the
"heights" of the pal-
isade in the former
city of Hudson. Cen-
tral Avenue was one of
the three commercial
arteries on which a
person could catch a
trolley north to the
county limit at Nun-
gessers Hotel or south
to Five Corners and
beyond. Courtesy,
Charles Balcer*

Bottom
*This wash drawing
by Danish architect
Detlef Lienau was
done circa 1850 as a
design for a house for
himself and his broth-
er, Michael, located at
the southeast corner of
Jersey Avenue and 3rd
Street in Van Vorst
Township (Jersey City
after 1851). Courtesy,
Jersey City Division of
Urban Research and
Design*

Colonel Samuel H. Lockett painted this View of the Morris Canal, Jersey City *in 1887. The canal was built to transport coal from the mines in Pennsylvania to the Port of New York, and Jersey City was its eastern terminus. This view shows the canal where it passed an inlet near Van Horne Street, looking west to the Johnston Avenue bridge, with the Passaic Zinc Works on the left, and the steeple of the Bergen Baptist Church in the far middle ground. The canal was landfilled in 1929. JCL*

The Edge Windmill *is based on an 1881 painting by Granville Parkins. Isaac Edge's grist windmill became a legend, having been sent by his father in Derbyshire, England, as a reminder of the old country. Edge erected it in 1815 at the end of a pier near Montgomery and* Greene streets. *It functioned until 1839, when it had to be dismantled to make way for railroad tracks. It was sent to Long Island, New York, where it burned in 1870. The romantic vista here is eastward toward lower Manhattan, with Robert Fulton's ferry seen at the right. JCL*

August Will painted this scene northeast from Cornelison Avenue near Montgomery Street, Jersey City, in 1899. The view is from the boiler room of the Jersey City Paper Company toward the Consolidated Traction Company powerhouse (left middle ground) and the elevated National Docks Railroad. The twin towers of St. Bridget's Roman Catholic Church (built in 1886) are at the left. The five towers of the Jersey City City Hall, seen at the right, were complete by 1897. The artist has located this new city hall too far to the south of St. Bridget's Church. New York City is a white silhouette on the horizon. This painting illustrates the main characteristics of Jersey City and Hudson County: the industry, the railroads, its political institutions, and its proximity to New York City. Courtesy, Jersey City Museum

Above
St. Henry's Roman Catholic Church is pictured in 1985 on Avenue C in Bayonne at 29th Street. Historian Daniel Van Winkle was inspired to say in 1924, "[it] is one of the most beautiful examples of church architecture in New Jersey." Photo by Joseph C. Brooks

Right
The First Baptist Church on Bloomfield Street, Hoboken, pictured in 1985, was built from 1890 to 1891. Photo by Joseph C. Brooks

Top
In 1870 architect Rich-
ard Mitchell Upjohn
designed this building
for the new Stevens
Institute of Technolo-
gy in Hoboken. The
general elegance of
proportions make this
building a fitting focal
point for the Hudson
Square park it over-
looks. Photo by Joseph
C. Brooks

Bottom
This 1985 photograph
shows Fire Engine
Company Number 17
at 106 Boyd Avenue,
Jersey City. Although
it was built in 1910, it
is similar in design to
firehouses built in the
last quarter of the
nineteenth century.
Photo by Joseph C.
Brooks

Right
Jackie Robinson, the Brooklyn Dodger great, broke the "color line" in organized baseball when he played against the Jersey Giants at Roosevelt Stadium in Jersey City in April 1946. At that time Robinson was a member of the Montreal Royals of the International League. One year later he moved up to the majors when he became a Dodger. In February 1998 this statue by Susan Wagner was dedicated in a ceremony attended by Robinson's widow, Rachel Robinson. Photo by William Tremper

Below
This brownstone church, pictured in 1985, is the Roman Catholic Church of The Holy Innocents in Harrison. It was begun in 1886 and dedicated in 1890. Photo by Joseph C. Brooks

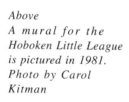

Above
A mural for the
Hoboken Little League
is pictured in 1981.
Photo by Carol
Kitman

Left
Bankers Trust of NY was
the first firm to sign a
long term lease for
Harborside Financial
Center. Located just
steps from the PATH
station and just three
minutes from the World
Trade Center, Harborside
proved to be a popular
location for other
businesses moving to
Hudson County. Photo
by Michael Lovero

Above
The Hudson County
Brownstone Revival
movement began in the
1970s and spread to
Jersey City. This home
at 916 Hudson Street in
Hoboken is typical of
the spacious brown-
stones near the water-
front. Photo by Joseph
C. Brooks

Right
After the opening of Hudson Boulevard in 1894, new housing for the wealthy was built along its route. This Georgian Revival house at 111 Gifford Avenue, Jersey City, is typical of these new suburbs. It was built circa 1902 for Sara Flemming, widow of famed criminal lawyer James Flemming. Photo by Joseph C. Brooks

Left
On high ground, on the major road from Philadelphia to New York, and near the Staten Island ferry, this house at 100 Broadway, Bayonne, is a reminder of circa 1860, when it was built. That was the time when a middle-class populace located themselves and developed their property at Bergen Point. This house was built by the Lord family on the site of the Bon Sejour Tavern. Photo by Joseph C. Brooks

This Queen-Anne style building was constructed circa 1875 and is an early example in the Hudson area of this English-originated style, so popular in all America from circa 1880 until about 1930. The style incorporates colorful and textural elements, such as leaded and stained glass, fish-scale shingles, and polychromatic brickwork. Photo by Joseph C. Brooks

Journal Square is pictured in this aerial shot of 1979. Courtesy, Jersey City Division of Urban Research and Design

The large West Side Park is in Jersey City at a central point on the Boulevard. Courtesy, Jersey City Division of Urban Research and Design

soon converted this most visible public service into a disciplined, well-equipped, and well-groomed department. His fight against street gangs, prostitution, and externally organized crime won the support of the reformers and of the city's wives and mothers. He would secretly turn over to the wives of disciplined policemen the fines which he had imposed for infractions of duty. In 1917 he and his entire slate were elected, and his fellow commissioners chose him as mayor, a post he held until 1947.

Once in the Jersey City mayor's seat, Hague moved swiftly to dominate the rest of Hudson County. His ally Patrick Griffin was elected mayor of Hoboken after that city adopted commission government in 1915, and Bernard McFeely, Griffin's successor, remained in the Hague camp from 1924 until 1947 with only one mild breakaway attempt in 1943. Hague relied upon Oscar auf der Heide from West New York to manage his interests in north Hudson and to attract German voters. By seating his candidates in key county offices, Hague quickly wrapped up the local scene. Mayors of other towns learned to cooperate if they wanted county projects or jobs for their own residents. By 1919 Hague moved onto the state stage and, when his man Edward I. Edwards defeated the Essex County nominee in the Democratic gubernatorial primary and went on to win the general election, the center of Democratic party power in New Jersey shifted from Newark to Hudson County, where it remained during Hague's tenure.

In June 1920, two months before the passage of the Nineteenth Amendment extending suffrage to women, Hague summoned Mary Norton to his office and charged her with the responsibility for organizing the women of Jersey City. Mrs. Norton had been working at a day-care center since the death of her only child and had occasional recourse to City Hall with appeals for funds and help. Impressed by her intelligence and demeanor, Hague selected this political novice to be vice-chairman of the State

Committee of the Democratic party. He backed her bid for election to the Hudson County Board of Freeholders, and in 1923 she became the first woman to hold that position in New Jersey. Then in 1924 Hague asked her to run for Congress. She won that election by 17,000 votes, and was reelected again and again with increasing majorities, serving a total of thirteen consecutive terms in the House of Representatives. Known as Aunt Mary to the Capitol Hill journalists, Mrs. Norton was the second woman to enter Congress and the first of the Democratic party.

Throughout her career as a New Deal Democrat, Representative Norton was loyal to her mentor. She stated, "Frank Hague believed in me. He never let me down. I don't believe many women who started working in politics back in the twenties could say that of their men leaders!"

During most of his years in office Hague had to deal with a Republican state legislature, but this was no insuperable handicap. By filling state boards and commissions with his appointees during the administrations of Democratic gover-

Above
Mary T. Norton, who represented Hudson County in Congress for 26 years, was a New Deal Democrat and an ally of President Roosevelt. This drawing by C. K. Bertram depicts her role as Chairman of the House Committee on Labor. Courtesy, JCPL

Opposite page
Exchange Place Area 1972: In the foreground is the rising frame of Paulus Hook Towers, a state-sponsored housing development. Also under construction, in the center, is 30 Montgomery Street, an office building. The old Harborside appears on the left, and the land closest to the river is used for parking. Courtesy, Jersey City Planning Division

nors such as A. Harry Moore from Jersey City and by horse trading and paying for votes on selected issues, Hague arrived at an understanding with the Republicans. It was a Republican state senate that confirmed the appointment in 1939 of Frank Hague, Jr., to the state's highest court despite the vigorous dissent of professional legal circles. Within Hudson County Hague's control of the local Republican party was complete.

Hague had an instinctive feel for the kind of public relations that would impress his constituents. He lured a heavyweight title fight between Jack Dempsey and Georges Carpentier to a temporary bleacher stadium at a site off Montgomery Street known as Boyle's Thirty Acres. Here, on July 2, 1921, the boxing world welcomed its first million-dollar gate; the unlucky fans who could not get tickets

could tune in their radios for the first broadcast of a boxing match. Hague regularly threw out the ball at the opening games of the Jersey City Giants of baseball's International League, and he persuaded businessmen to take season tickets. With no personal interest in the arts, he had some appreciation for their value to the city's image if not to its spirit, and he insisted upon superior quality materials and ornamentation for the public buildings erected during his administration. During the 1940s he appropriated funds to assist the Jersey City Philharmonic Orchestra led by J. Randolph Jones.

Hague's success was obviously dependent upon what he could do for people. Jobs for supporters who kicked back a percentage of their salaries, public contracts for contributors, and control of law enforcement, including selective disregard of the law of Prohibition, gave the machine much of its power. But when that power was threatened, Hague was firm and sometimes ruthless in squelching the opposition. This combativeness sealed his position and produced a closed society.

The first major challenge to Hague came in 1928 and 1929 when the local paper, *The Jersey Journal,* began printing satiric letters and then editorialized for Hague's opponents in the 1929 election. The other two major county papers, the *Jersey Observer* and the *Hudson Dispatch,* were solidly in Hague's camp. Hague's retaliation was severe. Public notices were no longer printed in the *Journal.* Newsdealers were visited by policemen and discouraged from selling the paper. Movie theaters were advised not to buy advertising space, and the newly opened area known as Journal Square was renamed Veterans Square although the name change never was accepted by the public. After the defeat of Hague's challenger, Robert Carey, the newspaper gave in to reality and ended its opposition. At the same time Hague fought off an attack from the legislature which appointed the Case committee to investigate the source of his wealth. A ruling by John Fallon of Hoboken, the state's vice-chancellor, held that the committee lacked jurisdiction and demonstrated the value of having appointees in high places.

A recurring thorn in Hague's side was Jeff Burkitt, a former riveter from the South, who made it his personal crusade to topple the Boss. Denied permits for public meetings, he would speak on street corners and then be routinely arrested. Though "built like a locomotive" Burkitt would often leave jail in a roughed up state. Others who suffered from speaking out were John Longo who was imprisoned on a charge of tampering with election registrations, a charge later overturned by the courts, and Ted Brandle, head of the iron workers' union who battled Hague in the early 1930s for condoning the use of non-union labor on the construction of the Pulaski Skyway. A confrontation at the site resulted in the death of one non-union worker and the arrest of union members on the charge of murder. To pay for their defense Brandle spent his fortune and lost the Labor Bank which he had built at Journal Square.

Hague's influence stretched into Hoboken where the family which controlled the Steneck Bank lost it in a political dispute and into Bayonne where allies of independent Mayor James Donovan were indicted. Yet his most publicized battles were with the new Congress of Industrial Organizations (CIO) and the American Civil Liberties Union (ACLU). When the CIO organizers tried to recruit in Jersey City in 1937, Hague denounced them as Communists and ordered the police to escort their speakers, including Norman Thomas, to the ferries for immediate transport to New York. The ACLU challenged the restrictive municipal ordinances regulating public speech and won a Supreme Court decision in 1939 to which Hague had to acquiesce. This widely publicized contest directed attention to Hague and Jersey City, and the national press began to describe him as a dictator. Although some residents were embarrassed by the disparaging criticism

of their city, others were affronted by the ethnic bigotry apparent in journals such as *The Nation,* which referred to the "peat bog elite," and they rallied around their leader. Thus the national criticism in some ways strengthened his hand at home. In the meantime, the CIO made its peace with Hague and supported him when he next ran for reelection.

With the carrot and the stick, with appeals to patriotism and pride, Hague reigned supreme. The question arises, "What did he do with his power?" For one, he became wealthy and made numerous trips to Florida and to Europe leaving the day-to-day administration to his talented second-in-command, John Malone. But his regime was too complex for the simple story of personal enrichment. In fact, Frank Hague made some

Above
This photograph is from around 1930, when it was still the custom to wear white shirts and suspenders even while digging ditches. These city workers are in Lafayette Park. JCL

Top
This view west over Kearny from the mid-1960s shows in the foreground the ramp of the Lincoln Highway bridge over the Hackensack River. Courtesy, Jersey Pictures

An aerial view, taken in 1948, shows the fourteen tall, brick and stone, Art Deco-style buildings of the Jersey City Medical Center—conceived by Frank Hague and designed by his official architect John T. Rowland. They were built from 1929 to 1941. The stepped building at right is the former Tuberculosis Hospital, and to the right of it is the Margaret Hague Maternity Hospital. In 1940 there were more births (5,332) in this medical center than in any other hospital in the United States. JCL

genuine contributions to the welfare of the people he ruled, and he had a vision of how the city could be improved. In the mid-1920s he decided to raze an entire block near the Hudson and Manhattan Summit Avenue station and by so doing created Journal Square, which he intended to be the city's commercial center. He backed Mary Norton's proposal for a county maternity hospital, which was named for his mother Margaret. After its 1931 opening it soon attained the lowest infant-mother mortality rate in the world. His genuine interest in health care prompted the construction of the massive municipal Medical Center and the adjacent county tuberculosis hospital named for its director, Dr. Berthold Pollak. Patients who could not pay were treated free. These medical services were a godsend to the average citizen who lacked health insurance and could not afford a private hospital, but they were expensive to maintain.

Another project dear to Hague's heart was his campaign to curb juvenile delinquency by means of an early intervention program designed to use the police and the schools to straighten out boys on the

verge of trouble. It was in the context of seeking jobs for unacademic youths, too young for work permits, that he made his famous statement, "In this case, I am the law."

Hague's ability to deliver the vote for President Roosevelt was rewarded with enormous largesse. All federal patronage jobs in New Jersey were cleared by Hague, not by the governor or senators. Roosevelt's aide, Harry Hopkins, gave Hague control over 1,800 Civil Works Administration jobs and appointed a Bergen County Hague man, William Ely, as head of the state's Works Progress Administration, which employed over 76,000 persons annually. Hopkins also stretched the law to allow WPA funds earmarked for labor costs to pay for equipment at the new Roosevelt Stadium. Both this structure and another Roosevelt Stadium in Union City were built with federal money which also covered most of the construction costs of the Medical Center. Hague also controlled the distribution of Federal Emergency Relief Aid. Without this help the burden of the Great Depression would have fallen more heavily upon the people of Hudson County.

During the 1940s the polished machine lost its fine tuning. Democratic governor Charles Edison would not take orders from Hudson County, and a proposal to adopt a new state constitution gained momentum despite Hague's opposition. On the local front mayors Joseph Stilz of West New York and Harry Thourot of Union City were showing signs of independence and Mayor Donovan of Bayonne was downright defiant. In 1946 Harrison elected young Frank Rodgers, a veteran who represented the new generation. Then in 1947, in a harbinger of things to come, Mayor McFeeley of Hoboken was defeated by a slate of three Italians and two Irishmen. At the age of seventy-one in June 1947, thirty years to the day after he became mayor, Frank Hague resigned and turned the office over to his nephew, Frank Hague Eggers. Whether Hague was too tired for the daily grind or whether he wished to marshall his remaining resources to fight the growing discontent is not known. Though out of office he was not out of the picture, but his time was running short.

The challenge came from one of his own lieutenants, John V. Kenny, also a son of the Horseshoe. Known as The Little Guy, Kenny's amiable style differed from Hague's earnest and aloof manner. He would stand on a street corner jingling coins in his pocket and wait for his favor-seeking neighbors to approach. "Johnny, the wife is sick." "Johnny, I've been laid off." "Johnny, the cops picked up my boy." Kenny realized that the time was long overdue to reward the Poles and Italians with places on the commission, and he used this strategy to win a May 1949 victory in what became locally as the "Wildest Election." The Hague-Eggers forces managed to retain control of county government for several more years, but were eventually ousted by the Kenny men. On January 1, 1956, Frank Hague died in his Park Avenue apartment in New York leaving a legacy of political intrigue perhaps unparalleled in America.

Three men who were important for Hudson County during the 1930s are pictured in this photograph. From left to right are Frank Hague, mayor of Jersey City 1917 to 1947; Franklin Delano Roosevelt, President of the United States from 1932 to 1945; and A.

Harry Moore, born in Jersey City and elected governor of New Jersey in 1925, 1931, and 1937. The photograph was probably taken in 1932 when the three met in the governor's mansion in Sea Girt for a campaign rally. JCL

XI

The Urban Challenge

The lower half of this 1965 photograph shows one-third of Jersey City's Hudson River waterfront, from Exchange Place (upper right, near the ship's prow) to the approach to the Holland Tunnel (lower left). The large warehouses near Exchange Place were built on landfill; the buildings around the park (lower left) constitute the Hamilton Park Historic District (built circa 1850 to circa 1900); the railroad lines are those of the Pennsylvania and Erie Railroads. In the foreground is the New Jersey Turnpike extension (opened in 1956) leading to the Holland Tunnel (opened in 1927). JCL

The flow of federal dollars cushioned the devastating effects of the Great Depression, but not even the Roosevelt-Hague alliance could ward off the factory closings and the layoffs which afflicted Hudson County during the 1930s. In this decade the county suffered the first reversal in its fortunes. Its population declined by 38,000 and its employment dropped a great deal. Two railroads, the Jersey Central and the Erie, went into working bankruptcy as freight and passenger traffic fell off drastically, and the other rail lines were crippled by severe losses. Private and public development programs were shelved when the world's capital supplies dried up. Nonetheless, the mixed industrial, transportation, and commercial markets of Hudson County and of the rest of the New York region fared better in these years than did the remainder of the United States.

Then came the world war which destroyed so many lives and scorched so many cities and rescued the American economy. As the men boarded ships for Europe, Africa, and the Pacific, orders for defense work poured into the factories, and soaring employment rolls attracted to the industrialized areas like Hudson County a large number of immigrants from the rural counties of New Jersey, from Appalachia, and from the South. The Kearny shipyards geared up,

Victory gardens bloomed, and the port went into overtime. Freight moved smoothly with none of the congestion that delayed shipping during World War I. With gasoline use restricted, the railroads were again in great demand, and their profits recovered. Soldiers were bivouacked in Hudson County parks and, as the fighting progressed, prisoners of war were detained in temporary brigs. The number of men and women from Hudson County who died while serving in the Armed Forces during World War II reached 1,623. The Wallace family of Hoboken suffered the most grievous loss when three brothers, Daniel, James, and William, died. Among the Hudson County heroes who fought so bravely, four received the Congressional Medal of Honor, Stephen Gregg and Nicholas Oresko from Bayonne and John Meagher and Francis X. Burke from Jersey City.

The Great Depression was ruinous and the war years cruel, but it was not these calamities but postwar prosperity, when hearts were light and full of hope, which bludgeoned Hudson County's economy and its spirit.

A new America was in the making after 1945. For the first time in the life of the nation, the majority of citizens had options and opportunities previously limited to the rich. War had taken people away from the familiar and opened their minds

Above
This photograph of August 1949 shows the last Hudson County trolley. In 1903 the Public Service Railway

Company bought all the small lines. Photo by Davis Studios, JCL

to new ways. The returning veteran could attend college tuition free; he could buy a home with a federally-backed mortgage; he could afford a car; and he could escape the working class for a white-collar job. These factors, plus the shortage of housing and the marriage and baby booms, opened up the countryside surrounding the cities and created instant suburbia remote from train connections and dependent upon automobiles. Government speeded the process by constructing the highways, bridges, and bus terminals that would make commuting relatively painless. Hudson County felt the brunt of this significant shift in population and employment as traditional patterns were altered permanently.

For a few years following the war, the rail lines held onto their business, but the changes in the economy threatened and ultimately destroyed these once haughty private empires. With gasoline cheap and plentiful travelers relied upon their cars, and shippers such as the Post Office turned to trucks and planes. The opening of the New York State Thruway in 1954 and of the Saint Lawrence Seaway in 1958 meant less traffic for the Erie, Lackawanna, and West Shore lines, and the shift to oil and gas for power and home heating destroyed the coal business for the Jersey Central and the Lehigh Valley. Even the mighty Pennsylvania, which termed itself the standard railroad of the world, suffered serious losses in both passenger and freight business. Rail management, in too many cases stuffy and unimaginative, met the challenge with too few successful innovations such as the piggyback truck service and with too much hand wringing and inertia.

Desperate, the rail lines resorted to mergers and track reduction. In 1960 the Erie and Lackawanna joined forces, and the Erie abandoned its Jersey City terminal and ferries to share the Hoboken quarters of the Lackawanna. The Pennsylvania eliminated its commuter service into Jersey City in 1961, and within a few years its station at Exchange Place and its trestle were razed. The state-sponsored

Aldene Plan made the Jersey City terminal of the Jersey Central obsolete in 1967. Bankruptcies became routine; even the merged Penn-Central could not escape. The answers were the nationalization of most freight service in the East, which occurred in 1976 when Conrail was formed and the takeover of passenger operations by the state and by Amtrak, which received heavy federal subsidies. When the New Jersey Transit Corporation was created by the legislature in 1979, only one active passenger facility survived in the county, the old Lackawanna terminal in Hoboken.

Even the Hudson and Manhattan tubes were in trouble. Falling into insolvency during the Depression and into bankruptcy in 1954, they ran with a disintegrating fleet that was nonetheless more essential than ever to the tens of thousands who used it daily, because ferry service was also dying. The final ferries between Hudson County and New York sailed across the Hudson in 1967. As part of a deal to erect the twin towers of the World Trade Center in downtown Manhattan, the Port Authority reluctantly took over the tubes in 1962 and rescued this vital operation, renamed the Port Authority Trans-Hudson System (PATH) with a multi-million dollar long-term renovation project.

With the decline in rail freight traffic came a concomitant drop in lighter and carfloat service. The once jammed Hudson River waters became quiet, and the whole marine shipping industry, reeling from the corruption portrayed in the film *On the Waterfront*, changed drastically as containers were introduced at Port Newark, across Newark Bay from Bayonne. In 1948 the Port Authority took over this municipal port and later bought adjacent acreage in Port Elizabeth where in 1962 it opened a huge modern containerport that was located strategically, not at a major rail terminal, but near Newark Airport and the New Jersey Turnpike.

While all these changes were occurring in transportation, Hudson County

Above
The Bergen Arches, circa 1910. The Erie Railroad steamed through this cut in the Bergen Hill until 1958. Now this roadbed is being considered for use as a highway of light rail line for traffic headed for Hoboken and downtown Jersey City. Courtesy, JCPL

watched its factories close. Industries that were household names looked for brighter prospects elsewhere. RCA and Otis Elevator left Harrison. Bayonne lost Ciba-Geigy and Hunt-Wesson. Lipton Tea, Todd Shipyards, and Tootsie Roll departed from Hoboken. American Can, Emerson, Lorillard, Swift, Westinghouse, and a myriad of smaller local establishments left Jersey City. Railway Express folded, and Seatrain Lines left Weehawken. Kearny lost its shipyards and, after the breakup of AT&T in 1984, its Western Electric plant. The loss of jobs, the collapse of the railroads, the shift in marine shipping from break-bulk to containers meant that in three decades Hudson County lost its traditional way of earning its living, and the process continues. Colgate-Palmolive, one of Hudson's oldest industries which moved to Jersey City in 1847, has announced that it will end manufacturing at this location in 1987.

As the jobs left, so did the people. Hoboken's Frank Sinatra was only the best known of the tens of thousands who found their main chance in other places. Not only did young couples move out when they married, but retired people took their pensions and headed for the shore communities in Monmouth and Ocean counties. The total loss of residents from 1930 when the total peaked at 690,730 to 1980 when it numbered 556,972 was 133,758, and the numbers do not reveal the changing nature of the population. Until World War II a working-class group of European immigrant stock

Opposite page, top
On October 7, 1948, President Harry S. Truman paid tribute to Congressional Medal of Honor winners (from left) John Meagher of Jersey City, Steven Gregg of Bayonne, Nicholas Oresko of Bayonne, and Francis X. Burke of Jersey City. The older man is World War I medal winner Frank Bart. Behind is Frank Hague. Photo by Irv Wagen

Opposite page, center
This aerial view of circa 1935 shows the central section of Hoboken's waterfront. JCL

In the city of Bayonne, at the southern tip of Hudson County, rises the steel arch of the Bayonne Bridge, pictured in 1931, the year it opened. Designed by the famous engineer Othmar H. Ammann, it spans the Kill Van Kull from Bayonne to Staten Island. One of several bridges erected by the Port Authority to link New York and New Jersey, it demonstrates the rising ascendancy of the motor vehicle over the railroad. The Bayonne Bridge is an elegant terminus of the boulevard, once called Hudson, now JFK, which runs the length of Hudson County. Photo by J. Byrnes. Courtesy, The Port Authority of New York and New Jersey

dominated the county. After the war the blend changed considerably. Several huge and significant shifts brought blacks, Hispanics, and then Asians to Hudson County.

Blacks, who had resided in Hudson County since the 1630s, were a small community until the end of the nineteenth century, when their numbers increased as they followed the railroads in search of work. For example, many sleeping car porters brought their families to Hudson County so that they would be close to home at the end of their runs. Throughout the first decades of the twentieth century, West Indians and southern blacks arrived in a small but steady stream. Clement Price, in his documentary history of blacks in New Jersey, *Freedom Not Far Distant,* includes testaments to the fairly free racial attitudes, for the time, that prevailed in Jersey City under Frank Hague. While the blacks as a group were economically deprived and generally confined to a ghetto, Jim Crow was less virulent than in other northern cities, and a few blacks held responsible municipal positions. Churches were the glue which joined many together and gave them hope. The need for workers in the humming factories during World War II induced many more blacks to migrate from the South and this movement continued throughout the

1960s. By 1980 blacks constituted 12.52 percent of the county with the largest number in Jersey City.

The first airborne migration, that of the Puerto Ricans starting in the late 1940s, introduced a new dimension into the population. Although they arrived cold with no predecessors to ease the way, the Puerto Ricans held United States citizenship, and so had the potential to become an immediate electoral force. In the first decades their political activity was most apparent in efforts to bolster their own culture and retain their Spanish language, and in the early years frequent flights back and forth to Puerto Rico nipped emotional ties to the mainland in the bud. Like all immigrants in the preceding century, the Puerto Ricans did not find a warm welcome in Hudson County. Several churchmen led by Father Joseph Faulkner, S.J., initiated activities to aid these newcomers, and federal programs and mandates have addressed their needs at least as much as have the traditional political solutions. Attempted coalitions with blacks have not endured although there are signs that a rebellion against gentrification has united these two groups plus low-income whites and tenants.

In 1960 the first of two large waves of exiles from Castro's Cuba arrived in Hudson County. Unlike the Puerto Ri-

This circa 1955 aerial view to the northwest shows Hudson County's Hudson River shoreline, excluding only Greenville and Bayonne. At the lower right is Ellis Island. The closeness of the island to the piers and shore of Jersey City (lower left) makes it clear how Hudson County was populated; Jersey City had a recruitment office on Ellis. The long tracks and train shed across the middle of the photograph are those of the Central Railroad of New Jersey, and the waterway just above those tracks is the Morris Canal (completed in 1836). The white building giving off smoke is Colgate's Soap plant, and the white ship is docked at Exchange Place, the eastern terminus of the Pennsylvania Railroad until 1910. JCL

cans who were concentrated in Jersey City and Hoboken, the Cubans moved to north Hudson County and crowded into Union City, West New York, and North Bergen. Within a few years the north Hudson County area became second only to Miami in its number of Cubans. Most were from the middle class with the entrepreneurial attitudes which gave them rapid financial success. One woman claims that she went to the same butcher and the same hairdresser and that her husband used the same auto mechanic in North Bergen as they had patronized in Havana. Despite their common language and Caribbean background, the Cubans and the Puerto Ricans did not cooperate for political ends. As they became naturalized, the Cubans ran for office with gusto, but they tended to split among the competing factions, and thus no single ticket claimed their allegiance.

By April 1, 1980, census day, 26.08 percent of the Hudson County population was Hispanic. In the summer of 1980 a Cuban boat lift brought another wave of refugees to America, and many found their way to north Hudson County to be near their countrymen. This second group included many young, unattached men without marketable skills who found assimilation difficult. The federal government stepped in with some assistance that was disbursed through church centers and through welfare agencies, and their condition slowly improved.

When Congress changed the immigration law in 1965, the doors were open to Asian and Middle Eastern immigrants who began to arrive and change the racial composition from a black-white polarity to a multi-racial wheel including Filipinos, Koreans, Indians, Pakistanis, Iranians, and Egyptians. They opened many retail businesses, worked in hospitals as doctors and nurses, and quickly bought homes. Portuguese immigrants, who settled in the Ironbound section of Newark in the early 1970s, started to move into Harrison, Kearny, and East Newark by the end of the decade. Vietnamese war refugees, Haitians, and Russians also arrived to make their home in the county.

This ethnic and racial mix has made

Hudson County a more tolerant community, if a less cohesive one, than it had been in the 1940s. For the majority it became easier to live and let live amidst the gamut of differing appearances, sounds, and styles than to pursue blatant racial prejudices and ethnic grudges. Religious leaders hammered away at the moral obligation to love one another, and state and federal policies pushed for school integration and affirmative action programs. As far as housing and employment are concerned, the blacks and the Puerto Ricans, as groups, are at the bottom, but many have purchased homes, earned college and professional degrees, and become solid members of the middle class. Substantial residential separation by race persists.

So Hudson County lost its railroads and its factories and replaced a significant portion of its population with a new multi-racial blend. Many untrained people arrived just as the jobs employing the unskilled were lost. The cost of municipal services rose at the same time that the tax base dropped off precipitously, while public service unions made their own demands upon the dwindling financial resources. Necessary repairs to the infra-

structure were deferred, and the cosmetic efforts to maintain the parks and streets were cut back severely. Never beautiful, Hudson County's public spaces became more dingy and shabby.

Decay infected the political process as well. The Kenny machine could not match the vigor that Frank Hague had displayed for over three decades. After completing one term as Jersey City's mayor in May 1953, John V. Kenny served only a few more months before resigning to devote his full time energies to being Hudson County Democratic Party chairman. The details and demands of the mayoralty irritated "The Little Guy." "I'm up to my a— in midgets," he complained. Kenny could not maintain the control of his predecessor, and recurrent challenges to his leadership cropped up during the twenty-two years Kenny was the boss. Hudson County was seen as corrupt as the machine faltered to its dismal conclusion in 1971 when eight politicians, including the mayor and the city council president of Jersey City, were convicted on federal charges of extortion and conspiracy. After being separated from the trial because of illness, Kenny pleaded guilty in 1972 to charges of in-

come tax evasion. Additional convictions of the mayors of Union City, Weehawken, and Kearny were obtained in the early 1980s. Counterbalancing these demoralizing events are the long public careers of Frank Rodgers, mayor of Harrison since 1947, and Paul Amico, mayor of Secaucus since 1964, who have demonstrated that longevity in politics is not synonymous with bossism. The people of Hudson County continue to be fascinated by politics and view each electoral contest with the enthusiasm of spectators at a title fight.

Murphy's law was at work; if anything could go wrong, it did. Seton Hall Medical and Dental College, started at the Jersey City Medical Center in 1956, was taken over by the state in 1965 and moved to Newark. War protests by college students and too frequent reports of the deaths of local men in Vietnam saddened and worried the people even as they paid tribute to their brave neighbors such as Father Charles Watters of Jersey City who was awarded the Congressional Medal of Honor posthumously for his courage while serving as a chaplain. The lowest psychological point was reached in the early 1970s, when the entire nation was troubled. Criminal convictions of politicians, a decline in services, climbing tax rates, crime, a diminishing population, and racial wariness all took their

toll. Even New York was enmeshed in its own financial crisis that brought it to the brink of bankruptcy in 1975. The urban areas of the northeastern United States seemed doomed to decline.

The future looked bleak and whatever stopgap measures existed were provided by the state and federal governments. Governor Brendan Byrne won a bitter battle in 1976 to enact a state income tax to finance the Public Education Law of 1975, a law mandated by court decisions in 1972 and 1973 in the case of *Robinson v. Cahill.* Kenneth Robinson, a child from Jersey City, was the plaintiff against the state in a case pleaded by a young attorney, Harold Ruvoldt, acting upon a commission from Mayor Thomas Whelan. To the surprise of all Ruvoldt succeeded in convincing Judge Theodore Botter and then the New Jersey Supreme Court that the existing method of school financing violated the state's constitution. The supreme court ordered the legislature to find a source other than the property tax to fund the schools. In effect, this meant that the cost of educating the poor was to be shared by all the residents of the state. Though no panacea for the urban school systems, the decision was a psychological as well as a financial lift that came at just the right time to give hope to a troubled people.

XII

The Meadowlands, Liberty State Park, and The Brownstone Revival

President Ronald Reagan and Archbishop Peter Gerety are pictured at the Church of St. Ann, Hoboken, on July 26, 1984. The occasion was the celebration of the feast of St. Ann by this predominantly Italian parish. The President is eating spaghetti without tomato sauce, because he is allergic to fresh tomatoes. The jars contain his favorite, jelly beans, and were a gift from Hoboken. Photo by Roy Groething. Courtesy, Jersey Pictures

A generation ago the Hackensack Meadowlands were the talk of the town and the toast of the state. On January 13, 1969 a jubilant Governor Richard J. Hughes, his muscles toned from twisting the arms of legislators, signed the Hackensack Meadowlands Reclamation and Development Act. The law established the Hackensack Meadowlands Development Commission (HMDC), giving it unprecedented power to regulate land use and distribute tax revenues within the Meadowlands district. Stoutly resisted by municipal officials defending home rule, the law was enacted after years of planning, studies by Rutgers University, and advocacy by the press. Hughes secured the crucial votes of Hudson County legislators by threatening to sit on their judicial and patronage appointments.

At stake was a 19,730 acre marshy tract, larger than Manhattan, stretching along both sides of the Hackensack River and incorporating parts of 14 communities, ten in Bergen County and four within Hudson County: Kearny, Jersey City, Secaucus, and North Bergen. In the 18th and 19th centuries the Hackensack meadows consisted of dense cedar swamps and stretches of salt hay and grasses. Although the cedars had begun to die from natural causes, the nearby residents accelerated their decline, felling

the trees for logs and burning the swamps to flush pirates and highwaymen from their lairs. Damming of the Hackensack at Oradell in 1922 increased the salinity of the river and doomed any plant and animal life that could not thrive in tidal water. The tall, tough phragmites reed took over to become the dominant growth.

During the 1800s several investors sank fortunes into the soupy soil. In 1816 the three well-connected Swartwout brothers of New York erected 7 ½ miles of dikes and dug 120 miles of ditches to drain thirteen hundred acres in Secaucus for farming and grazing. But the brothers had bad luck. Exceptionally high tides in 1819 cascaded over the dikes inundating their crops with salt water. Then they detected tunnels in the dikes through which water was pouring back onto the reclaimed soil; constant repairs could not match the pace of destruction. Burrowing muskrats were the culprits.

When John Swartwout died in 1823, his estate was held hostage to his investment. Samuel abandoned the losing venture, and, in 1826, sold his desolate acres to Bergen Township for a farm for the poor. Decades later Hudson County used this land for its extensive welfare and correctional complex at Snake Hill. Robert, however, persisted into the 1840s, becoming more crazed as success

eluded him. Failing again and again and
estranged from his children who resented
the loss of the family's wealth, he died in
1848, still cherishing the hope that some
new technique would rescue his reclamation projects and redeem his life.

The next attempt to drain the meadows
was financed by Samuel N. Pike, a
distiller from Ohio, best remembered as a
builder of opera houses in Cincinnati and
Manhattan. Like many a successful Mid-
westerner with unfulfilled social and
financial aspirations, he moved to New
York. There he joined forces with
Spencer B. Driggs who believed he could
defeat the muskrats. Driggs' break-
through was the iron dike, guaranteed, he
maintained, to thwart burrowing. In
1866 Pike purchased 3,500 acres in
Kearny and North Arlington and employed a battalion of laborers to plant the
dikes. Fields of corn were sown, but the
stalks, though tall and plentiful, were
stunted by the excess of salt and nitrogen
in the soil and failed to produce ears.

Following Pike's death in 1872 the
reclamation project tapered off as the
Pennsylvania Railroad bought prime
sections for a price higher than any
farmer could afford. Sufficient tillable
fields remained to sustain some farming
for almost fifty years. Early in the

twentieth century the lower portion of the
Pike property became the heart of the
south Kearny industrial area.

During the optimistic 1920s planners
recognized that the potential of the meadows far exceeded their drab reality. The
Regional Plan Association made its initial
foray into the discussion in 1929 when it
proposed extensive reclamation, directed by
a public agency, for housing, recreation,
and industry. The Port Authority and
others in the transportation field recommended a railroad transfer station near the
intersection of Jersey City, Secaucus, and
North Bergen, but the independent rail
companies vetoed this idea.

In 1928 New Jersey's legislature
appointed Lt. General Edgar Jadwin, a
veteran of the Army Corps of Engineers,
to head a Meadow Reclamation Commission. General Jadwin prepared a fifty-
year program for 40,000 acres between
the city of Hackensack and the Amboys.
Anticipating by thirty years the relocation of the port of New York to Newark
Bay, he proposed a design based upon the

swap of an enormous quantity of land. Material dredged to create a deep-water channel would be deposited in the meadows to create dry land for industry; shipping, housing, and recreation. Jadwin underscored the importance of state action to coordinate and override, when needed, the diverse interests of the many individual property owners and municipal jurisdictions in the district. But the work was for naught, shelved by the reality of the Great Depression.

Though they had thwarted professional planners, the meadows beguiled visionaries. From his bed at St. Barnabas Hospital in Newark the Reverend Doctor William P. Taylor, Rector Emeritus of St. Paul's Episcopal Church in East Orange and a champion of universalism, spent his final months on earth penning *A Permanent, Unifying, Ever-Perfecting World-City on the Meadows.* In this 1936 pamphlet Dr. Taylor outlined his dream: broad and noble boulevards, a triumphal bridge, great theaters for drama and films of "world import," a sports stadium, and conference buildings, expressive of their home locale, for every state of the union and every nation of the world.

Finally, to cap this most fanciful of plans and the last of the pre-war decade to see the light of day, Taylor proposed the World Building, a reproduction of the Parthenon, erected to house the headquarters of all world organizations and situated on the Meadowlands' very own Acropolis, Snake Hill.

What really happened is that truck depots, generating stations, and industrial plants located on the perimeters of the Meadowlands. The post-war shift from rail to road and the opening of the New Jersey Turnpike in 1952 enhanced the value of the meadows as a distribution center. The impact of the Turnpike went beyond opening the area to interstate trucking. It chopped off a chunk of Snake Hill, exerted pressure to close the pig farms of Secaucus, and demonstrated the feasibility of a relatively new technique for building on saturated soil. Charles Noble, the Turnpike's chief engineer, sank sand caissons down to

bedrock to drain the water and create a firm support for the roadway. In the 1970s the designers of the Meadowlands sports complex used the same construction method.

A destructive storm in 1950, mosquito control ditches, berms, fill, rail embankments, pipelines, and industrial effluent all altered the terrain and water flow. The greatest blight came from unregulated junking of household waste and construction rubble. When the state imposed a 1959 deadline forcing towns to close their open dumps, the procession of garbage trucks headed for the meadows turned into a stampede. Ten years later the Meadowlands received 40% of the waste generated in New Jersey, plus thousands of tons from New York. Littered with waste, scarred by frequent and uncontrollable grass fires, coursed by waterways foul with filth, the meadows had become a swampy slum with garbage as the growth industry.

Some children in Secaucus and Kearny became meadow rats, fishing, trapping, and exploring the spooky byways. But for most of the people of Hudson County

The Urban Pool, Diving from an Old Hoboken Pier, 1970s. For generations fearless swimmers used the Hudson River as their swimming pool. Photo by William Tremper.

Above
Waiting to Enter the Meadowlands Exposition Center, Secaucus, 1999. This exposition and convention center is located at the Plaza at the Meadows, another Hartz devel-opment in Secaucus. Office buildings, movie theaters, shops, and a number of hotels fill the Plaza area. Photo by Michael Lovero

Right
Harmon Cove Condominiums and an Outlet, Secaucus, 1999. The outlets in Harmon Cove draw shoppers from New Jersey, New York, Pennsylvania and points beyond. Tour buses are often seen pulling up to the fashion, home furnishings, and giftware stores. Then their travelers, laden with shopping bags, head for one of the new hotels in Secaucus for a good night's sleep before another day at the outlets. Photo by Michael Lovero

the meadows created a barrier, separating them psychologically as well as physically from the rest of the state and reinforcing their identification with New York. To the east rose the glistening spires of Gotham; to the west, the dismal swamps. If Hudson County residents wanted to see major league sports or buy fashionable clothes or book first class facilities for their dinners and dances, they went to Manhattan.

In the years following the establishment of the HMDC, transportation and distribution facilities on the west side of North Bergen extended into the meadows, and huge mail centers opened in Kearny and Jersey City. No town experienced so

dramatic a change as did Secaucus where Hartz Mountain Industries took the lead. A major producer of pet supplies based in Harrison, Hartz Mountain was founded in 1926 when Max Stern imported singing canaries from his native Germany. Leonard Stern, Max's son, diversified into warehousing and, in 1969, bought a 750-acre tract of barren land in Secaucus for a distribution park. Producers of clothing and gift items soon discovered that bargain hunters would flock to their warehouses in search of markdowns. Thus was born outlet shopping.

Naming the area Harmon Cove, Hartz added office buildings, a hotel, over 1200 townhouse and high-rise condo units, and Meadowlands Hospital, originally known as Riverside. Hartz acquired additional land on the north side of Route 3, for the mixed-use Harmon Meadow development. In 1986 WWOR, the newly assigned VHF television station for New Jersey, moved to Harmon Cove as did MSNBC eleven years later. With hotels and houses, corporate buildings, movie theaters, shops, and restaurants the little town with the aboriginal name has become a thriving commercial and

residential center, even as its older neighborhoods, situated on islands of upland, retain their quiet appeal.

While construction progressed, the HMDC tackled pollution by capping landfills, collecting and treating leachate, and ending the dumping of household garbage. Though still far from pristine and needing much remediation, the district is obviously cleaner than in the dark days of the 1960s. Since 1969 75,000 jobs have been created in the Meadowlands district.

Even as the HMDC was setting up shop, changing attitudes about the environment began to influence Trenton and Washington. By the mid-1980s laws

barring intrusion on wetlands stalled development. The Meadowlands became a fierce battleground in the land use wars. A draft Special Area Management Plan released in 1995 called for no net loss of wetland values to be accomplished by building in selected zones and by replacing phragmites in other areas with higher quality plant life. In 1997 a Memorandum of Understanding between federal and state agencies provides guidance in the areas of wetlands mitigation and ecological restoration. Environmentalists continue to oppose any intervention, insisting that new construction be directed to central cities. However, planners say that developers are the only

Central Railroad of New Jersey Terminal and Tidewater Basin, Jersey City; November 1961. Passenger rail and ferry service of the Jersey Central ended in April 1967. The coal and freight operations ended in the early 1970s freeing the land for Liberty State Park. Lining the left side of the Tidal Basin are the finger piers of the Lehigh Valley Railroad, a major coal carrier. Courtesy, Port Authority of New York and New Jersey

Inset
The Embryonic Liberty State Park, late 1970s. The Jersey Central Terminal, the train shed, the ferry house, and the Railway Express building, which runs along the north side of the train shed, are all that remain of the vast railhead in this late 1970s picture. All the empty land shown was created by the railroad from landfill. In subsequent years the ferry house and the Railway Express building would also be demolished as Liberty State Park was developed. Photo by Michael Lovero

Grain Elevator at National Dock, Black Tom, Jersey City; January, 1964. Coal, grain, petroleum, soap, coffee, livestock on the hoof, and many other commodities were handled on the working waterfront of Hudson County. This grain elevator was located on what is now the southern boundary of Liberty State Park, near the boat ramp and parking lot. Twelve years after this picture was taken this site was being prepared for the June 1976 opening of the park. Courtesy, Port Authority of New York and New Jersey

Below
The Seawall and Walkway at Liberty State Park, 1999. The best viewing place in the county to see Manhattan, Brooklyn, the Hudson River, Ellis Island, and the Statue of Liberty. Courtesy, Liberty State Park Development Corporation

ones with pockets deep enough to fund the needed cleanups, while the residents and mayors of towns in the district resist any change that will increase traffic or add any more expensive pupils to the school rolls. The future of the Meadowlands will depend upon resolution of these competing interests.

Meanwhile, on the east flank of Hudson County, along the shorefront near the Statue of Liberty and Ellis Island, Liberty State Park opened on Flag Day in June 1976, just in time for the Bicentennial festivities on July 4th. Limited at first to a 35 acre corner near the site of the 1916 Black Tom explosion, the park soon expanded northward across the old Jersey Central yards up to the Tidal Basin, where coal barges once jammed the piers of the Lehigh Valley Railroad.

As early as 1912 the consultant who prepared Jersey City's first planning study had recommended a park along the Hudson River, but the railroads monopolized waterfront property and would yield nothing for recreation. In 1958 Morris Pesin, a Jersey City merchant, and Tom Durkin, a *Jersey Journal* reporter, paddled a canoe through the shallow waters between Black Tom and Liberty Island to dramatize Pesin's intriguing new idea: a small waterfront park with a pedestrian causeway linking Jersey City to the Statue of Liberty. This eight and a half-minute voyage propelled Pesin on a crusade on behalf of Liberty State Park that lasted thirty-four years until his death in 1992.

While Pesin kept his plan before the public eye, other forces ultimately produced a much larger park. In 1954 the federal government had closed its

alien detention center on Ellis Island and two years later put the property up for sale. But the government could find no acceptable buyer willing to deal with the thorny tangle of competing claims by New York and New Jersey to jurisdiction over Ellis. Concluding that the island should remain in federal hands, Washington considered an immigration museum but adamantly refused to proceed until New Jersey agreed to clean up its waterfront less than a quarter of a mile away. When the state gave assurances in 1965 that it intended to relocate existing rail operations and create a park along the waterfront, Congress authorized $6 million for preliminary work on Ellis. To set the park in motion, Jersey City donated 156 unconnected acres, many underwater.

*Left
Liberty Science Center,
1999. Not only does the
Science Center draw
visitors from the region
and tourists from afar
to view its exhibits and
enjoy its IMAX Dome
theater; it also hosts
conferences and meet-
ings for businesses and
organizations. Courtesy,
Liberty State Park
Development Corpora-
tion*

*Opposite page middle
The Liberation Monu-
ment in Liberty State
Park, 1997. Natan
Rapoport created this
sculpture as a memorial
to the Holocaust. It
depicts an American
soldier carrying a
rescued victim of a
WWII death camp and
stands on the South
Overlook section of the
park with the Statue of
Liberty in the back-
ground. Photo by
Daniel Beard*

*Bottom
Liberty Science Center,
Jersey City, 1999. Here
are a few of the 1.5
million people who visit
Liberty Science Center
each year. The Center
is filled with multimedia,
hands-on exhibits with
special features such as
a 100-foot long Touch
Tunnel and a Square
Wheels and Driving
Science Home where
kids can use their feet
to power pistons and
move a car. Photo by
Michael Lovero*

From the mid-1960s through the early 1970s both city and state officials issued designs for an elaborate ribbon park with a twenty-story observation tower, but they could do little more than stage press conferences until the region's deteriorat-ing rail freight services were consoli-dated. Although the Aldene Plan of 1967 had brought an end to the Jersey Central's passenger and ferry services, it was not until 1973 that the changing fuel market forced the shutdown of coal operations. At that point all of the railroad land went on the market.

Still, the park was delayed as concerns about its cost mounted. New Jersey held limited Green Acres bonding funds, while Jersey City had qualms about the loss of potential ratables. In 1973 hope surged for a massive Liberty Harbor develop-ment that called for landfilling the cove south of Black Tom to create a new industrial/distribution sector. It also envisioned 20,000 units of housing along both sides of the Tidewater Basin and across most of the western side of the

current park. The park would be limited to a 400-acre belt along the water's edge. But money was tight, infrastructure and site preparation costs were enormous, and the market was too uncertain. The failure of Liberty Harbor doubled the land available for the park to 800 acres.

A 1974 deal between Governor Brendan Byrne and Mayor Paul Jordan secured the green light. Construction began in January 1976 and has been ongoing as the park gradually changes. As part of a harbor cleanup, rotting piers and other marine debris were removed.

Right
The Northeast Section of Hoboken. This photo from the early 1980s gives an idea of the density of the city known as "The Mile." In the foreground is the Maxwell House Coffee plant with its "Good to the Last Drop" sign visible to river traffic and to New Yorkers. In the 1970s Hoboken began a Brownstone revival that attracted homebuyers who favored urban living close to Manhattan. Photo by Michael Lovero

The Jersey Central terminal building and several ferry slips have been meticulously restored and accommodate tourist ferries to Ellis and Liberty islands. A walkway atop a seawall provides unparalleled views of the New York skyline, and a marina on the north end plus a launch dock on the south attract boaters and those who enjoy looking at boats. In 1993 Liberty Science Center opened on the site of the old Jersey Central round-house, near Exit 14B of the Turnpike. It is devoted to informal science and tech-

nology education through demonstrations and hands-on exhibits.

The park quickly became a focal point for ceremonies, concerts, and festivals. On Labor Day 1980 Ronald Reagan launched his successful presidential campaign at the park in the shadow of the Statue of Liberty. Even the en-trenched Democratic politicians of Hudson County felt a measure of pride because the county finally had a setting worthy of its vista, a place to show off.

Like any major public work, Liberty State Park aroused controversy. What should the park look like and how should it be used? A theme park, a doll museum, and a golf course were proposed. Of these only the plan for a golf course on 225 acres had any staying power, and it evoked prolonged, heated discussions between those who favored open space and those who sought an adult recreation missing in Hudson County. Environmen-talists stressed the bird, marine and wildlife, while other opponents dismissed golf as a rich man's pastime. It was a classic case of the Greens versus the Suits. The foes of the golf course mus-tered more forces than did its proponents, and in 1995 Governor Christine Todd Whitman opted for the open space position. Subsequently the state devel-oped a $10 million green park plan that includes a thirty-seven acre lawn for picnic tables and park benches and a twenty-one acre wildflower garden.

*Left
Grundy Park in the
Winter, Jersey City,
1990. Stretching out
into the Hudson River in
an inverted L shape, this
park at Exchange Place
attracts office workers
and Jersey City resi-
dents, plus photogra-
phers from around the
world eager to capture
the famed New York sky-
line. In the summer the
stage at the end of the
park accommodates
noontime concerts.
Photo by Michael
Lovero*

*Opposite page bottom
Abandoned Pennsylva-
nia Railroad Ferry
Landing at Exchange
Place, Jersey City, circa
1970. Even as the
Twin Towers of the
World Trade Center
rose across the Hudson,
the old ferry terminal
at Exchange Place
symbolized the decay
of the Jersey City
waterfront. On the
right is the pier where
Wilson Line showboats
once boarded passen-
gers bound for Rye
Beach. By 1986 a new
city park, named for the
late City Historian,
J. Owen Grundy, would
open up this location.
Courtesy, Jersey City
Public Library*

The pleasures of vibrant urban life did become apparent on the streets of Hoboken, a 1.3 square mile city with block after block of well preserved brick and brownstone homes. Coinciding with a national interest in historic preservation, the old buildings of Hoboken appealed to a new group of homebuyers and commanded prices high enough to surprise their owners, but lower than those offered in Manhattan and Brooklyn Heights. Hoboken residents griped about the yuppies invading their territory, but, as they looked at the fate of other cities struggling to survive without new blood, the gripes were muted. No longer a declining port city, Hoboken has acquired a Left Bank atmosphere, as students, artists, tourists, and locals mingle at the fashionable music clubs, restaurants, and galleries, and Friday night on Washington Street is livelier than the Jersey shore on a summer weekend.

The Brownstone movement in Hoboken spilled over to its neighbor, Jersey City. When City Historian J. Owen Grundy organized a Brownstone Revival meeting in 1972, an overflow crowd at the Five Corners library heard experts praise the choice homes located so close to the PATH lines to New York. This was a novelty for Jersey City; outsiders were making favorable comments about their tough old town. Mayor Jordan and his successor, Thomas F. X. Smith, promoted the idea by supporting historic designation in the downtown section. By the mid-1980s the city led the state in the number of official historic sites and saw a number of abandoned factories and warehouses transformed into offices and housing, thanks to the tax credits available for rehabilitation of historic structures.

People began to heed the optimists. The success of the Meadowlands and the appeal of historic buildings raised hopes for better days ahead. One abandoned railhead had become the state's most popular park, and rumors floated of interest in the Pennsylvania and Erie properties. Soon all eyes would be on the Gold Coast. As Governor Hughes had predicted in 1969, New Jersey would be a contender.

Left Bank Rising

Early in the 1980s, soon after he became mayor of Jersey City, Gerald McCann stood at a window high in the World Trade Center and peered intently across the Hudson at his hometown. "I won't be happy," he said, "until Jersey City has a skyline to match New York."

Well, it's not Skyscraper City yet, but Jersey City does have the three tallest buildings in New Jersey, and plans are on the drawing board to build even higher. North of Jersey City, from Hoboken to North Bergen, parks, housing, and offices are replacing the abandoned remains of the industrial past. The biggest news in Hudson County is the stunning transformation underway along the Hudson River waterfront.

Jersey City's first commercial center was Exchange Place at the foot of Montgomery Street, a landfilled area created by the New Jersey Railroad in the 1850s. Flanked by factories, piers, and railroads, Exchange Place attracted banks, law offices, and a few firms that processed securities. Its heyday lasted until the 1920s when Journal Square emerged as the hub of the city. The Pennsylvania Railroad stopped running ferries from Exchange Place in 1949 and ended commuter trains in 1961. Through the 1950s the Wilson line ran excursion boats, but this service also petered out. Until 1988 Colgate-Palmolive continued

production at its plant in Paulus Hook, sending tank cars across Montgomery Street on their way to the rail yard at Harsimus Cove, but, overall, Exchange Place was a has-been with prime land, right at the water's edge, used for parking. In the 1970s two subsidized apartment buildings went up on Montgomery Street just west of Exchange Place. The fact that large lots with wide lawns and street level parking could be used for income-based housing demonstrated that land values were low.

Exchange Place may have lost its luster, but it retained its prime asset, a location directly across the Hudson from lower Manhattan. One of the stalwarts of the city, the First Jersey National Bank, located at Exchange Place since 1864, moved its management quarters to a new building at 2 Montgomery Street in February 1969. Two months later the Ukrainian National Association unveiled plans for a 15-story office building next door at 30 Montgomery Street.

These signs of life were promising but the advent of the Gold Coast, as the revitalized Hudson County waterfront came to be known, occurred in 1982 when a partnership headed by Michael Sonnenfeldt and David Fromer purchased the bankrupt Harborside, a reel-to-keel terminal erected for the Pennsylvania Railroad in 1929. Harborside was a

Above
The Exchange Place PATH Station and Harborside Financial Center Photographed from Grundy Park, 1990. To foster the renaissance at Exchange Place, the Port Authority erected a new PATH station building, shown here in the foreground with Harborside Financial Center in the rear. The old Erie PATH station at Pavonia was also renovated and renamed after Newport development began. Photo by Michael Lovero

Right
Colgate Tank Car Headed for the Harsimus Cove Freight Yard, Jersey City, 1986. Until the Colgate-Palmolive plant closed in 1988 scenes like this were routine. Here a tank car turning off Hudson Street crosses Columbus Drive bound for Harsimus Cove. Slightly visible on the top left is the Bankers Trust building at Harborside and on the right the rising frame of Exchange Place Centre. Photo by Michael Lovero

structural behemoth, three connected buildings strong enough to support railroad cars and trucks with 1.9 million square feet of leasable space, stretching along the river for the length of four city blocks. After signing the deed for $26 million, the new owners presented the city with a check for $1 million in back taxes.

Sonnenfeldt's interest in Harborside began as a teenager when he worked as an office boy at the terminal and continued through graduate school where he wrote his master's thesis on the site's potential. Reasoning that easy access to Wall Street and low costs for utilities, rent, and taxes would attract insurance and financial firms, Sonnenfeldt and Fromer renamed their property Harborside Financial Center. When they signed Bankers Trust of New York to a long-term lease for 385,000 square feet, they proved that businesses would move to Jersey City.

Encouraged by the auspicious start at Harborside, Thomas J. Stanton, Jr., chairman of First Jersey National Bank, announced that the bank would erect a new office tower on an empty lot for-

merly occupied by Pennsylvania Railroad offices. When it opened in 1989, Exchange Place Centre, standing 495 feet tall from its base to the top of its spire, ranked as the tallest building in New Jersey. (Through the mergers in the banking industry First Jersey National became part of Nat West and subsequently Fleet Bank.) Remembering his family's roots in nineteenth century Jersey City when "No Irish Need Apply" signs were nailed to factory doors, Stanton was a force for tolerance and inclusion as well as a persuasive advocate for his native town. In 1999, in recognition of his moral and financial leadership, Jersey City dedicated a portion of Exchange Place to Tom Stanton's memory.

The improvement of Exchange Place continued in the mid-1980s with a redesigned PATH station and the new Grundy Park. At Columbus Drive and Washington Street Evergreen International, a shipping line based in Taipei, erected the Evertrust building, and several blocks west, at Grove and Columbus, the Cali Realty Corporation signed the Pershing Division of Donaldson, Lufkin, and Jenrette and NTT Data Communications of Japan as tenants for its new International Financial Center. Currently known as Mack-Cali, the firm acquired Harborside in 1996.

The closing of the massive Colgate-Palmolive plant brought an end to perfumed air in Paulus Hook and introduced the development known as Colgate Center. The 1992 opening of 101 Hudson Street, the first stage in Colgate Center, brought Merrill Lynch and Lehman Brothers to Jersey City. Standing 550 feet tall, with forty numbered floors, 101 Hudson won awards for its architectural excellence and took the honors for tallest structure in the state away from both Exchange Place Centre and a newer contender, the 37 story, 528 foot tall, Newport Office Tower. The Colgate clock, famed as the world's largest single-faced timepiece, still keeps on ticking from a perch on the ground facing the river.

In 1986, with the aid of a $40 million Urban Development Action Grant, ground was broken for Newport, the largest development along the waterfront. Located on 600 acres once occupied by the Erie Railroad, about half a mile north of Exchange Place, Newport is a mix of housing and office towers, street level stores, an international food market, and a regional shopping mall, all enlivened by a marina, a health club, a hotel, restaurants, and movie theaters. It is a joint enterprise of Melvin Simon & Associates, a leading developer of shopping malls, and the Lefrak Organization, headed by Sam LeFrak, the family's patriarch, and his son Richard. The elder LeFrak, who made his name in the New York City housing market, has staked his fame on Newport, the crown jewel in his empire. The Newport properties have introduced firms such as Brown Brothers Harriman, First Chicago Trust, and the USA Network to Jersey City and are the largest taxpayers, contributing $14 million a year to the municipal coffers.

Situated next to the Holland Tunnel, with a PATH station in its midst, Newport attracts empty-nesters returning to the city after years of child-rearing, young people from the suburbs eager to be near Manhattan, local residents looking for a spiffier address, and émigrés from New York seeking more bang for their housing bucks. In an article in *The New York Times* of September 13, 1998, a new resident of Newport explained why she was happy with her family's move from Brooklyn: "First of all, the view" and then she concluded her list of reasons with the comment, "And when you go out at night on the promenade there are tons of couples with their children. You feel like you're living in a yacht club."

The Gold Coast glittered in north Hudson as well. In 1981 Arthur Imperatore, a West New York native and the founder of A-P-A Transport of North Bergen, purchased 360 acres of railroad land in West New York and Weehawken for a new community, Port Imperial. Hartz Mountain Industries, fresh from its

success in the Meadowlands, acquired the old Seatrain terminal in Weehawken for its Lincoln Harbor development. After signing Paine Webber to a long-term lease in 1986, Hartz created a complex of four office buildings, shops, restaurants, a hotel, and a marina. Riva Point, luxury condo housing, opened in 1990 along a 980-foot pier originally used by Seatrain for container operations.

Indeed housing was proving as popular as commercial development near the waterfront, with the view of New York a major selling point. It was this view that had attracted tenants to the post-war apartments erected atop the Palisades in Union City, North Bergen and West New York, to the posh Galaxy complex in Guttenberg, and to Half Moon Harbour,

Exchange Place Looking West from Grundy Park, 1993. Exchange Place Centre in the foreground and 101 Hudson rising tall on the left have dramatically altered the landscape. Along with Newport Office Tower, they are the tallest buildings in New Jersey. Photo by Communipaw Communications, Courtesy, Jersey City Public Library

formerly Roc Harbour, on the North Bergen waterfront. In the 1980s new high-rise condos were completed in Hoboken and work began on Portside overlooking the Tidal Basin in Jersey City. Converting abandoned factories into housing was the route taken at Clermont Cove, Brunswick Laundry, and Dixon Mills in Jersey City and at the Lipton Tea and Keuffel and Esser plants in Hoboken. The most imaginative housing development was Port Liberté at Caven Point in Jersey City, a mix of townhouses and apartments rising next to canals through which a resident could steer his boat to dockage at his own front door.

Sick to death of looking at rot on the waterfront, most of the people of Jersey City greeted these developments warmly. The Gold Coast provided amenities previously missing in the city plus a little glitz and glamour and many more jobs. But some did dissent. In the mid-1980s the fear was abroad that developers would drive out the poor and the middle class. That perception, fueled by condo conversion mania and escalating home

prices throughout the city, contributed to the defeat of Mayor McCann in his 1985 reelection bid. A few objected to the tax abatements awarded to most new projects or opposed the design of the Newport garage or protested against increased traffic. Joe Duffy of the Historic Paulus Hook Association didn't like the idea of 101 Hudson at all. "Too big," he insisted. Instead he wanted Colgate to erect four log cabins.

Waterfront plans met much more resistance in north Hudson where concerns for esthetics and congestion drove the debate. With its piers forsaken by the shipping lines, Hoboken seemed a natural for development, but the joint plan of the city and the Port Authority for offices and housing was stymied by those who preferred parks and open space along the river's edge. Hoboken held two referenda, one in 1990 and the second in 1992. Each time the development proposals were narrowly defeated. In Weehawken and West New York objections to buildings high enough to impinge upon the view from the heights slowed and altered

Lincoln Harbor and so delayed Imperatore that he gave up his dream of an elegant, European style community. Instead, he created a marina, a shorefront restaurant, and a golf range and concentrated upon his growing ferry business.

While the changes along the waterfront were not universally welcomed in Hudson County, they caused great distress in the Empire State. Bidding wars erupted in the 1980s and 90s when American Express, NBC, CBS, the commodity exchanges, and even the New York Stock Exchange announced that, no kidding, they were very seriously thinking of moving to Hudson County. After a few false alarms even the starry-eyed optimists in New Jersey realized they were being used to wring concessions from New York. A Jersey City Stock Exchange seemed as improbable as a Saks-Journal Square. The "Masters of the Universe," newly enriched by financial incentives, stayed put in Manhattan, but

Portside as Seen from Liberty State Park, 1999. These two residential towers, one 19 and the other 25 stories, are located on the southern rim of the Paulus Hook section of Jersey City, overlooking the Tidal Basin and Upper New York Bay. Planned in the 1980s, Portside languished during the recession of the early 1990s. The Jersey City School Superin- *tendent considered acquiring Portside I for a school and administrative center, but the neighborhood objected. As the market improved in the mid-1990s the first tower proved so successful as a rental property that Portside II was constructed and quickly filled. 101 Hudson stands on the right in this view. Photo by Michael Lovero*

the exodus of other top-drawer firms so threatened the Big Apple that its mayor, Edward Koch, posed for three full-page ads in *The New York Times* in July 1987. Armed with hammer and nails Koch was pictured progressively boarding up the Holland Tunnel. "New Jersey? No Way!" he proclaimed.

What Mayor Koch could not achieve with his tool kit and lumber, the recession of the early 1990s did accomplish. On February 8, 1993 *Crain's New York Business* asked, "What Gold Coast?" No new construction was planned, and developments started in the 1980s sputtered. Portside's condo tower remained unfinished, the piles for its proposed twin poking up in mute witness to the stalled market. Port Liberté fell into the hands of the Resolution Trust Corporation.

Above
An Outdoor Café on the Plaza at 101 Hudson Street, Jersey City. The Gold Coast has introduced new restaurants, marinas, hotels, and theaters, plus a touch of the Left Bank. Courtesy, 101 Hudson Leasing Associates

Lower left
NOL Center and 90 Hudson Street, Exchange Place, Jersey City, 1999. Neptune Orient Lines, a shipping firm based in Singapore, rebuilt the former Commercial Trust Company building on the right. Hartz Mountain Industries is building the office structure on the left with Lord, Abbett, a mutual fund manager, as its principal tenant. Photo by Michael Lovero

But the lull lasted just a few years. As the economy rebounded, Neptune Orient Lines gutted and rebuilt the former Commercial Trust Bank at 15 Exchange Place and created a colonnaded entrance on a plaza where trolley cars once turned around. Joseph Barry, head of the Applied Companies and publisher of weekly newspapers in Hudson County, had gained his expertise by building and managing affordable housing in Hoboken and Jersey City. In the 1990s he moved into the high end of the market by rescuing Portside and Port Liberté. From Newport to Paulus Hook new apartments, hotels, and offices have been rising at a non-stop pace. In late 1997 and again in 1998 Hartz paid $10 million an acre for land within Colgate Center to erect twin 12 story office buildings at 70 and 90 Hudson Street. With Harborside filled and with a tenant base that has broadened to include technology and Internet firms, Mack-Cali is planning an additional 3.8 million square feet of office space west of Harborside and is weighing a 56 story American Financial Exchange to its north. Newport is building anew, and Metropolitan Life is moving employees to 2 Montgomery Street after adding a floor and a half to the former First Jersey National Bank building.

North Hudson's waterfront also bounced back in the mid-1990s. From Weehawken north to Guttenberg Roseland Properties and K. Hovnanian are building town house developments known as Bull's Ferry, Jacob's Ferry, The Landings, and Riverbend. Imperatore and Roseland have teamed up to create Port Imperial South, and Hartz has expanded its hotel at Lincoln Harbor. However, citizen challenges to high-rises continue to wend their way through administrative and legal tribunals, so the future configuration of the north Hudson waterfront remains uncertain.

After a long period of internal debate, with Mayor Anthony Russo taking a pro-development stance and the Coalition for a Better Waterfront lining up as watch-dogs, Hoboken agreed to three major initiatives. In the north, on the site of the old Bethlehem Steel Shipyards, Joseph Barry is building The Shipyard, a large residential complex with shops and a new home for the Hoboken Museum. Close by, the empty Lipton Tea factory is being converted to 540 housing units known as Hoboken Cove. Maxwell House shut down in 1992, but the plant still stands and efforts are being made to attract offices and light manufacturing. Between First and Fifth streets work has begun on the south waterfront project that will feature commercial and residential high rises on the upland and recreational facilities on the two piers. There is even a proposal by the owner of the New Jersey Devils hockey team to build an arena over the Hoboken train terminal.

At the former Greenville Yards in Jersey City, where the Port Authority runs an auto marine terminal, Tropicana-Dole opened a distribution plant in 1992. Each week trains from Florida bring orange juice to Jersey City where it is packaged for the Northeast, the largest market for orange juice in the nation. Hudson Eagle built a distribution center nearby for those with different tastes in beverages. In March 1999, ground was broken for a Foreign Trade Zone at the Greenville Yards with the Summit Imports Corporation on tap to be the first company located within this zone. At the industrial park near Liberty State Park Ritter-Sysco opened a distribution center, and the New York's *Daily News* invested $200 million for its new printing plant.

While the Hudson River waterfront from Jersey City north commands attention, it is just a segment of the bigger picture. In south Kearny, where the Hackensack and Passaic rivers empty into Newark Bay, River Terminal constructed warehouses and distribution facilities on the site of the World War II shipyards and has acquired the former Western Electric plant for future development. Harrison, once a manufacturing powerhouse, lost many of its factories in the past thirty years and is striving to augment its economic base. Restaurants, sports, and entertainment complexes are high on its agenda for a dormant industrial sector along the northern waterfront, directly across the Passaic River from the Performing Arts Center in Newark. Harrison also hopes to convert an abandoned Worthington-Dresser plant into a sound stage.

Bayonne, Hudson County's second largest city, enjoyed a prosperous industrial ring along its waterfront for over a century, but in recent years it has lost its leading petroleum firms and faces the challenge of attracting new businesses to its extensive waterfront.

The heart of the city is filled with well-tended family homes. Broadway, a commercial concourse running north-south for more than forty blocks, remains a strong shopping center similar to Kearny Avenue/Frank E. Rodgers Boulevard in west Hudson and Bergenline Avenue in north Hudson. A stable community, well liked and well cared for by its residents, Bayonne has scant room in its established neighborhoods for additional growth beyond its 1990 population count of 61,444. In this respect it resembles Union City, the third most populous city in Hudson County with 58,012 residents and the only municipality without a waterfront.

Bayonne has a few aces up its sleeve. A golf course is planned for an old municipal landfill recently designated as a Waterfront Recreation Zone. In 2001 the Army will close the Military Ocean Terminal, and the city is studying how best to use this 445-acre bonanza. Under consideration is a deepening of the channel on the north side of the terminal for a possible expansion of Port Jersey, the harbor's largest privately owned containerport that opened on the Bayonne-Jersey City border in 1972. The Terminal is expected to welcome a new museum, the battleship *U.S.S. New Jersey*. Although the Pentagon will make the final decision on the permanent location of the nation's most decorated vessel, a state commission has selected Bayonne over Jersey City and Camden as New Jersey's berth for its namesake battleship.

The Peninsula City should also feel the impact of the Hudson Bergen Light Rail Transit System, scheduled to begin

The Miss New Jersey with Passengers for Ellis and Liberty Islands, Liberty State Park, 1999. All year long these ferries run from the restored Jersey Central ferry slips in Liberty State Park to the Statue of Liberty and to the Immigration Museum on Ellis Island. Photo by Michael Lovero

service between 34th Street in Bayonne and Exchange Place in March 2000. With a projected cost of $1.2 billion, the Light Rail is the largest public works project in New Jersey and will ultimately run from 5th Street in Bayonne to Ridgefield in Bergen County, with a spur to the west side of Jersey City. Conceived as a way to comply with clean air laws, the Light Rail will provide a north-south public transportation artery and is expected to increase real estate values along its route. One likely beneficiary is the Martin Luther King Drive hub redevelopment that is bringing stores, a supermarket, restaurants, and a new post office to a Jersey City neighborhood eager for a commercial boost.

The Light Rail has its critics, particularly among those who live on Essex Street in Jersey City, where the tracks run very close to homes. The rest of the county awaits the line with curiosity, hoping it will diminish traffic on streets laid out in the pre-automobile era. Just as the Light Rail is reminiscent of the trolleys, which last ran in Hudson County in 1949, so do the new ferryboats recall the railroad ferries that made their

Building the Hudson-Bergen Light Rail Transit System, 1999. Workers on the tracks at the Danforth Avenue station of the Light Rail line. The Light Rail is scheduled to open between 34th Street in Bayonne and Exchange Place in March 2000. When completed the line will run from 5th Street in Bayonne to Ridgefield in Bergen County, with a spur from the west side of Jersey City. Photo by Michael Lovero

final crossings in 1967. From a 1986 start between Port Imperial in Weehawken and 38th Street in New York, Arthur Imperatore's fleet, NY Waterway, has grown to nine separate routes. Ferries also run between Liberty State Park and Ellis and Liberty islands, and a little yellow water taxi transports passengers to New York from both Newport and the Tidal Basin.

Other transportation initiatives under consideration include a Turnpike ramp on the Secaucus/Jersey City border that would tie into the Secaucus rail transfer station. The ramp would serve Allied Junction, a proposed commercial development to be situated around the transfer station, and link to yet another proposal known as the Bergen Arches. The North Jersey Transportation Planning Authority has committed funds to determine the feasibility of converting the old Erie Railroad right of way through the Bergen hill into an east-west highway for passenger cars headed for Hoboken and downtown Jersey City. By removing local traffic from the roads that feed the Holland Tunnel, Bergen Arches would speed access and reduce congestion, especially at the notorious Charlotte/Tonnelle circles. The study will also consider adapting the Bergen Arches for a light rail line or for new rail freight tracks.

Like most of America, Hudson County has experienced a significant drop in its crime rate. In the war against crime East

Newark introduced a novel weapon, street cameras linked to police headquarters. Another major concern of urban areas is the quality of education; here Hudson County scores mixed results. Union City's schools have been applauded for their technological leadership, and throughout the county districts are gearing up to provide Internet connections. In 1989 the State of New Jersey assumed responsibility for the Jersey City School District, the first state takeover of a large public system in the nation. Authority was vested in a state-appointed superintendent with the school board's powers greatly curtailed. Citing improvements in the dropout and absentee rates, the Superintendent of Schools stated in January 1999 that the takeover may be nearing an end, but he would not specify a pullout date until test scores rose. On the good side of the ledger, *New Jersey Monthly* magazine, which publishes an annual evaluation of schools in its September issue, rated McNair Academic High School in Jersey City as tops in the state in 1998.

In the past decade the two county educational institutions have grown in stature with expanded facilities and programs. The Hudson County Schools of Technology enroll high school and adult students seeking the skills required for the workforce of the future. With its campuses joined by a fiber optic interactive television network, the Schools have a waiting list of applicants eager to enroll. One of the components, the High Tech High School, twice received the prestigious Star School designation awarded by the New Jersey Commissioner of Education, the only school in the state to be so honored. Hudson County Community College, centered upon a growing campus at Journal Square in Jersey City, offers associate degrees and certificate programs and has experienced a rate of growth higher than any other community college in the state with a 1999 enrollment of 4000 students.

Stevens Institute in Hoboken continues to draw undergraduate and graduate students interested in engineering and allied fields. St. Peter's College in Jersey City is expanding its campus, adding dormitories and a pedestrian bridge across Kennedy Boulevard plus a new parking facility with retail shops near McGinley Square. Jersey City State College acquired a new name and status in 1998 when it officially became New Jersey City University. Like St. Peter's it is revamping its campus, with a newly wired library at its center.

On the housing front the county provides an Affordable Housing Trust Fund with assets of $40 million that has produced 2,000 rental units. This Trust Fund is the largest local housing initiative in the nation and has won numerous awards for its imaginative and effective approach to providing housing for those who cannot afford to buy their own homes or pay premium rents. The state and federal governments have also been active in the housing field, funding apartments for seniors and providing subsidies that enable families of low and moderate income to achieve home ownership. Market housing has succeeded at the base of the Palisades on Bergen Ridge Road in North Bergen and at Society Hill on the former site of Roosevelt Stadium in Jersey City. Several blocks away at Franklin Park, 225 one and two family houses sold quickly at market prices on land where the Van Leer Container factory once stood.

All the additional housing units along the waterfront and throughout the city suggest that the Jersey City will continue to see its population rise, as it did in 1990 when an increase of 5,000 to 228,537 reversed the downward trend of the previous fifty years. The April 2000 census is expected to record a population ranging between 240,000 to 250,000 and may push Jersey City ahead of Newark to become New Jersey's biggest city.

Politics, as usual, have been a mix of stability and volatility. The Silver Fox of Hudson County, Frank E. Rodgers, stepped down in 1995 after having served as mayor of Harrison since 1947, an American longevity record. Raymond McDonough became his successor. Paul

Amico ended his twenty-eight year tenure as mayor of Secaucus in 1991 and was succeeded by Anthony E. Just, Sr. The past twenty years have been notable for the rise of Hispanics as a force in local politics. Puerto Ricans fill important slots in Jersey City's government, and Cuban-Americans hold three major offices in Hudson County. Albio Sires is mayor of West New York, Rudy Garcia heads Union City, and Robert Menendez, the county's first Hispanic member of the House of Representatives, has risen quickly in the Democratic caucus to the fourth ranked position in the party's Congressional hierarchy. In the redistricting that followed the 1990 census, a portion of Hudson County is now represented by its first African-American Congressman, Donald Payne, whose base is Newark but whose constituency includes parts of southern Jersey City and northern Bayonne.

After a change at the top in each term in the 1980s Jersey City cast its ballots for Bret Schundler in a special mayoral election in 1992. An articulate Harvard graduate, Schundler gained recognition as an opponent of the tax revaluation that set the city reeling in 1988. Schundler's election shattered two common pieties. Raised in Westfield, New Jersey, he could not claim the status of a lifelong Jersey City resident, and, *mirabile dictu*, he was

St. Peter's College Plans Pedestrian Bridge, 1998. County Executive Robert C. Janiszewski and the Reverend James N. Loughran, S.J., the president of St. Peter's College, shake hands as they review the college's design for a bridge across Kennedy Boulevard. At the right is Joseph V. Doria, Jr., an administrator at St. Peter's until July 1998 when he became mayor of Bayonne. Mayor Doria is also a member of the New Jersey State Assembly, where he is the leader of the Democrats. Courtesy, HC Executive's Office

Right
New Jersey City University, 1999. In 1998 Jersey City State College attained the status of a university and marked the occasion with a new name, New Jersey City University. The building pictured, Hepburn Hall, is the original Gothic tower on the growing campus. Photo by Louis Tiscornia

Below
Port Liberté, Jersey City, 1999. The most visually attractive housing development on the waterfront, Port Liberté was rescued from the doldrums of the early 1990s recession by Joseph Barry, head of the Applied Companies. Barry completed the unfinished units, is constructing new town houses and apartments, and plans to add a golf course. Photo by Michael Lovero

a registered Republican, the first to occupy the mayor's chair since Mark Fagan moved into City Hall in 1913.

Schundler proved his staying power by winning reelection in 1993 and again in 1997. He has fought to keep the lid on property taxes while achieving an unprecedented 100% collection rate and has been an advocate for school choice in a city with many private and several charter schools. In tribute to the harmony apparent among a population of enormous racial and ethnic diversity Schundler calls Jersey City a "Slice of Heaven," and he has devoted much of his energies to highlighting the cultures of the city's exceptionally varied citizenry.

With the waterfront responsive to market forces Schundler has been paying attention to other sections where growth and rehabilitation need a helping hand. He introduced Neighborhood Improvement Districts for enhanced delivery of services throughout the city and has sponsored Special Improvement Districts for Central Avenue, Historic Downtown, McGinley Square and Journal Square. Funded by extra assessments on property owners plus an inflow of cash through the Urban Enterprise Zone program, the Special Improvement Districts finance landscaping, façade facelifts, and improved security and maintenance. With brick-paved sidewalks, attractive lighting and landscaping, new stores and office buildings, plus the growing campus of Hudson County Community College, Journal Square is poised to resume its

status as the city's center. No one will relish the rebirth of the Square more than Colin Egan, the master sergeant of the restoration of Loew's Jersey Theater, a former movie palace with a sumptuous baroque interior. Like Father Kevin Ashe who has revitalized the Park Theater in Union City, Egan is striving to create a cultural destination and a showplace for local and big-name talent.

In downtown Jersey City Charles Kessler, founder of an advocacy group known as Pro Arts, has collaborated with Robert Cotter, head of the municipal planning office, to establish an eight-block live/work district for creative artists. Already 200 artists have set up studios at 111 First Street, while across the street in an eight-story brick warehouse at 110 First Street a non-profit housing/studio cooperative is being developed. Retail shops supporting the arts will be added on the street level, and a Left Bank ambience will truly pervade the streets of Hudson County.

Robert C. Janiszewski, County Executive since 1988, speaks about Hudson County with the fluency of a professor and the authority of a prelate and takes particular pride in the achievements of the Affordable Housing Trust Fund and in the progress of the Schools of Technology and the Community College. During his tenure the county's parks have been repaired and upgraded, and a new correctional facility in Kearny has replaced the old Pavonia Avenue jail. Infrastructure improvements include rebuilding the Newark Avenue bridge near Dickinson High School, replacing the narrow cobblestone road leading to Harrison with a modern highway, and reconstructing the 14th Street viaduct connecting Union City and Hoboken. Kennedy Boulevard from North Bergen south to Bayonne has been repaved, its curves realigned as needed, and new signage added.

Much of the work of county government involves securing and administering state and federal funds for programs that run the gamut from AIDS to roads to the arts to welfare. Through the Hudson County Economic Development Corporation the county serves a special role working with its communities to encourage business growth. From 1995 through 1998 the number of jobs in the county rose by 20,000, and unemployment dropped to the lowest rate in decades. In January 1999 the state approved the Strategic Revitalization Plan that will guide Hudson County through the first decades of the 21st century.

In his 1998 book, *New Jersey's Multiple Municipal Madness*, Alan Karcher observed, "One cannot spend a day in Jersey City, nor for that matter in any part of Hudson County, without being impressed by the vitality and vibrancy that seem to push up from the pavement." With construction cranes aloft and with sidewalks alive with people from around the globe, Hudson County is on a roll. Even the United States Supreme Court has contributed to the momentum. On May 26, 1998 the Court ruled that the landfilled portion of Ellis Island, roughly 90% of its total area, falls under the jurisdiction of New Jersey, not New York. So, Hudson County enters the new millennium with forty-six square miles on the mainland and twenty-four more acres on the island where the ancestors of so many county residents first set foot in America—Ellis Island, New Jersey, zip code 07305.

Press Conference May 26, 1998: Supreme Court Decides Most of Ellis Island Is in New Jersey. Mayor Bret Schundler of Jersey City addresses a press conference on the day the U.S. Supreme Court decided that the land-filled portion of Ellis Island, nearly 90% of the total area, falls under the jurisdiction of New Jersey. Surrounding Mayor Schundler are retired Congressman Frank Guarini, who initiated legal action to assert New Jersey's claim in the 1980s, and Jersey City Councilmen Arnold Bettinger, Fernando Colon, and William Gaughan. Photo by Alton O'Neill

Chronicles
of
Leadership

This circa 1900 photograph shows a jolly group of Dutch or German ship officers in their cabin while at Hoboken's piers. Hoboken became established as a transatlantic port from about 1863, when the North German Lloyd and the Hamburg-American steamship lines located there. By the turn of the century the city was world famous as a port of entry to a continent. JCL

During the 1630s the first immigrants challenged the native Indians for the right to farm the land that was to become Hudson County. These pioneers set the agricultural pattern that would dominate the northeast section of the Garden State for two centuries. Not until the railroads and the Morris Canal arrived in the mid-1830s did urbanization and industrialization take hold. Then, like Rip Van Winkle, Hudson County awoke from its bucolic sleepiness, and, eyeing the progress of its neighbors, plunged into the competitive fray.

Encouraged, financed, and to some degree coerced by outside investors eager to do business in the Port of New York, the people of Hudson County dotted the shores of their rivers with factories, docks, and railroad terminals. By the 1880s a continuous commercial line stretched along the Hudson River, and tight clusters of industry flourished near the banks of the Passaic in west Hudson County.

Waves of immigrants settled in Hudson County to man the new factories, dig the sewers, staff the trains, and move the freight. So rapid was the pace of change in the years between the Civil War and World War I that the evolving political, social, and physical structures were strained, often beyond the breaking point.

Following the Depression and the brief revitalization of the 1940s, Hudson County suffered severe shock in the postwar years as plants closed, railroads stopped, and residents moved out in droves. Nonetheless, in the midst of a gloomy decline, public and private investment during the 1970s started a chain of events that has already altered the county significantly and promises to continue to do so.

Today the Meadowlands, Liberty State Park, and, above all, the Hudson River waterfront are magnets for hope. The contemporary economic mix includes traditional manufacturing along with new jobs in banking, financial services, and retailing and additional employment in health care and education. With so many changes in its economy and population, the future of Hudson County is certain to be as lively as its past.

The organizations whose stories are detailed on the following pages have chosen to support this important literary and civic project. They illustrate the variety of ways in which individuals and their businesses have contributed to the county's growth and development. The civic involvement of Hudson County's businesses, institutions of learning, and local government, in cooperation with its citizens, has made the community an excellent place to live and work.

ALLIANCE CAPITAL

Alliance Capital Management L.P. is a leading global investment management firm built on entrepreneurialism, creativity, and success. In the 27 years since its founding as an institutional pension fund manager, Alliance Capital has become one of the largest publicly traded investment management firms in the United States, serving institutional clients and individual investors around the world.

Alliance Capital's global presence extends from its world headquarters in New York City to 32 cities in 20 countries on six continents. And Alliance Capital prides itself on the fact that, around the globe, all investors—large institutional clients and individuals—receive the same

Alliance Capital Management world headquarters in New York City. Photo © David Lubarsky

high-quality investment expertise and service. In 1971, when Alliance Capital was founded, institutional investors were its core client base. In the late 1970s, when the mutual fund business, in general, and the money market business, in particular, took off in the United States, Alliance Capital made a strategic decision: in addition to serving institutional clients, Alliance would enter the cash management services field by offering money market funds to individual investors. In 1978, Alliance introduced its first money market fund, and in 1983, Alliance offered its first load mutual fund to the public.

This strategic decision gave Alliance responsibility for providing a high level of customer service to individual investors and the many financial intermediaries serving these individuals. To accomplish that

mission, Alliance formed its transfer agent and shareholder servicing subsidiary, Alliance Fund Services, Inc. (AFS), on November 15, 1983. AFS would manage all the shareholder record-keeping, transaction processing, dividend distribution, tax reporting, and portfolio accounting services for all of Alliance Capital Management's mutual funds, and serve as a shareholder service center for Alliance fund shareholders and their financial advisors.

Initially, AFS was located in the Wall Street area of New York City, close to its parent company. As Alliance Capital Management expanded its mutual fund business and built its client base and assets under management, AFS grew from fewer than two-dozen people to a staff of close to 200; the time had come for AFS to move to larger, customized quarters. In 1987, Alliance Capital opened its doors in Hudson County, when AFS moved its operations to a state-of-the-art facility in Secaucus, New Jersey.

By the end of its first full year in Hudson County, AFS could assess, with great pride, Alliance Capital's growth in the mutual fund industry, and its own growth in servicing Alliance's mutual fund business. Mutual fund assets under management had increased from $1.4 billion at year-end 1983 to $8.9 billion at year-end 1988, which represented 25 percent of total client assets under Alliance's management. Individual shareholders serviced by AFS had grown from a start-up base of a few thousand to over 460 thousand accounts. Ten years later, at year-end 1998, mutual fund assets under management at Alliance Capital had reached $118.6 billion, which represented 41 percent of total client assets under Alliance's management, and AFS was servicing approximately 3.7 million shareholder accounts.

Alliance Fund Services, Inc., in Secaucus, New Jersey. Photo © Anthony D'Elia

From the day AFS opened its doors, it has been committed to providing the same quality service to individual mutual fund investors as Alliance had long provided its large institutional clients. In fact, AFS's stated mission has been "to be recognized by our clients as the leading service provider in the global investment management industry." Quality is the watchword at AFS, which sets the industry standard for courtesy, efficiency, accuracy, and reliability.

Over the years, AFS has sustained its focus on providing high-quality service to its clients, on doing things right, and on continually improving the process. It has achieved its mission by investing heavily in its greatest resource—its people—and by constantly leveraging new technologies. And this effort has positioned AFS as an industry leader.

Much of AFS's success can be attributed to its culture, which embraces quality service, innovation, employee development, and teamwork. Almost all of AFS's senior management started with the company some twelve years ago, with the move to Hudson County. A large percentage of senior management spent significant portions of their careers within the organization, and they have developed, perpetuated, and passed down AFS's culture to the current AFS organization. At AFS, there is a history of real pride and a true sense of belonging, held together by reliance on organization-wide dedication to providing the best service in a supportive environment that fosters teamwork and individual growth.

Inherent in AFS's culture is its explicit dedication to giving back to the communities in which its employees live and work. AFS employees participate and provide leadership in volunteer organizations and serve on community boards. AFS-sponsored teams and sports events help raise money for local charities. Local high school and college students participate in AFS's summer internship and co-op programs, and many AFS employees are recruited from the immediate area. In 1998, AFS was named "Charitable Organization of the Year" by the Meadowlands Regional Chamber of Commerce for its support of local charities in New Jersey. And AFS expects to continue to be a vital contributor to Hudson County.

As we ready to enter the millennium, Alliance and AFS stand strong on their record of achievement and in their commitment to lead the way in the global investment management industry.

BY DESIGN, LLC

By Design, LLC exhibit to demonstrate to their department store customers suggested ways to display merchandise.

Using her 10 years of related import and wholesale experience, Ms. Jay Lee Choi jumped into her role as head of By Design, LLC in 1994. Partnering with an established European-based firm, Jay Lee launched By Design, LLC with only 3 employees. Her premise behind starting this company was that By Design, LLC would offer the best possible quality for the best possible price.

Now, five years later, By Design has 80+ employees in NYC and NJ and has become a leading supplier of women's apparel, specializing in sweaters, knit tops, and sportswear. By Design, LLC markets 3 lines: Debbie Morgan, a missy line that is targeted to certain department stores, By Design, a junior line, and Carolyn Taylor for By Design which markets missy and woman fashions.

By Design's products can be found in leading department, specialty, and mass merchandisers throughout the United States and Canada such as, Federated Department Stores, May Co., JC Penney, Sears, and Dillards.

By Design has brought fashion European style into the American middle market. The focus is to supply quality fashion knits to the moderate and mass market using yarns that look expensive, but at good prices. For example, the company features chenille, rayon chenille, acrylics with rayon finishes, thermal knit, and high twist acrylic yarns. The company

also takes advantage of their European affiliates which feed them information about trends; therefore they are always observing what styles are doing well in Europe and adapt that to the American market. The advantage is they not only constantly get information but they receive confirmation as well. The company uses this knowledge to create unique details and fit to give time honored basics a fresh and updated look for customers who desire high quality, fashion basic clothing at competitive prices.

As By Design, LLC continues to grow, Jay Lee has an aggressive plan in the works to expand worldwide through internal expansion and mergers and acquisitions. In 1999 the company updated their computer system to a state-of-the-art network and installed their in-store shop and fixture program, whereby participating department stores set aside floor space highlighted by distinctive fixtures dedicated for the exclusive sale of the company's products by the retailer. This program enables the retailer to create an environment consistent with the company's image and at the same time increases customer product recognition and loyalty because of the retail customer's familiarity with the location of the company's products in the store.

Production of By Design's products occurs all over the world and the company ensures that it gives back to these countries. Not only does this sourcing of goods ensure jobs in third world countries, they have gone the extra mile by making donations to help establish schools in these areas. They also perform charity work in the United States, including donating money and new clothing to the area communities' police and fire squads.

Because of her generosity and success, Jay Lee has been recognized as one of the 500 most successful women in the U.S. and has also appeared in the Ernst & Young's top entrepreneur registry. Jay Lee credits much of her company's strength and success to its people who work there and their extraordinary work ethic. It is a very healthy atmosphere and everybody motivates each other. Everyone is a team player.

By Design, LLC has accomplished outstanding growth, and Jay Lee is well on the way to taking this company international, all the while remembering that her people are her most important assets.

DIFEO & SALERNO DUANE AUTO DEALERSHIPS

The first DiFeo Buick showroom opened in West New York in 1954.

When you sell over 100,000 automobiles and generate nearly $1 billion annually in revenues, your operation is obviously running on all cylinders. But the success of the Difeo automotive family comes as no surprise to most Hudson County residents, some of whom are now coming up on their fourth generation of buying cars and trucks from one of the family's dealerships.

Sam Difeo, the patriarch of the clan, was born in New York City during World War I, and relocated with his family to establish a retail bakery business, Difeo Pastry, which the family operated from 1913 until it was sold in 1945. While working at the bakery Sam gained experience in the automotive business by buying and selling used cars until 1945, when he obtained his first new car agency, a Willys-Overland franchise located on fifth street in Jersey City.

Four years later he purchased a Chrysler-Plymouth dealership in Linden, but returned to Hudson County in 1954 to open the first Difeo Buick in West New York, site of the old Cleary Buick. Difeo Buick marked the beginning of a succession of auto dealerships that were established by the rapidly growing family business. In 1963 a Difeo Buick dealership opened on Communipaw Avenue in Jersey City, and since that time, with his sons, Joseph, Sam, and Dennis, and his daughter, Cecelia, Sam has managed ten additional dealerships in Jersey City alone. They include Hudson Toyota, Park Pontiac, J&F Oldsmobile, J&S Ford/Isuzu, Difeo Volkswagen, Difeo Subaru, Difeo Mitsubishi, Difeo Hyundai, Difeo Nissan, and Difeo Jeep, Chrysler Plymouth.

In 1990, Difeo joined forces with Salerno Duane, an automotive group operating in Morris, Sussex, and Union Counties to form Saturn of Jersey City. The dealership opened in April of 1990 with 12 employees, and since then has opened up Saturn of Englewood and recently built Saturn of Paramus. The Saturn operation now employs close to 100 people in Hudson and Bergen Counties. Equally important, Saturn has recognized the importance of community involvement in Hudson County. Two childrens' playgrounds have been constructed in Jersey City by the Saturn retail facility over the years, as well as hosting an annual blood drive, Thanksgiving food drive, numerous community functions, such as teach your children to read day, and recycle a bike day for less fortunate children.

In 1994 Salerno Duane, owned by Jim Salerno, his son Michael, and Chip Duane became a partner in Difeo Mitsubishi, and also added Subaru and Kia automobiles to the stable of automobiles retailed in Hudson County. Jim Chip and Michael brought with them over 80 years of combined automotive experience and a long list of community achievements with them to Hudson County. Salerno Duane owns and operates five other new car dealerships in the area, representing eight manufacturers.

The Difeo family sold several franchises to publicly held United Auto Group in 1992, but remains a partner in a Ford, Buick, Pontiac and GMC truck facility in Jersey City as well as the above mentioned franchises in Jersey alone. These operations employ nearly 200 people and generate over $100 million in annual sales in Hudson County. The family also holds interests in a dozen other automotive ventures in the tri-state area.

The continuous dedication of the Difeo and Salerno Duane family to the community is being reinvented on almost a daily basis. It is this attitude, backed up by pro-active steps that keep people coming back to do business with these dealerships as much as the pricing and commitment to service. Their dedication to worthwhile causes is legendary.

Sam Difeo has been an active member of the Boy Scouts of America, the United Way, the Elks Club, and the Dante Aligheri Society. In 1981 he received the coveted *Time* magazine Quality Dealer Award at the National Automotive Dealers Association Convention, and the following year he received the Boy Scouts of America Distinguished Citizen Award. His children have also been active in local causes, serving on the boards of the Kiwanis Club, Rotary Club, and the Boys Club, along with local hospitals and colleges.

This activity has been perpetuated by Salerno Duane through innovative efforts at Saturn of Jersey City, targeting the youth of the area, as well as championing the cause of battered women in Hudson County by teaming up with a local crises center to help raise awareness of the issue throughout the county.

The Difeo and Salerno Duane dealerships remain committed not only to the automotive business in Hudson County, but also the larger social issues that face us all. This type of action will ensure that their business will survive and prosper along with Hudson County long into the 21st century.

FOODMART INTERNATIONAL OF JERSEY CITY

Foodmart International might be short on history, but it's long on space, and success. Since its opening in late 1997, the super-sized grocery store has become a vital ingredient in this community of varied ethnic groups. In its 138,000-square-foot location, the Jersey City supermarket offers an extensive array of foodstuffs for a variety of Asian and Hispanic cuisines, along with the usual American fare.

The store's success is due to the determination of founder Lewis Wu, who comes from a family of grocers in Manhattan's Chinatown district. He faced heavy criticism about the store's size, and fierce competition from three major supermarkets in a five-block area when the store first opened. "The predictions were that we'd close within six months. One and one-half years later, we're up and running, with plenty of customers to keep us growing."

The huge store, with its artfully designed specialty booths and enormous selections of fresh produce, live seafood and fish, calls to mind an indoor street market. Neighborhood children peer at the wide variety of live fish and seafood swimming in big tanks. Customers can choose from more than 15 different types of live fish and seafood, including lobster, dungenness crab, Long Island crab, striped bass, mullet, catfish and tilipia, a fish shipped in from farms in Philadelphia and Florida.

Another favorite gathering place at Foodmart International is the bakery section, where its homemade red-bean-filled buns are always popular. Asian shoppers, who make up 25 percent of Foodmart's clientele, can find

ingredients for Korean, Japanese, Chinese and Philippine dishes. The six aisles devoted to Asian food feature large sections of tea, soy sauce, rice, noodles and Japanese dumplings, as well as other items for Oriental households. "Our tea section is 64 feet long and the soy sauce section is also 64 feet long," says Wu. For customers who are too busy to prepare their own meals, Foodmart International offers a variety of prepared foods in addition to a Chinese restaurant in the store itself.

Hispanic customers comprise 55 percent of Foodmart's shoppers and have five aisles of foodstuffs to select ingredients for South American regional cuisine. If customers need help with reading the language on the labels, Foodmart International employs multilingual employees who can converse in Chinese, Korean, Japanese, Spanish, Portuguese and Tagalog. Wu is proud of the community harmony that prevails at the supermarket. "Satisfying both Asian and Hispanic customers can be tough, but in our store there's plenty of room for everyone."

Wu's father and uncle opened the first supermarket run by the Wu family in Manhattan in 1973. At the age of six, Lewis joined the family business. "When I started at dad's place,

In its 138,000-square-foot location, the Jersey City supermarket offers an extensive array of foodstuffs for a variety of Asian and Hispanic cuisines, along with the usual American fare.

he'd pay me five dollars a day to sweep the floor," he recalls. Like all the Wu grocers, Lewis is passionate about providing the best selection for his customers, at low prices. By 1991, the Wu family had opened its fifth grocery store, all within the same Chinatown block. After Wu supervised the opening of the 12,000-square-foot store in 1991, he was ready for an even bigger challenge.

It took him several years to find the right site, but when Wu learned that the warehouse owned by Kmart in Jersey City was vacant, his vision of providing specialty foods for many different cuisines all under one roof, moved closer to reality. Lewis took over the lease in July of 1997, renovated the empty warehouse and opened Foodmart International on December 8, 1997. Now that the Jersey City supermarket is successful, Wu is already looking at other locations to open a second store. His additional expansion plans include development of a website where his customers can find their ethnic favorites under one virtual roof.

LOUIS GARGIULO COMPANY, INC. GENERAL CONTRACTORS

In 1936, Louis Gargiulo left Sorrento, Italy for America with his wife, who was nine months pregnant, and their three children. The American economy was experiencing the ravages of the Great Depression. The only available construction work was plaster patching. Louis Gargiulo completed this "patching" work with the same philosophy as he did all of the company's future projects. *All work was completed with first-class workmanship—with attention to detail and putting the company name and reputation behind every project.* Louis Gargiulo supported his family on a $6.00 daily wage, he made patching plaster. From this humble beginning the foundation of a reputable general construction firm was established.

Louis Gargiulo Company, Inc. continues to be owned and operated by the son and grandson of Louis Gargiulo, 63 years later. The firm specializes in industrial, commercial and municipal construction, primarily in northern New Jersey.

In 1947, Anthony Gargiulo joined his father full-time in the family business. Through the '40s and '50s, the company flourished and established itself within the community. In 1947, Aetna Casualty Insurance Company began underwriting construction completion bonds for the firm. The bonding allowed the firm to bid for larger construction contracts. The bonding has been a mere formality, since Louis Gargiulo Company has never failed to complete a project.

The company's labor force completes demolition, carpentry, concrete, and masonry work. In 1984, a subsidiary, G & T Mechanical Contractors, Inc., was established to provide plumbing, sprinkler and heating, ventilating and air conditioning (HVAC) work. In-house control of the many phases of a project allows for more competetive bidding and better results in meeting completion dates.

The company has continued to grow over the years, and is now in its third generation of family ownership. Beginning in 1936, from a daily wage of $6.00—average sales have grown from $3 million in the early 1980s to over $10 million in the 1990s. The corporate philosophy is controlled growth with a quality product. The 63 years of progress is a result of the pride and the interest taken by both the owners and the company employees, some who have been employed by Gargiulo for almost 40 years.

Anthony Gargiulo has also taken an active role in many community and charity organizations. He served as a member of the board of trustees for St. Francis Hospital in Jersey City for ten years, the last four as its president. He was the United Way Man of the Year in 1984, and is currently still serving on the board of trustees for both the Cement Finishers Union of Hudson County and the statewide board for the Bricklayers Union.

Historic 100 year-old City Hall roof restoration project, Jersey City.

Anthony Gargiulo, 1948, in front of a recently completed masonry project. Inset: Louis Gargiulo, founder, 1942.

The company has completed construction projects for many industry leaders, including: Exxon; Bendix; Block Drug Co.; Ciba Giegy; ITT; Muellers Macaroni; Sea-Land; and Tropicana. The firm took great pride in its 1996 historic restoration of the 100 year old-roof at City Hall in Jersey City. Current projects include an $8 million Community and Recreation Center, which will be home to one of Jersey City's Charter Schools in the fall of 1999. The community center is progressing as a design/build project where Louis Gargiulo Company has full responsibility for all architectural and engineering design as well as construction of the project.

Louis Gargiulo Company looks forward to the next millennium and the challenges and opportunities of future construction projects. In a time when too many firms, especially in the construction industry, solve their problems using bankruptcy laws, the 63-year history of Louis Gargiulo Company is a tribute to the philosophy of its patriarch.

GENERAL PENCIL COMPANY

In this age of corporate buy-outs it is rare to find a company that has not only survived over a century, but is also still family-owned and operated. General Pencil Company, based in Jersey City, New Jersey, has managed to not only survive, but to use its history and tradition to grow and thrive. General Pencil has worked to preserve its American-made tradition, and its brand products have come to mean quality and value. General Pencil takes pride in making high-quality handcrafted pencils and it takes pride in the people who make them. The family tradition of pencil-making actually goes back further than the company's date of establishment.

Edward Weissenborn learned the art of pencil-making in Germany, working for the I.I. Renbach Lead Pencil Co., and in 1854 he came to America to establish his own factory. Using his engineering background, he assisted in the design and construction of the Civil War battleship, the *Monitor*. Then in 1860, he founded a pencil factory in Hoboken, NJ. This was the American Lead Pencil Company.

American Lead Pencil quickly earned a reputation for producing quality pencils. It received hundreds of letters praising its product, including ones from four members of President Lincoln's cabinet: Secretary of War E.L. Stanton, Treasury Secretary Hugh McCulloch, Navy Secretary Gideon Welles, and the First Assistant Postmaster General, A.M. Randall. There were also letters of commendation, dated 1866, from Governer R.E. Fenton of New York and Mayor John T. Hoffman of New York City.

Weissenborn sold American Lead Pencil in 1885. Four years later, Edward's son, Oscar A. Weissenborn, began making pencils

Factory building with two insets, Edward Weissenborn (first generation) at the upper right, and Oscar Weissenborn (second generation) bottom left.

in a large room of the family home in Jersey City. He did this because it was impossible at this time to buy pencil-making equipment, so he set up his own machine shop. The following year Oscar rented a floor over a grocery, and in 1891 he rented an old mansion for a factory. He called this operation the "Pencil Exchange." In 1914, he moved into his own factory in Jersey City.

World War I nearly killed the fledgling Pencil Exchange. The British blockade made it impossible for pencil manufacturers to get lead (what is today called graphite cores) from Germany. And then the British put into effect

Oscar Weissenborn (center), working in the Machine Shop. (circa 1910)

an Orders-in-Council prohibiting American importers from obtaining any German products—even if they were paid for with American money and were awaiting shipment in neutral ports.

In 1915, Oscar Weissenborn took charge in presenting the views of the U.S. pencil industry at an emergency meeting of importers held at the McAlpin Hotel in New York City. He called the British order, "the most outrageous invasion of the rights of the United States of America in its peaceful trade relations in non-contraband articles, being a curtailment of the commerce of the sea, contrary to all international law and custom."

His speech was widely quoted in the American press, and it came to the attention of the British authorities. Weissenborn went to Washington to plead his case at the British Embassy, but the British were adamant, and the American pencil manufacturers could not get their

The employees of General Pencil Company.

graphite cores out of Germany. So Weissenborn experimented and came up with a way to make his own graphite cores.

It took Weissenborn 30 years to build up his business, and in December 1923, his operation became the General Pencil Company. In 1927, his son Oscar E., entered the family business. In the 1950s and '60s his sons, Oscar A., Frederick Hill, and James S. became officials in General Pencil.

In 1965, James Weissenborn expanded the General Pencil sales, marketing and distribution operations to California, to service the growth of customers in the Western States and internationally. In 1992, the fifth generation of family pencil-makers, his daughter, Kate Weissenborn, joined the family business to run the sales and marketing operations.

General Pencil Company has been making fine quality artist pencils used by U.S. Presidential portrait artists, as well as by beginning artists, for over 110 years. It supports local schools, by donating pencils and erasers and by giving "factory tours" for educational purposes. General Pencil also supports Youth Art Month, to help preserve and build art and drawing programs in schools across the U.S.A.

For five generations the Weissenborns have been manufacturing high quality pencils in the U.S.A. General Pencil currently employs over 70 people from neighboring communities, including Bayonne and Hoboken. Several of them are second-generation General Pencil employees.

Today, with brand-name products sold all over the world, General Pencil still makes over 90% of its products in its Jersey City factory. Several employees have been with the company for more than 20 years. This kind of experience and loyalty helps General Pencil survive and succeed. General Pencil Company celebrated its 110th anniversary in 1999, making it the oldest pencil company still manufacturing in the U.S.A. Tradition and quality are the heart of General Pencil. Its success also comes from the innovation, creativity and involvement of the family pencil-makers, as well as the extended family of dedicated employees.

General Pencil continues to create high-quality pencils and creative products that are used and trusted by artists, draftsmen and crafters all over the world.

The Finishing Department (circa 1915), showing employees sorting and examining products for quality control.

HERZOG HEINE GEDULD

Each day, more shares of stock change hands on the Nasdaq stock market than on any other stock market in the world. About half of those transactions are executed by Jersey City trading firms. Herzog Heine Geduld, a leading Nasdaq market maker located in the city's prominent Newport Tower, itself accounts for 6-8% of Nasdaq's daily share volume.

Herzog Heine Geduld, established in 1926, has been a part of Nasdaq's explosive growth since its inception in the early 1970s. The firm's talented veteran traders are armed with the latest technology to execute the trade orders of financial institutions.

The firm also is a member of the New York Stock Exchange, and its OES Division maintains a presence on all U.S. exchange floors to accomplish electronic orders, executions and services for the professional community in equities and options, integrated to all automated exchange and other electronic clearing systems.

Through its Private Client Group, Herzog Heine Geduld provides a full range of brokerage services to individual clients by

John E. Herzog.

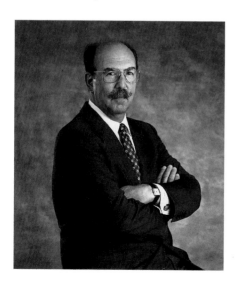

way of its offices in New York City, Rhinebeck, NY, Miami and Philadelphia. The firm also provides fully disclosed clearing and execution services for brokerage firms, banks, insurance companies and other institutional investors, and custodial services for self-directed IRA, Keogh and other retirement accounts.

The firm attributes its amazing success to its commitment to customer service. Herzog Heine Geduld's philosophy of customer service means understanding customer needs in the present, working hard to satisfy those needs, as well as anticipating how their customers' needs will change in the future and seeking innovations that will accommodate those changes. Technology has always been an important part of the Nasdaq marketplace. Herzog Heine Geduld continually pioneers new technological solutions with an eye toward how the new technology will provide better service to clients.

As with many great American success stories, Herzog Heine Geduld's history begins with a 14-year-old Hungarian immigrant, Robert I. Herzog, stepping off a boat in 1915 not far from Newport Tower. Robert held a succession of office jobs and, in 1926, at the age of 25, entered into a series of partnerships, starting with the establishment of Parmer, Herzog & Chadwick, a general brokerage business.

Robert Herzog's first steps toward building a Wall Street firm came just as the American capital markets began to evolve from being the playground of the elite few to being truly accessible to the broad population. The firm's history has reflected that evolution to date—its financial fortunes tracking the prosperity of the public at large with the emergence

Robert I. Herzog, founder.

of a large middle class, but successfully navigating the choppy waters of the roughest periods, when many of its competitors left the business.

The fledgling firm weathered the Great Depression with great difficulty and then embarked on several decades of modest growth —reflecting a very conservative business strategy. Herzog expanded his operation, by then called Herzog & Co., in 1933 with a four-person trading desk for over-the-counter stocks. By November 1961, the firm still traded just 44 stocks.

E.E. ("Buzzy") Geduld.

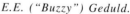

Trading floor at Herzog Heine Geduld.

The following decade saw the steady growth of Herzog & Co. as a market maker. The firm was immensely strengthened in this regard with the addition of brothers Irwin and E.E. "Buzzy" Geduld as partners. In 1976, Herzog & Co. merged with Heine Fishbein & Co., a New York Stock Exchange member firm, became a full clearing member of the exchange, and took the name Herzog Heine Geduld. At the time, the firm employed 40 people, had $1 million in capital and made markets in 800 stocks. By the early '80s, it had grown to 260 employees, boasted $11.5 million in capital and made markets in 1,800 stocks.

In 1995, Herzog moved to its current state-of-the-art facilities at Jersey City's Newport Center, where its Nasdaq trading desk and other operations units are housed. Of the firm's 700 employees worldwide, 500 are located here. Today, Herzog makes markets in more than 5,500 stocks and has more than $165 million in capital.

The firm remains privately held and is led by E.E. Geduld, as President and CEO, and John E. Herzog (Robert's son) as Chairman.

Herzog Heine Geduld has pioneered many of the financial community's most significant changes. For instance:

• In 1968, the firm was among the first of the over-the-counter companies to install computerized bookkeeping, a great step forward from the past when a firm's accounts were posted manually or on bookkeeping machines.

• In the early 1970s Herzog Heine Geduld instituted a policy of trading new issues, and then quickly became the industry's specialist—still trading virtually all Nasdaq new issues and secondary offerings today.

• In 1971, the firm became a founding subscriber to the Nasdaq Stock Market, an electronic exchange that revolutionized the trading of over-the-counter stocks. Originally proposed as a quotation system, it quickly became a trading market, and HRZG - Herzog became a national trading firm in short order. The development of Nasdaq encouraged capital formation in fledgling companies, particularly in the high-tech sector. Many of these companies, such as Microsoft, Intel, Cisco, and more recently, Yahoo, have become major commercial powers in the American corporate landscape.

• The company was among the first to hire women on the trading desk and remains active in the recruiting of women for trading positions, a classic male stronghold.

• Herzog Heine Geduld was the first trading firm to introduce the use of a computerized trading system—COLT—for Nasdaq stocks, in 1983. The system was then purchased by a number of the largest trading firms.

• In 1984, Herzog Heine Geduld pioneered Auto-Ex, a computerized interface that permits its customers to transmit Nasdaq orders electronically. At the present time, Herzog Heine Geduld receives approximately 90% of its orders through electronic interfaces.

• In 1997, the firm expanded its philosophy of customer service to Europe by establishing Herzog Heine Geduld International, a London company, to make markets in the stocks of companies listed on the new pan-European EASDAQ exchange, as well as in stocks quoted on the London Stock Exchange.

Herzog Heine Geduld is a progressive, innovative leader, always on the cutting edge of new technology, ever prepared to engineer new solutions, constantly seeking ways to provide better service to its clients. Its success and growth over many years have made it possible to provide jobs for many people, training them and offering them career opportunities in a field of increasing importance to the nation. The firm's strategy has worked since 1926. It will undoubtedly serve them well in the years to come.

Herzog Heine Geduld is proud to be headquartered in New Jersey, and looks forward to many years of productive growth in Jersey City.

HOUSING AUTHORITY OF WEST NEW YORK

Founded in 1949, as an interim solution to provide low-cost housing, the Housing Authority of West New York in Hudson County, New Jersey is still in the business of offering shelter and support to township residents. This year marks the 50th anniversary of the award-winning Authority that was established by members of the Town Committee of West New York to provide "safe, clean and decent housing and a new life for low income and elderly residents."

Subsequent to its establishment in 1949, the Housing Authority persevered through some difficult early years, under first Executive Director Charles Dobbins. After protracted negotiations concerning land acquisitions, the first apartment building operated by the Housing Authority—Palisade Gardens—with 36 family units, was opened in 1952.

With a continued need for low-cost housing in its community, the Housing Authority erected seven more buildings during the next nine years: Park East Gardens with 84 units; Sunset Gardens with 82 units, now renamed the Joseph "Whitey" Pizzuto Building to honor the chairman of the Board of Commissioners during the 1960s; Sunshine Garden with 81 family units; Otis Gardens with 99 senior units; the McGowan Building with 36 senior units; the FDR Building with 103 senior units; and the Kennedy Tower, built in 1963 with 199 senior units. In 1962, the Housing Authority also purchased Fillmore Gardens, a veterans housing complex built in 1949. Fillmore Gardens now contains 45 units of mixed housing, senior and family.

Another notable director was Alma Majiocchi, who joined the agency as a clerk in 1949, and was

F D R Building, 6100 Adams Street, West New York, also houses the senior building office.

appointed executive director in 1984. During her tenure, she maintained and upgraded the projects owned by the Housing Authority. The Authority continues to work in close partnership with community officials of the township of 45,000, including the Mayor and members of other community and state organizations. Mayor Albio Sires and Chairman of the Board of Commissioners Gene Martorony, collaborate with the Housing Authority's current Executive Director Robert A. DiVincent to expand services and build an enduring network of community for the residents.

"We want to go beyond safe, clean and decent housing and say, 'What more can we provide?'" Under the present leadership, the Authority has developed a comprehensive approach to bettering the lives of its residents. "You have to understand the people, where they came from and where they are going." In partnership with Mayor Sires, Chairman Martorony and other community members, the Housing Authority offers a variety of social services, including child care, transportation for

seniors, citizenship classes, financial assistance for Welfare to Work participants, a "study buddy" program and after-school computer classes. Children of residents study with their after-school mentors, high school volunteers from the National Honor Society. Residents work together with the Authority to plan and participate in these programs.

Two very visible signs of that participation are the "Children First" childcare centers established by the Housing Authority in 1998. Through its interaction with Welfare to Work participants, the Authority realized that single-parents needed good, affordable childcare. The infant center, located in the FDR Building, provides care for 20 infants. The "waddler and toddler" program is also housed in a senior residence, where residents enthusiastically share their time by helping the staff care for 36 children. The newest childcare initiative from the Authority provides much needed childcare for residents of both housing and the surrounding communities, in partnership with North Hudson Community Action Program.

Services for the Housing Authority's senior residents include: citizenship classes, which recently featured an 80-year old graduate, and transportation to medical appointments in the Authority's van. The Housing Authority views the senior residents as essential parts of its vision to build a responsible community with active participants of all ages. Since many of the older residents speak only Spanish, the agency initiated "English as a Second Language" classes for residents, taught by other residents. The Director listens to language tapes as he commutes to work, "my Spanish is improving, their English is improving, together we make it work."

As the residents take a more

Front building: Joseph "Whitey" Pizzuto Building, a family unit building at 590-62nd Street. Pictured to the left rear is a senior building, the McGowan Building at 6300 Adams Street, both in West New York.

active role in building their community, positive change is occurring in both the buildings and the residents of the housing projects. The Director has witnessed improvement not only in the outside appearance of the buildings, but also in the interaction with tenants, "It's more cooperative and less adversarial." During his daily visits through the apartment buildings, the Director knocks on doors as he checks on problems and people throughout the projects. His open-door policy makes him available for tenants to share their good news as well as their complaints. "People come in to invite me to their daughter's First Communion, or to tell me that their son was accepted at Penn State. They're coming out of their shells, and telling us their problems and their successes."

The innovative programs at the Housing Authority of West New York earned the agency special recognition from the Federal Housing Commission in April 1999. Secretary of Housing and Urban Development (HUD)

Andrew Cuomo presented the Authority with an award at a ceremony in Washington, D.C., with Assistant Secretary Harold Lucas also in attendance. The Housing Authority of West New York was one of only two Housing Authorities from the state of New Jersey to receive recognition at the ceremony.

Improving its current housing stock is an ongoing goal of the Housing Authority. The Authority is also working with the Town of West New York to investigate the possibility of constructing additional units for lower income families. As the Housing Authority expands its mission to build community along with safe, clean and decent housing, all aspects of life for the residents will continue to improve. The number of residents on welfare is dwindling, and tenant participation in activities and programs continues to grow. As the Housing Authority of West New York enters its next 50 years of service, the Director remains optimistic about its future: "I think we're definitely moving in the right direction."

OFFICE OF THE HUDSON COUNTY EXECUTIVE

While county government in New Jersey dates back over 320 years, the history of the office of County Executive in Hudson County has roots that stretch back only to the mid-1960s. The modern leadership and activist county government that have been the hallmark of current County Executive Robert C. Janiszeski have only blossomed in the past decade.

In the late 1960s, the State Legislature conducted a study commission to modernize municipal and county governments and make them more accessible to the public. A referendum was placed on the ballot to reorganize the County under the Optional Charter Law of the State of New Jersey. On November 3, 1975, the citizens of Hudson County voted for a County Executive at-large and a Board of Chosen Freeholders elected by geographical district, officially adopting what is known as the County Executive Plan under the Optional Charter Law.

While some have likened the County Executive position to an "elected CEO type," the County Executive post was created by Hudson County (and four other New Jersey counties) to improve the accountability of county government and make it more responsive to the public. Today, the County Executive is responsible for the day-to-day operations of the County and acts in an executive capacity similar to that of a Mayor or Governor.

Hudson County's first County Executive was Edward Clark of Bayonne. He served in office as County Executive until a Jersey City resident and former State Assemblyman, Robert Janiszewski, challenged him and won in the June 8, 1987 primary election. On November 3, Janiszewski easily defeated a Republican challenger to become the second County Executive in Hudson County history.

With the County's infrastructure in disarray, property taxes spiraling out of control, and a county bureaucracy that was not responsive to the needs of its community, Janiszewski realized that a long-term, top-to-bottom overhaul of the County government structure was desperately needed. By investing hundreds of millions of federal and state monies in the County's roads, bridges, parks and buildings, Janiszewski restored the County's infrastructure to its best condition in nearly 40 years. By reducing the County workforce some 40 percent, privatizing the management of two long-term care facilities that were in danger of decertification, and by turning around the old County "vo-tech" into one of New Jersey's ten best public schools (the Hudson County Schools of Technology), Janiszewski ushered in an unprecedented period of activism in local government that has received accolades across New Jersey and the nation.

In 1988, the County's park system, which dates back to the early part of the 20th century, was falling apart and was plagued by disuse, crime and abandonment. Janiszewski tapped the state's Green Acres program to provide over $30 million in capital improvements to the County's eight parks. In 1997, Laurel Hill Park in Secaucus was formally dedicated,

County Executive Robert C. Janiszewski (right), inspects new athletic fields at Mercer Park, located on the Bayonne-Jersey City border, with Hudson County Parks Division Chief Thomas McCann (center) and Freeholder Bill Braker (left) in August 1998. Since 1989, the County has invested over $30 million in its park system, restoring the beauty of historic structures and upgrading all of the parks' athletic and passive recreation facilities. Hudson County's eight parks total over 716 acres and range in size from 2.6 acres (Columbus Park, Hoboken) to 167 acres (James J. Braddock North Hudson Park, North Bergen).

becoming the first new County park in over 80 years.

Janiszewski has also received state and national recognition for establishing the nation's largest local affordable housing initiative, the Hudson County Affordable Housing Trust Fund. By using both the trust fund and federal HUD dollars, Hudson County plans to break ground on its 2,000 units of affordable housing by the year 2000, building more of these units over the last ten years than all other counties in New Jersey combined.

This year, Janiszewski will be seeking his fourth consecutive term. If elected, he will have the distinction of being the longest-serving County Executive in its brief history in New Jersey.

CITY OF JERSEY CITY

Since early in its history, Jersey City has been home to rows of beautifully-restored brownstones. The houses pictured are typical of the carefully-restored brownstones which many downtown residents today proudly call home.

Liberty State Park on the Jersey City waterfront is appropriately named. Miss Liberty holds her torch high only a few hundred yards from its shoreline. Ellis Island is even closer, connected to Liberty Park by a vehicular bridge. Sadly, most Americans don't know how close Jersey City is to these two hallowed reminders of our American freedoms. But they're learning.

Jersey City has enjoyed a pretty good reputation from the start. When Henry Hudson sailed into the area on Sept. 12, 1609, his mate wrote in the ship's log that it was, ". . . a very good land to fall in with, and a pleasant land to see." National business and financial firms are "falling in" with Jersey City in record numbers today, and the city's changing skyline, facing New York's, is breathtaking.

Jersey City is the capital of Hudson County, the smallest in area of New Jersey's 21 counties. Yet, after the 2000 census is completed, it is anticipated that Jersey City will forge ahead of Newark as the state's most populous city. It already has the most diverse population ethnically, as befits the home of Ellis Island.

On November 22, 1630, the earliest known conveyance in what is now Jersey City, was established. Its first settlement was on the waterfront at Communipaw (the Dutch version of the native inhabitants' name for the area). The first house was built there in 1633 for Jan Evertsen Bout, superintendent of the colony, by then called Pavonia. In May 1647, Peter Stuyvesant became Director General. It is his statue that stands proudly, peg leg and all, at Bergen Square, where in Stuyvesant's time a log structure served as New Jersey's first church and school, and where a school has stood ever since.

For nearly 200 years, much of what is now Jersey City was part of Bergen County to its north. In 1838, Jersey City was separated from Bergen, and began expanding on its own, reaching its present size in 1873, when the township of Greenville merged with the city. Thirteen years later it became famous nationwide, when thousands of people packed the shoreline for the "unveiling" of the Statue of Liberty. The crowd was bigger 100 years later, on the Fourth of July, 1986, when the world's tall ships sailed by, the Boston Pops played in Jersey City (setting Bostonians on their heels), and the fireworks display offshore was said to be the nation's biggest and best ever.

Since July 1, 1961, Jersey City has functioned under a Mayor and Council form of government, with six ward council members and three elected at-large. It replaced an unwieldy, five-member Commission form of government under which commissioners in effect served in both the executive and legislative branches of government. The *Jersey Journal* spearheaded the change.

Its Gold Coast, seven miles of Hudson River waterfront, is giving Jersey City what could be America's fastest-growing skyline. Thanks to relentless and joint-efforts by local people in government, business and finance, Jersey City is now attracting the attention of the nation's investors. They are becoming aware of its convenient location, extensive transportation system and the prosperous economy that makes Jersey City an excellent place to work and live. They're learning that Jersey City businesses pay less than half the taxes and utilities that their competitors pay in New York and other cities in its metropolitan area. Jersey City is already in step with the year 2000.

Jersey City's more than century-old City Hall serves as the home to the Mayor's Office and the Municipal Council. Local residents may obtain copies of ordinances, pay their taxes, or visit with constituent services representatives at this historic 280 Grove Street site.

LIBERTY SCIENCE CENTER

Science centers are now common sights in America's urban landscape. Liberty Science Center (LSC) is situated in Liberty State Park, next to the Hudson River in Jersey City. As a new type of museum over the past thirty years, science centers are places of multimedia experiences to explore the science and technology that pervade society. Core roles are to be a field resource for the formal educational system and a worthwhile venue for family outings. Used in these contexts, visits are often memorable, sometimes transformational, moments in personal journeys of lifelong learning. Science centers are also important players in urban revitalization by adding to the quality of life, knowledge level, and economic development through tourism. For its part, LSC has been among the leading proponents for a new consciousness of relevance in how science

A westward view of LSC under construction in 1992. The facility was conceived as an anchor attraction for Liberty State Park and now attracts 750,000 visitors annually. Photo by James Payne, LSC

centers can best serve their communities and expand the public's perception of culture to include science and technology with the arts and performing arts.

Liberty State Park was originally a tidal bay turned into a landfill site, then a busy industrial hub served by the Morris Canal and the Central Railroad of New Jersey, and a famous place for the immigration of many millions of Americans. It was visionary thinking indeed that led to the establishment of this large area as a state park in 1976. Located in the midst of the country's largest metropolis, it certainly has incredible assets—views of Ellis Island, the Statue of Liberty, Manhattan skyline, the Hudson River entering New York Bay with its passenger and commercial shipping, and under a busy airspace between Newark, Kennedy and LaGuardia Airports. Today, Liberty State Park is New Jersey's most visited park.

Located at the park's northwest corner next to the NJ Turnpike extension and a station along the new NJ Transit light-rail system, the $68 million LSC is a landmark

175,000 square foot building. Capital funding was made possible through a successful public-private partnership. Opening its doors to the public in January 1993, LSC instantly became New Jersey's most popular museum, and is today regarded as among the nation's most innovative science centers for its educational programming. March 1999 included a fanfare for the five-millionth guest.

The idea behind Liberty Science Center, a private not-for-profit organization, was underway by the early 1980s. Driven by a mounting concern over national news that school science test scores were declining, and mindful of the workforce needs of New Jersey's high volume of major industries, the Research and Development Council of New Jersey nurtured the climate of corporate support. Newark's *Star-Ledger* newspaper, especially the late Mort Pye, promoted the concept in the public arena. In orderly terms, chairs of LSC's Board of Trustees during the first dozen or so years have been: Dr. Robert A. Fuller, now retired in Toronto; the late Thomas J.

Stanton Jr., who contributed a tremendous breadth of community and business contacts; Joseph D. Williams, chairman emeritus of Warner-Lambert Company, who spearheaded the capital campaign; Dr. John S. Mayo, president emeritus of AT&T Bell Labs; and currently, Robert J. Dougherty, Jr., president and CEO of PSEG Energy Holdings, Inc. The board has consistently been a senior executive group drawn from the region's leading industries, as well as its higher education, government and other community organizations. Josh Weston, LSC trustee and honorary chairman of Automatic Data Processing, Inc., chairs an Advisory Council composed of some twenty or so leading corporate CEOs. Much of LSC's staff, both employees and volunteers, each totaling more than two hundred, lives in Hudson County. Design and construction of the new facility were overseen by Charles "Chuck" Howarth, now a museum consultant based in California. Since 1996, Dr. Emlyn Koster, a geologist and previously head of two major science museums in Canada, has led a new era of institutional advance.

LSC offers interactive exhibitions and varied programs on three floors, concerned with the environment, health and invention. It also houses the nation's largest dome IMAX theater and an unusual 3D-laser theater. Frequently in the evening and overnight, LSC turns into a camp-in and award-winning facility rental venue. Overall, LSC's mission is to be a lifelong public resource for interactive exploration of science and technology. Principal strategies include: playing an active role in area improvements; attracting an even larger audience; accelerating the renewal of the thematic learning

experiences it offers; stabilizing its funding through a diverse portfolio of earned and contributed revenues; and expanding appropriately in mission-critical ways. LSC has succeeded in becoming a unique resource for schools through its on-site programs as well as traveling and electronic outreach options. Surveys confirm that LSC is one of the metro-New York area's most well-known family destinations. Its president and CEO is sought after nationally and internationally as a board member, author and speaker. In New Jersey, Dr. Koster is on the board of directors of the State Tourism Industry Association and Hudson County Chamber of Commerce, on the Board of Regents of St. Peter's College, and is an adjunct faculty member of two universities.

In Hudson County, LSC is home to a novel middle school called Explore 2000 as part of its Schools of Technology. For Jersey City Public Schools, 60% of the 32,000 students use LSC annually, as do scores of its teachers for professional development purposes. LSC is also pleased to service a major

Young minds explore energy resources in an interactive exhibition. Part of LSC's upper environment floor, this project was made possible by a generous grant from Exxon. Photo by David Wagner, Virtually Real

contractual request from the state government to assist with science education at all grades in at-risk public school districts. It is also proud to be an invited signatory on New Jersey's declaration for diversity, with other business leaders. Through the films it premieres, the conferences it hosts, the dignitaries it greets, and the electronic links it makes with places as varied as Trenton, Toronto, Los Angeles and Santiago, Chile, LSC helps bring Hudson County to the world. Nationally, a strong, combined focus on educational reform, science and technology, inner-city renaissance, inclusivity of all who comprise society, as well as the many particular attributes of LSC's site, all bode well for the future. Liberty Science Center is proud to be where it is, helping where and when it can under its particular mission of relevance to the community-at-large.

MATSUSHITA ELECTRIC CORPORATION OF AMERICA

Drive along the New Jersey Turnpike at night, near Exit 16W, and the logos shine like beacons, with the Manhattan skyline as their backdrop. Affixed to the facade of the corporate headquarters buildings, the five-foot-high neon letters spell out "Panasonic" in brilliant blue, visible from miles away.

But while motorists cruising through the Meadowlands may immediately recognize one of the world's best-known brand names, they likely aren't as familiar with the remarkable 40-year story of growth and success that has placed Panasonic/Matsushita among the leading electronics marketers in the United States, and made it one of Hudson County's largest employers.

And amazingly, it all began back in the era of Eisenhower, poodle skirts and sock hops—with just three employees.

In 1959, Japan-based parent Matsushita Electric Industrial Co., Ltd., decided to establish a company to sell products in the enormous U.S. market. The first Matsushita Electric Corporation of America (MECA) office, in Manhattan, was staffed by an American salesman, a Matsushita employee from Japan and a secretary. The first product was a small transistor radio. From this modest beginning the company made rapid strides. In 1961—with its workforce having expanded to 20 employees—it adopted the "Panasonic" brand name. The first Panasonic television, a black-and-white model with a 14-inch diagonal screen, followed in 1962.

One year later, with annual sales reaching the $10 million mark and 65 employees in its ranks, the company shifted its headquarters to New York's Pan Am Building. MECA remained at this location for a dozen years, during which time its sales advanced toward the $500 million mark and the number of its employees passed 5,000.

By the mid '70s, the dizzying pace of the company's success had made it too large for the confines of the Pan Am Building. After careful consideration, Matsushita decided to relocate its North American headquarters across the Hudson River, to Secaucus, NJ. On a 50-acre site that was undeveloped marshland, the company arranged for the construction of a three-story administrative building and an expansive warehouse facility. In 1975, with the Meadowlands Sports Complex rising just a stone's throw away, MECA employees moved to their glistening new corporate campus on Meadowlands Parkway, just off of Route 3.

"Working in Manhattan had its advantages," remembers Weehawken, NJ-resident Justin Camerlengo, who joined MECA in 1973 and is now president of its Panasonic Corporate Enterprises Company. "But relocating to the new headquarters in Secaucus was really a wonderful time for us. Suddenly we had this modern office complex. It really hammered home the point that Panasonic had become a leader in the U.S. electronics industry. And, of course, our business has enjoyed impressive growth since then."

Having relocated its base of operations to New Jersey, the company's expansion continued

The Panasonic corporate campus in Secaucus, NJ, as it appears today.

unabated. By 1977, sales reached $1 billion; by 1981 they topped $2 billion. To commemorate this continuing success, a $1 million grant was provided to the prestigious Massachusetts Institute of Technology in 1976 to endow a chair of engineering in medicine. This was followed five years later by a $1 million grant to Harvard to create a chair in leadership. In 1984, as sales soared past $3 billion and the North American workforce topped 7,500 employees, Matsushita celebrated its 25th anniversary by contributing $10 million to establish the Panasonic Foundation to foster educational reform in U.S. public schools.

Matsushita's success swelled the ranks of its employees in the U.S., Canada and Mexico, and the capacity of the administrative building in Secaucus was soon overwhelmed. But rather than undertake another relocation, MECA elected to remain in Hudson County by expanding its existing campus. In 1985, a new four-story structure was completed directly adjacent to the original office building. The project left MECA headquarters with the three-building layout it boasts to this day—the impressive series of off-white structures now so familiar to drivers who frequent Meadowlands Parkway and the Turnpike's western spur.

As the '80s progressed, Matsushita bolstered its North American manufacturing presence by establishing a series of new factories in Tennessee, Washington, Georgia, Ohio and elsewhere. In 1988, MECA achieved a milestone as it began exporting Illinois-made Panasonic televisions to Japan. That same year, Matsushita donated $1.5 million to Pacific University in Oregon to establish the Pacific Intercultural Institute and Foundation.

With the '90s came accelerated manufacturing expansion—plants sprung up in a number of U.S. states, and in Mexico as well—and also the advent of research and development facilities. Today, the hub of Matsushita's U.S. research network is based in Princeton, NJ, while its highly successful advanced television lab is located in Burlington County, NJ. Corporate contributions also continued, as in 1991 Matsushita gave $1.25 million to the University of Pennsylvania's Wharton School and $1 million to help establish the New Jersey Performing Arts Center in Newark, NJ.

MECA's Kid Witness News hands-on video education program —which now boasts more than 200 participating schools in 39 U.S. states—was established in 1989. But as the program expanded from its very first participant school, in Weehawken, to dozens and then hundreds around the country, local schools continued to be well-represented. Of the 23 New Jersey schools currently participating in KWN, 10 are located in Hudson County. With so many of MECA's philanthropic and outreach activities focused on the Meadowlands and surrounding communities, the company has indeed woven itself into the local fabric. A high percentage of Panasonic's approximately 2,000 Secaucus-based employees reside in the county.

For MECA, the present is indeed quite bright. There are now 23,000 employees across North America, and sales for fiscal 1998 reached $8.1 billion. Whatever future challenges lay ahead, there's no doubt that being based in Hudson County has played a key role in the company's continued success.

"For 25 years now, we've conducted business from headquarters in the New Jersey Meadowlands, and doing so has helped shape the nature of our company and contributed to its achievements," explains Yoshinori Kobe, MECA chairman. "Being in Hudson County gives us access to a sizeable pool of talented, well-educated employees, and puts us in close proximity to multiple international airports. On top of that, we're just a few miles from New York City, the financial capital of the world. All things considered, it's hard to imagine a better location for our company."

Construction underway on the four-story "North Building" on Panasonic's 50-acre corporate campus in Secaucus, NJ. The structure (seen here looking toward the northwest) was completed in 1985.

MAYO, LYNCH AND ASSOCIATES, INC.

In 1951, Joseph Lynch, a young engineer, partnered with a college colleague and started a firm which has become a fixture in the Hudson County business landscape. Mayo, Lynch and Associates, Inc., provides engineering, architectural and planning design services to municipal, commercial and residential clients. A component of success is the ability to stand the tests of time. Mayo, Lynch and Associates has met the challenges of more than four decades of change, in development, new technologies, governmental regulations, and economic and political tides.

Throughout these changes, Mayo, Lynch has held the respect of the communities it has served and its peers in the profession, many of whose principals have served apprenticeships with the firm, or who still maintain an active association with MLA. Joseph Lynch understands the value of long-term relationships.

The son of a proud longshoreman and long-time union delegate, Lynch was born in West New York and has since lived and worked in Hudson County. He attended parochial schools in Union City and received his degree in 1948 from Stevens Institute of Technology, after an interruption in his education due to service in World War II. At Stevens he met Leonard Mayo, his eventual partner for more than twenty years. Mayo, an engineer and architect, is now retired.

Entrepreneurship came early to Lynch, who began working at the age of fourteen, and was a freelance electrical and mechanical contractor during his undergraduate days. His first job after graduation was with the O'Kane Marine Repair Company in Hoboken, and by the time he was 26 years old, he was supervising over 200 mechanics. In 1951, he and Mayo founded the

Union Hill Shopping Plaza, urban renewal site, Union City.

firm, working nights while they retained their day jobs. A year later the pair decided to devote all their efforts to the new business, and in 1953, officially incorporated the name. One of the firm's first local jobs was commissioned by Leo Smith of the original Mount Olive Baptist Church.

Lynch and Mayo established their credentials on the national level as design engineer and architect for two Air Reduction Company plants, one in Texas and one in California. In 1955, MLA entered into a joint-project with Bowe Albertson for work on the Hoboken Sewage Treatment Facility, the first of many such treatment facilities it would design. They include: the Secaucus Treatment Plant, which

Konoko Graphics Inc., facade restoration and total interior rehabilitation, Hoboken.

ran smoothly for over 20 years until parts replacement and updating were required; the North Bergen Central Treatment Plant, the first of its kind in the nation, in which secondary treatment was accomplished for about $10 million dollars, less than 33 percent of the nationwide average; and in Jersey City, where Mayo, Lynch's expertise as a consultant put the plant back in operation after seven years of failure. Many of these facilities have since been upgraded due to the environmental regulations and expanded development promulgated since their inceptions, and Mayo, Lynch was involved in many of the required upgrades. At the time of design, these projects represented the latest in innovation and technology.

Mayo, Lynch and Associates was involved in low-income and affordable housing before the terms were common. The firm prepared the application for federal funding of the Hoboken Model Cities program, a pilot program that enabled the federal government to test its myriad of programs all at once in an urban setting. In addition, the company provided services for the newly-established Applied Housing Associates, who has since successfully rehabilitated over 2,500 housing units. The Hudson County landscape is dotted with MLA's projects, including Unico Towers

senior citizens housing in Jersey City, Marian Towers senior citizens housing in Hoboken, the Secaucus Swim Center, the Boulevard East Promenade in West New York, the Hoboken branch of First Jersey National Bank, and the Secaucus and West New York branches of Plaza National Bank.

Its services have also been in demand outside Hudson County. Mayo, Lynch and Associates was the architect and designer of Mater Dei High School in Monmouth County and the Clemente/Shalom housing project in Newark. The firm has designed or composed spillways and dams, incinerators, energy audits, transportation and roadway systems, land-use controls, master plans, and zoning ordinances for cities and towns throughout New York and New Jersey, including Hoboken, North Bergen, Secaucus, Roosevelt, Goshen, Marlborough, Neversink, New Paltz, and in Delaware and Sullivan counties. The company has been involved in solid-waste facilities projects in Beacon and Newburgh in New York, and New Haven, Norwalk, and Stratford in Connecticut.

Staying-power is predicated on an ability to meet new challenges. Changes in water and waste treatment and environmental requirements prompted MLA, in conjunction with the City of Jersey City, to organize a sludge treatment research project with Stevens Institute of Technology, Brooklyn Polytechnic, and Merchant Marine Academy professors. The group has received two federal patents to date dealing with the removal of PCBs.

Change is also evident in the profession and in the firm. In the face of such change, Joseph Lynch, a professional engineeer, licensed land surveyor and planner, has closely watched the evolution of his

craft. New technology has brought new challenges. A mimeograph machine was a modern office addition in the early days of the firm, while computers are now located on every desk and digital 3-D images join the ink drawings in file drawers. Computer models are the new tools of the trade, and new senior staff supervise today's projects, under Lynch's expert guidance.

Seamus Cunningham, a key member of the firm, holds an honor's degree in economics from Queen's University in Belfast. Seamus has considerable experience with governmental policy and process. He has worked closely with Lynch for the past 20 years, and has prepared major treatment and infrastructure projects for review and approval with regulatory agencies.

Lynch's daughter Grace, an architect and planner, joined the firm more than fifteen years ago, after receiving her degree from the Cooper Union. Grace heads the architectural division and has been the lead architect on projects which have varied from treatment plant structures and Housing Authority improvements to single-family homes. Grace has amassed considerable experience in the design of school facilities, historic restoration projects and planning studies. School projects include new early childhood facilities and major renovations and additions, some utilizing modular construction. Her architectural restoration work ranges in size from a Hoboken rowhouse (a new storefront for Shipco Transport received an award from the

Wastewater Treatment Plant, West New York.

Historic Commission), to comprehensive terracotta and masonry facade restoration programs for North Bergen Schools. Planning efforts in joint with colleagues include Master Plans in New Milford, Boonton, and Hamburg (which received an award for its Community Design), and a Main Street Improvement project in Paterson, which included planning studies and the design of new street lighting and pedestrian improvements, soon to be realized.

John Curry, a professional engineer and planner, heads the engineering division. John received a degree in mechanical engineering from New Jersey Institute of Technology, and has considerable design-build experience with large industrial and commercial projects. Prior to joining MLA, John had overseen projects in Illinois, Georgia, Alabama and New York. John has been the lead engineer for MLA on projects such as the Woodcliff Treatment Plant in North Bergen, and storm and wastewater studies for Jersey City drainage sub-basins utilizing an EPA computer model (SWMM). He provides architectural engineering expertise in mechanical, plumbing and electrical disciplines, as well as planning review.

Joseph Lynch is hoping that Grace, John and Seamus will continue to build another generation of Mayo, Lynch and Associates. As one of Hudson County's foremost and well-respected engineers, Lynch has provided a stable foundation.

MECCA & SON TRUCKING

Jerry Mecca started life with the disadvantages of having lost his mother when he was only nine days old, and growing up in extreme poverty. In fact, when Jerry was just five years old, the *Jersey Journal* wrote an article about him being the poorest boy in Jersey City.

However, it was this very adversity that provided the strong driving force to initially work just to survive, and then, to build. While in public school, Jerry would look out the window, watching the trucks go by and dreaming of someday owning his own trucking company. Prior to

quitting high school, he earned money doing such odd jobs as bicycle repairs, cleaning yards and basements, raking leaves, snow shoveling, and even scavenging garbage to find anything of value. With savings from these endeavors, along with some money from the sale of an old car given to him by his father, he had enough cash to purchase an old truck and start his business, at the age of seventeen.

Being so young and obviously inexperienced to prospective customers, it was very difficult for Jerry to find accounts. At this point, he asked his father, "Leo," to help him with his sales calls. At the time, Leo was employed at P.J. Schweitzer as a papermaker, but did agree to find time for these calls with Jerry.

This started a string of successes, with Leo passing as the owner, and his son Jerry at his side. The first of their accounts was Paper Novelty Manufacturing Company. Here such items as Christmas tree balls, party items, and other seasonal goods were picked up at the manufacturer and delivered to Paper Novelty on Morton Place in Jersey City. This was followed by Allgood Terminal, and Goodman Furniture. Interestingly, in 1985, Jerry and his wife Helen purchased Allgood Terminal and Goodman Moving & Storage Company, both owned by his original account and friend, Alfred Goodman and Family.

At the age of 18, Jerry was able to secure his second truck and his first employee, Johnny Olsen.

Jerry operated the business out of his father's home at 143 Bayview Avenue, in Jersey City. The trucks were parked in a lot adjacent to his house.

Jerry Mecca with new Mecca trailer, 1998.

Jerry Mecca, founder of Mecca & Sons Trucking.

In 1956, Jerry made his best decision—marrying Ms. Helen Critelli, originally of Jersey City, but living in Fanwood, NJ at the time. Jerry first met Helen while renting space in a building owned by Helen's family, where she was an office employee. Prior to renting this space, Jerry would literally stay up all night with blowers to keep the contents of Toni Company hair products from freezing in the cold outdoors.

On June 4, 1956, Mecca & Son Trucking was incorporated, followed one month later by Jerry and Helen's marriage on July 7th. Helen often joked that she, "married notes payable," as the earlier years were consumed with making monthly payments. However, what they truly started was a partnership for life, together building a diversified and successful group of companies, and a family of five children.

Soon after the marriage, real estate became a favorite pastime of the Meccas, with the purchases of a Warehouse at 14 Florence Street, a cold water flat at 25 Fairmount Avenue (their first home) and vacant lots on Corneilson Avenue.

During the 1960s, as the trucking business expanded, they first complemented it with the addition of warehousing, with a separate corporation at 14 Florence Street, where operations were consolidated. Employment had grown to 12, with Johnny Olsen and all original employees still on board. While jobs were plentiful at this time, employees looked upon Jerry as family, due to the special bond that he developed with them and their customers. This developed from the respect and love that grew out of working together as a team. It was a friendship, rather than the typical relationship with owner/worker, or customer/supplier.

While the business was consuming—sometimes around the clock six-days-a-week for Jerry, and a demanding work schedule for Helen—a beautiful family of two daughters and three sons, was started. His daughters Peggy and Anna were literally raised in the office, as Helen continued to work during this period. It was only when the boys were born that Helen took some time off to raise the family. She later returned to full-time employment, where she still continues to work along with her entire family.

Interestingly, one of the first new ventures that Jerry conceived of and started over 35 years ago, as the first of its kind, was a gas station/snack bar/car wash, all at one location. This company was named the Clean-O-Mat Corporation.

As his business interests were flourishing and his children were growing and working within the various companies, Jerry felt that Jersey City was not being led in the proper direction. In 1984 he decided to help restore city government to a dedicated, honest and tolerant team that would rebuild and heal the wounds. To this end, he threw his full support behind Anthony Cucci, with not only the maximum allowable financial contribution, but also with a campaign effort that had Jerry shaking every hand in Jersey City while talking about the virtues of new government. With this effort came the unfortunate attacks on Jerry that he was only doing this to receive favors, but those who know Jerry only laughed at the idea. The

Jerry and Helen Mecca, center. Left to right, Anna, Jerry Jr., Lenny, Michael and Peggy.

political advertisement below, paid for by *The News Shack,* and reported in its entirety, sums up what Jerry is "all about," and how respected and loved he is.

From 1984 to the present, Jerry and Helen have continued to

Merry Christmas to Jerry Mecca.

Tomorrow, I'll have the Christmas lights on, the kids will be around to pull out the trees and the "Drummer Boy," along with Mahalia Jackson—"Happy Birthday Dear Lord" will echo thru-out the "Junction"—a so called ghetto area. It's 11 P.M. as you try to mentally warm yourself from the 7° temperature.

The Christmas Trees stood like toy soldiers waiting for their night-time shelter to arrive. The "eighteen cats and two dogs" would play amongst and between the spiritualistic aroma of the evergreen pine. Symbolically, the trees echoed the struggle of the people of Jersey City. No, there was no corporate artificiality about these trees. Their traditionalistic roots were deep in Christian Principles.

A neighbor passed, "Jerry, bring the trailer tonight?" Yep, he told me at 6 A.M. this morning he'd be there. Twelve years, Jerry Mecca has always kept his word. The trailer for the next thirty days would be donated free by Mecca Trucking.

At 11:30 P.M. the 40-footer would swing wide into Prescott Street. Jerry would jump the curb twice and with laser precision back and drop the box in a minute. A tired "little boy" who struggled the old-fashioned way; his eyes would be drowsy, his hands would be grease-dirty. An Italian, who earned every penny from sweat, toil, long hours—he would emerge from the "rig" and humbly say, "Gee, sorry I'm late." Jerry Mecca has always kept his word. Merry Christmas, Jerry.

From
The Christmas Tree Man
"At the Junction"

---

expand their business horizons with such diversified enterprises as: coffee warehouses certified by the NY Board of Trade; an investment in a nursing home; a major cocoa grinding operation (built from scratch); the purchase of a marina and warehouse in Bayonne; and an injection molding company. Jerhel Plastics, Inc., with over 300 employees, has its corporate office at 63-69 Hook Road, Bayonne. This location is the original Ceiba Geigy building, now owned by Jerry and Helen. Also in this building, is Accem Warehouse, owned by the Meccas. This warehouse provides a cooler, as well as ambient storage mainly for food items, in over 180,000 square feet, and is operated by his son, Jerry Jr.

Jerhel Plastics, which is now the Mecca's largest operating company, serves the cosmetic industry with a wide range of injection and blow molded products such as compacts, powder boxes, soap dishes, combs, bottles, etc., with a Who's Who list of customers. Jerry's daughter Anna and son Lenny both work at

---

Jerry and Helen Mecca.

Jerry, center working on foundation for Cocoa Mills. Circa 1970s.

---

this operation. His other son, Michael, and daughter Peggy, along with his wife, Helen, operate the original Mecca & Son Trucking.

With all this, Jerry still continues his unending search for the next challenge.

MACO OFFICE SUPPLIES

Maco Office Supplies was established in 1952 in Jersey City, NJ, and moved to its current location at 1000 Kennedy Boulevard, Union City in 1961. Maco began as a full-service stationer providing business stationery including logo design, general merchandise, office machinery and furniture. Maco Office Supplies quickly became well-known in the area, and began establishing commercial accounts that remain its customers today. As the area began to grow economically, more businesses were coming to Hudson County. By 1961, within 10 years of its establishment, the company moved to a 5,000 square-foot building. Four men, Harry Casner, Harry Goldberg, Charles Kreitman and Sidney Reissman, would run MACO for the next 27 years. Together, they built a successful business well known throughout Hudson County.

In 1978, Sidney Reissman, the last surviving partner died. With less than a year remaining at Boston University to complete his

degree, Sidney's son, Ricky left school to return to NJ and assume the role of General Manager. Maco had operated primarily as a commercial source providing daily deliveries, with only a small retail business. But as the area grew, the retail business increased significantly. Plans were outlined to open a showroom/retail store.

In 1986, the retail store opened, with a purple and peach color scheme. It was met with excitement and praise by the local community. A glass, diamond-shaped display case welcomed customers as they entered. A 40-foot counter provided an ample customer service area, with cubicles creating workspaces for employees. The exterior was redone, and the mansard roof prominently displayed the letters: MACO.

Also in 1986, Ricky married Sharon Giannattasio, who joined the Maco staff. Initially, Sharon worked in the retail store and currently designs office interiors. She was responsible for expanding the furniture sales division. Ricky's sister, Carol, came to work at the store too, and is now responsible for developing and maintaining commercial accounts.

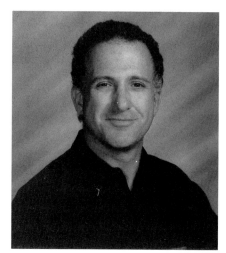

Richard S. Reissman.

Throughout Maco's history, two employees have played integral roles in the company's development. Norma Messina has served as bookkeeper for over 35 years, and Irene Gerding has been Maco's billing clerk for over 25 years. Another important figure has been Gilbert Sunshine, Maco's accountant for nearly 50 years. In 1987, Paul Ostrow joined the company, significantly increasing commercial sales in both Hudson and Bergen counties.

"Maco has been providing quality products and office furnishings for almost half a century," says Ricky Reissman. "We have watched our customers' businesses grow over the years and are proud to have helped them. We have been a part of our customers' success through our commitment to customer service, prompt deliveries and innovative products."

In this marketplace where similar businesses are being devoured by the giant superstores, Maco has established itself by providing superior customer service at competitive prices.

The retail store's debut in 1986.

NEW JERSEY CITY UNIVERSITY

Friday, May 29, 1998, is the birthday of New Jersey City University. On that day the New Jersey Commission of Higher Education acted on a formal petition that designated Jersey City State College a comprehensive university and approved the change of name.

Dr. Carlos Hernandez, president of NJCU, describes New Jersey City University as "a place where the American Dream is alive and well. It is a place where the dream is spoken in many languages and has many cultural contexts. It is an institution that will always be committed to offering its students the opportunity to realize that dream. It will continue to address the needs of nontraditional students

The Gothic Tower of Hepburn Hall is a campus landmark. Constructed in 1929, this architectural gem is a replica of a fourteenth-century Norman cathedral. Photo by Bill Wittkop

and will forge ahead as the premier cooperative education institution in New Jersey."

As Jersey City State College, in fact, the institution had already been functioning as a university. It would have had university designation for at least ten years in no fewer than 48 states. The change of designation, therefore, does not require any immediate changes in academic program. But changes that will enhance the institution's ability to carry out its traditional mission are coming.

The mission of NJCU, which can be summed up as access and excellence, has lasted through the institution's many transformations. "University designation places us in a unique position to solidify our goals, refine our strategies, and explore new areas of inquiry and involvement," Dr. Hernandez explains.

New Jersey City University was chartered back in 1927 and opened as the New Jersey State Normal School at Jersey City in 1929. It was built to accommodate 1,000 students and an eight-room demonstration school in its one building,

Most students at New Jersey City University are commuters who work or have family responsibilities. Study lounges in the Gilligan Student Union provide NJCU's non-residential students with a comfortable haven in the midst of campus activity. Photo by Steve Jordan

Hepburn Hall, on ten acres on what was then Hudson Boulevard. The institution was renamed New Jersey State Teachers College at Jersey City in 1935 and Jersey City State College in 1958, becoming a liberal arts institution in 1968. Throughout these changes it has remained a place where all students who have the intelligence and motivation to benefit from higher education are welcome.

Today, almost 10,000 students, served by 800 employees, attend New Jersey City University, which is situated on an attractive 46-acre campus in the Greenville neighborhood of Jersey City. NJCU continues to face the challenge of providing the best possible higher education to a varied and broad spectrum of people, a rainbow population that is a microcosm of the world.

The new designation is a launch-

Above:
The Electronic Learning Laboratory is one of many resource centers that are available to NJCU students. A number of academic computer labs and terminals are located across the campus. By August 1999, when the University's Irwin Library is completely renovated, the building will be a state-of-the-art information center designed for the technology age. Photo by Bill Wittkop

Below:
Whether scholars or practitioners, NJCU faculty members are outstanding professionals. They are devoted teachers who nurture students in an exceptional university environment that links academic exploration in the classroom with cooperative education experiences in all fields of study. Photo by Steve Jordan

ing point from which, according to Dr. Hernandez, "the institution will focus on what the basics of a liberal arts education should be at this point in American higher education and at this point in the country's history, when urban living and diversity are the rule rather than the exception."

"This institution, which has always played an important role in the development of the Jersey City community, will take a leadership role in advancing partnership strategies, community service, and the celebration of diversity and civility," Dr. Hernandez explains.

"As Jersey City becomes the largest city in the state as well as the economic engine for development," he adds, "we must be prepared to assist as well as benefit from our position and historic presence." The NJCU Center for Public Policy and Urban Research, established in 1996, will play an important role in this initiative by conducting basic and applied research on issues related to urban education, urban development, and public policy.

The academic administration of the University has been restructured

to include three colleges: the College of Education, the College of Professional Studies, and the College of Arts and Sciences, in addition to the divisions of Graduate Studies and Continuing Education.

The University plans to develop new graduate and undergraduate degree programs and will eventually offer doctoral degree programs. Presently, 25 undergraduate degree programs and 24 graduate programs are offered. NJCU full-time faculty members number 235, and more than 70 percent of them have doctoral degrees or the highest degrees in their fields.

Technology will become increasingly central to both the content and the delivery of NJCU academic programs. The master of arts program in educational technology is NJCU's first degree program in which all courses may be taken online. The Irwin Library will reopen in September 1999, completely renovated to provide students and faculty with the latest technology in electronic research and learning.

The Library renovation is just one of many changes in the physical plant now underway or planned. Fries Hall is being renovated to become a new media and performing arts facility, and the campus is being relandscaped to provide more trees, plantings, and outdoor seating. In a later phase of its master plan, the university will develop the 13-acre site known as the West Campus, located between West Side Avenue and Route 440. These changes will provide a significant stage in campus revitalization.

New Jersey City University is poised to make a difference in Hudson County, New Jersey, and the nation. NJCU is a dynamic institution that proudly maintains the Gothic tradition of making a difference in the lives of those it touches.

PROVIDENT SAVINGS BANK

One cannot write the history of Jersey City or Hudson County without including the story of The Provident Savings Bank, the first savings bank in the history of New Jersey. The three entities were born at the same time; Jersey City was incorporated in 1838, Hudson County was created as a separate entity from Bergen in 1840, and The Provident Institution for Savings in Jersey City was granted its charter in 1839.

Provident did not actually open for business until the administration of its second president, Dudley S. Gregory, in 1843. The delay was due, in part, to the public's distrust of banks resulting from the Panic of 1837, in which hundreds of commercial banks had collapsed and individuals and businesses suffered great losses. The idea of a mutual savings bank in·which income and profit

Provident Savings Bank first headquarters building at Plymouth and Washington Street, Jersey City.

were to be applied and divided among depositors was a new one.

The 1839 charter, combined with sage leadership of the bank's incorporators was first begun by President John F. Ellis, and would stand the institution and its depositors in good stead through panics, wars, crashes, down markets and depressions. The new bank's aim was to serve the wage earners and families of its community. Mr. Gregory, who was also Jersey City's first mayor, would steer the Provident from first day deposits of $227 in 1843 to assets of $3.5 million 33 years later in 1873.

The earliest mutual savings banks were often named for the people they served: "mechanics," "farmers," "seamen" and, simply, "people's." Provident was to become known as 'The "Old Beehive" in admiration of the thrifty life of the bee. It never forgot to guard the savings of its depositors. When the Panic of 1873 shuttered many financial institutions, the Provident continued to pay its dividends. In 1876, the New Jersey Legislature passed an act that required all state savings banks to live up to standards that had long been set for the Provident by its charter of 1839.

In 1893, despite a gold and silver panic, President Isaac I. Vanderbeek, who followed Andrew Clerk and David Smith, paid dividends for the 50th consecutive year. Freeman A. Smith, Edward W. Kingsland, and George R. Perkins, all civic and business leaders of the community, shepherded the bank through the turn of the century and into a time when Jersey City was becoming the nation's 17th largest city. When Mr. Perkins' term began in 1910, assets had reached $16 million.

James B.Throckmorton became President in 1916 and guided the bank safely through the Jazz Age, the Holland Tunnel to Manhattan, the Crash of 1929, the Bank Holiday,

Chairman, Chief Executive Officer and President Paul M. Pantozzi, The Provident Savings Bank.

and the Depression. As banks around it failed, the Provident remained healthy. In fact, it was one of the first banks permitted to reopen after President Roosevelt closed all banks in 1932 to get the system running again. At the bank's 100th anniversary in 1939, with continuation of uninterrupted dividends, Mr. Throckmorton announced an innovation—its first branch office opened at Bergen and Harrison Avenues.

Existing regulations prevented savings banks from opening branches outside their home cities, thus limiting the expansion efforts of Presidents George R. Beach, Karl A. Schwotzer and William Neumann, Jr. But Mr. Neumann did strategically position two branches near the Bayonne city limits to encourage out-of-town depositors to cross the municipal border and take advantage of the Provident's stability and services. By 1964, when a fifth branch opened, the Provident had 68,000 depositors and had become one of the state's leading providers of residential mortgages, helping more New Jerseyans to realize the American dream of home ownership.

In reality, it was Kenneth F.X. Albers who captained Provident during its most dramatic growth period—the decades of the 70s and 80s. In 1970, The Provident Institution for Savings officially became The Provident Savings Bank and for the first time in its history expanded beyond the city by opening new branches in West New York and Union City. In 1978, Congress eased some of the regulations that had long reined in the thrifts and in 1982, the banking industry was further deregulated. The Provident, at last, could sell a fuller range of financial services to increase banking and investment options for its customers.

The era of expansion continued as The Provident established a statewide presence, with offices in the Delaware Valley, Bergen and Essex Counties and in the shore area. As the popularity of the shore grew, the "Old Beehive" was readily accepted by expatriates of Hudson County, many of whom referred to the shore as "Jersey City South." From 1970 to 1987, under Mr. Albers, a bank with a main office and five branches and assets of $233.9 million grew to 35 branches with assets of $1.25 billion.

In 1983, Mr. Albers and James K. Feely, president of the Bloomfield Savings Institution, successfully merged their two organizations into a billion dollar-plus bank—Mr. Feely, becoming the bank's 14th president and Mr. Albers, the first Chairman of the Board and Chief Executive Officer. The two banks shared the same principles of service to the community and the fit was ideal.

More changes in the banking industry were becoming visible. The convenience of driveup banking, started in the 70s, was followed by the "ATM" in the 80s. The Provident was one of the first in the state to offer 24-hour automated teller machines. Computer-age "cash cards" and space-age technology were becoming previews of future banking.

In 1989, on the 150th Anniversary of the Provident, Paul M. Pantozzi became its 15th President, having joined the bank as a teller in 1963, six months after graduating from high school. With Pantozzi as Chairman, Chief Executive Officer and President, The Provident approached the Year 2000 with more than 50 offices in 10 counties throughout the state and assets of over $2.4 billion. Under Pantozzi's guidance, The Provident weathered the merger craze of the 90s, recognizing that mergers and consolidations of many local banks had created new opportunities for community banks such as The Provident. Customers, reacting negatively to the out-of-state takeovers of their local and regional banks, responded positively to

Provident's new corporate headquarters, 830 Bergen Avenue. A local landmark structure, crowned with a 30 foot high clock tower, redesigned and built in 1987. It is a tribute to the growth of The Provident and the vitality of the Jersey City community.

Provident's more personalized approach. While The Provident traditionally catered to the individual and his banking needs, it now focused new energy developing products and services for commercial business and real estate customers. In effect, The Provident became a full service bank—a bank for all seasons. In 1999, over 150,000 individual and business customers selected The Provident as their bank of choice.

Chairman Pantozzi looks ahead to "customer-centric" banking—a bank that will never forget to look back—secure in the knowledge that the strength of a financial institution is rooted in the approval and loyalty of its customers. The words that described the Provident in 1839 still apply: strong, secure, stable, dependable and absolutely safe. The bank that first pledged "to maintain the highest degree of safety and to pay the highest dividends consistent with that aim" looks past the Millennium to continued dedicated service to residents and businesses of New Jersey. The thrifty life of the bee is a lesson for every century.

READY PERSONNEL SERVICES/READY TEMPS, INC.

Officers (l to r): Denise Arthur, president; Josephine Brescia, comptroller; and Jean Frank, vice president.

The history of Ready Personnel Services/Ready Temps, Inc. is hardly the classic account of bricks, mortar, expansion, and a climbing sales curve on a visual chart. It is, instead, the story of Denise Arthur, a schoolteacher who decided to make a career change by plunging into the male-dominated personnel field long before the advent of women's liberation or equal opportunity. Five years after that momentous decision, Arthur, armed with a $10,000 loan and the entrepreneur's dream, opened Ready Personnel Services and began a business that would eventually catapult to the forefront of its field.

Arthur discloses that while she enjoyed schoolteaching, it somehow lacked the ultimate challenge to satisfy her drive for accomplishment. After leaving the field of education, she became the franchise director for a Manhattan-based personnel firm, earning her dues as she spent nearly 35 weeks a year on the road covering all 50 states.

Her role with that firm included responsibility for basic advertising, employee relations, acting as director of sales, and keeping abreast of the general market pulse. After five years Arthur decided to take the giant step and opened her own firm in June 1974 at 26 Journal Square in Jersey City. The loan that was used to launch the business was paid back in six months.

At the outset the firm operated as a family enterprise with Arthur's mother and father helping to sort mail and do the bookkeeping. The business, in fact, was named after her father, Clayton Ready. The name "Ready" ultimately did more than just identify the business. The new firm determined that the candidates it sent to corporate clients were honest, enthusiastic, and thoroughly screened—in a word, "ready" for employment.

Business grew at a rapid pace. In 1975, just one year after its opening, Ready Personnel took on Jean Frank, who now serves as vice-president and general manager of the permanent placement side of the business. Within eleven short years another eleven employees were added, and in June 1985 Ready Temps, a temporary personnel service, was added to the corporate structure. Ready Temps operated in the black before the year's end. To add to its already high penetration of the market, Ready became known for providing legal secretaries and paralegal personnel.

However, the firm did experience some hard times. Recessions twice

The original Ready Personnel/Ready Temps management team (l to r): Annette Amoroso; Jean Frank, vice president; Denise Arthur, president; and Clayton Ready, comptroller.

during the decade resulted in depressed markets, high rates of unemployment, and hiring freezes. But the good experiences always stand out. In Arthur's case it was the story of an applicant, a welfare recipient, with excellent secretarial skills, who hadn't utilized her talents for a long period of time. Ready got the applicant a babysitter, bought her some clothes, and gave her carfare to the interview. That was fifteen years ago, and today the woman is director of operations for a large local firm.

As Arthur watched the Downtown Waterfront grow she realized that was where the Ready Organization belonged. Ready Personnel and Ready Temps relocated to the Atrium at Harborside Financial Center in 1993. The gentrification of Hoboken also was intriguing. This would be a perfect location to attract skilled and educated job seekers. A storefront office was opened at 51 Garden Street (corner of Observer Highway) in Hoboken in 1996. This office is managed by Marie Russo.

In 1998 Ready Personnel/Ready Temps, Inc. celebrated 25 years in

Ready Personnel/Ready Temps Hoboken office.

Ready Personnel & Ready Temp's staff in their office. Left to right: Renee Gaughran, Fran Lecowitch, Josephine Brescia, Jean Frank, Denise Arthur, Marie Russo, Linnette Torres, Victoria Bing and Lucretia Amaker.

business. They billed three million dollars in sales with volume growing due to repeat business and Ready's excellent reputation.

Arthur is quick to acknowledge that it is her staff that makes this happen, not herself alone. That staff of 11 females is certainly loyal. Vice President Jean Frank has been with her for 24 years, Comptroller Josephine Brescia for 21 years, Delores O'Keefe for 16 years, Temporary Coordinator Victoria Bing for 14 years and Permanent Specialist

Fran Lecowitch for 12 years.

Denise recognizes that the collective attributes of her staff, such as being committed, intelligent and intuitive have helped Ready succeed in this extremely competitive industry. She notes that "ours is not a clear cut, black-and-white business. It is the ability to find that special quality in someone that will make a difference to one of our clients." She continues, "that's fun and very rewarding!".

Honesty, quality, and the insistence on only putting its best applicants forward have helped to establish Ready Personnel Services/Ready Temps, Inc. as the most reliable service of its kind in Hudson County.

Ready Personnel is located in the Harborside Financial Center, 145 Plaza Two, Jersey City, NJ and at 51 Garden Street, Hoboken, NJ.

RECYCLING SPECIALISTS, INC.

Recycling Specialist's ("RSI") mamouth 60,000 square-foot, eight + acre facility was erected in 1987, in response to the New Jersey Mandatory Source Separation and Recycling Act. The Act required homes and businesses to separate all recyclable materials from their waste stream so that New Jersey, as a whole, would dispose less solid waste, and ease the burden on the state's few remaining landfills.

RSI's founders were familiar with disposal of solid waste, having been in the waste business in New Jersey as owners of Classic Sanitation Co. of Saddlebrook, New Jersey ("Classic"). Recycling Specialists recognized the birth of a new industry, and RSI was formed on January 7, 1987. RSI met the need to process the materials that were once delivered to landfills and which, due to the Act, would require processing for return to market as a recycled raw material. Hence, brothers Frank Chiaia and Ralph Chiaia, and brothers David Granatell and Michael Granatell, invested approximately $7 million into this new industry by purchasing the eight + acres of

The front of the facility in Jersey City.

land at 375 U.S. Truck Route 1 & 9 South in Jersey City, abutting the Pulaski Elevated Highway. Its tooling facility with two Mosley balers, a paper sorting system, and a glass, aluminum, metal and plastic sorting system, made RSI one of the nations largest state-of-the-art recycling centers. Since 1987, the facility has processed over three million tons—nearly 750 tons of materials per day. But for recycling, these materials would have been disposed in a landfill or in an incinerator.

RSI offered to businesses a dumpster for cardboard to be placed alongside of the waste dumpster. The dumpsters were color-coded

The plant loaded with material to process.

beige for corrugated. At the time all dumpsters offered by RSI were beige for corrugated. Similarly, the cardboard collection trucks were beige. Presently, RSI also has white dumpsters for commingled (glass, aluminum, plastic, tin, and metal) and has blue dumpsters for high grade paper. The tonnage of material that RSI collects is insubstantial in comparison to the tonnage that is delivered to RSI from municipal curbside collections. The environment is far cleaner today thanks to these municipal governments and their citizens that separate their paper and their commingled (glass, aluminum, plastic, tin, metal). In 1989 RSI acquired Hackensack Paper, formally of Division Street in Jersey City. Hackensack Paper collected and recycled primarily high-grade paper such as computer paper and white ledger. With this acquisition, RSI was better able to serve its corporate clients who sought greater reduction of waste and higher rebates for their recycled tonnage.

In 1991, RSI installed a Mc MRF 300 sorting machine to automatically sort commingled glass, aluminum, metal, and plastic.

The machine sorted 4.5 tons per hour. It utililzed a trommel for separation of broken glass; an air classifier to separate light materials such as plastic and aluminum from heavy materials such as glass; a magnet for metal and an eddie current for removal of aluminum. 1991 also brought the addition of a new shareholder, Mr. Joseph Carbone. Prior to Mr. Carbone's arrival, the company had been owned only by members of the Chiaia and Granatell families. Today, the company remains owned by David and Michael Granatell, Frank Chiaia, his daughers Christina and Catherine, and Joe Carbone.

In 1998 the company replaced the Mc MRF 300 with a new sorting system which increased the through-put from 4.5 tons per hour to 16 tons per hour. The machine is a larger version of its predecessor, also utilizing magnets and an eddie current. However, the new machine has neither a trommel, (it uses finger screens to sort broken glass), nor an air classifier, (it uses a destoner and air knife to sort aluminum and plastic from unbroken glass.)

Two new Moslely Balers, 1987.

The company hopes to have a newspaper recycling system and a concrete recycling system in the near future, as well as a pulverizer to create sand from its broken glass by-product.

RSI's location in Jersey City is key to its existence, as its central location is just minutes from the Hudson River Crossings and major highways, such as the Holland Tunnel, Bayonne Bridge, Route 440, the New Jersey Turnpike, the Garden State Parkway, Route 280 and Route 78. Towns in Hudson, Union, Essex, Bergen, Passaic and Morris Counties find RSI a convenient market source for processing their recyclables. Similarly, NYC has utilized RSI's facility.

Jersey City not only provides a central location and convenient access, but has an abundant population of hard working, competent and conscientious people. RSI is immensely grateful for the hundreds of employees who have contributed to her growth and have become a substantial part of her existence and success. RSI is equally grateful to play a small part in Hudson County's rich history.

Some of the employees of RSI.

TOWN OF SECAUCUS

Geological upheavals and the slow transformation of land through erosion and weathering produced the strange geographical location in which the Town of Secaucus now stands. Less than a million years ago, mammoth glaciers, which once covered all of New Jersey, retreated to leave the fossils of dinosaurs, crocodiles and huge turtles lying under the soil of sandstone and shale.

Today, a Secaucus landmark, Laurel Hill, previously named Snake Hill, due to the inordinate numbers of snakes inhabiting the area, is a peculiar rock mass believed, by geologists, to be the stump of a volcano which long ago erupted to form the Watchung Mountains.

Secaucus was, and is today, an island surrounded by water—the Hackensack River, streams and creeks. Present-day evidence shows that the area was also home to large cedar forests. In the early years, the Lenni-Lenape Indians inhabited the area. The Lenape tribe remained in the Hudson area until the late 1700s, when they moved westward. They were mostly dependent on hunting and gathering shellfish for their food supply. From their language comes the name Secaucus. While we are not certain of the original meaning, it probably had something to do with the area's association with snakes or marshes. While the Hackensack Indians didn't have permanent villages in Secaucus, they lived nearby and traveled through the area. Many of their narrow trails became paths for settlers, and finally broadened into the roads and streets of today.

The first Europeans to explore and settle the area were Dutch. Exploration began in 1621 and by 1629 colonists were encouraged to

The Municipal Building was constructed during 1909 by building contractor John J. Hoffman at a cost of $26,100. This building was demolished in 1977 by the previous administration, and an ultra modern building now stands on the site.

settle. At first, the relationship between the settlers and the natives was friendly. After some unfair dealings with white traders, the relationship turned hostile. Peter Stuyvesant, Governor in 1647, tried to remedy things in 1658, with a treaty between the two groups. The land Stuyvesant negotiated for coincides with today's Hudson County. Secaucus is first mentioned by name in the treaty, referred to as the "Islandt Sistakes"—one of the many spellings that would be adopted for the area. Other names included Cekakus, Cecaicos, Silkackes, and Sekacus.

To protect themselves against further Indian attacks, the settlers took the Governor's advice to build fortified villages. One of the first villages was Bergen Township, today Bergen Square in Jersey City. The township held in its outskirts several smaller settlements, including Bayonne, Hoboken, and Secaucus. The boundaries of Secaucus then, are similar to the boundaries of today.

By 1833, Secaucus was on its way. Railroad tracks were laid in town, and by December trains began operating. As a point of

interest, the original bridge over the Hackensack River, in Secaucus, some 1700 feet in length, connecting Hudson and Bergen Counties, is reputed to be the first railroad draw-bridge constructed in the United States.

The second half of the 19th Century saw Secaucus grow in three directions: a) the development at Snake Hill which included a County tuberculosis hospital, an Almshouse, Lunatic Asylum and Penitentiary, along with other County buildings; b) the establishment of the foundry and Sauer Island colony; and c) the general influx of German immigrant farmers. By the 1870s Germans constituted 90% of the population.

The 20th Century found Secaucus maturing politically, and taking an interest in its own destiny. Feeling too removed from the political scene and unhappy about certain taxes in North Bergen Township, of which Secaucus was part, Secaucus broke from North

Secaucus Plaza Center—Veteran's Memorial Plaza.

Bergen and became the Town of Secaucus on January 23rd, 1900.

By this time, Secaucus had established itself as a major farming area, due to the very fertile land. With its close proximity to New York City, it was easy and profitable for farmers to sell their products. Over the years, farming included hog, vegetable and flower farms. Hog-raising alone constituted close to 200,000 hogs annually, which amounted to 50,000,000 lbs. of pork per year. This made Secaucus a major food producer for the war-effort during World War II. However, the post-war period saw the demise of much of the farming in Secaucus. The New Jersey Turnpike came through Town in the early fifties, buying out farms in its path. The '50s and early '60s saw the boom of single-family housing throughout town.

Those years also witnessed Henry Krajewski, a pig-farmer, campaign on the "Poor Man's Party" line for Secaucus Councilman, Hudson County Freeholder, New Jersey Governor, U. S. Senator and 3 times (1952, 1956 and 1960) for President of the United States! Krajewski is remembered for carrying a piglet under his arm while campaigning, and for his 1960 slogan, "No Piggy Deals in Washington!"

The 1960s saw the development by Hartz Mountain Industries of many warehouse and distribution centers for major clothing manufacturers. Eventually, these warehouses opened their doors to the general public, selling clothing at wholesale prices, thus making Secaucus a significant off-price merchandise outlet center in the Metropolitan area.

Secaucus today is a vibrant suburban community, 5.89 square

Trolley Park—end of Paterson Plank Road, where once was the oldest bridge crossing over Hackensack River to go to Bergen County. Restoration completed by Mayor Just.

miles, with 15,000 residents. During the work-week the town welcomes between 45,000 and 50,000 people who are working and shopping. The town is a thriving, growing, modern community, much sought after for its well-maintained residential neighborhoods, excellent municipal services, lowest tax rate in Hudson County, outstanding recreational programs, a great school system, and many lovely parks. The community predominately consists of one and two-family homes, with some hi-rise, condo, town-house, and senior-living units. The town fathers take great pride in holding on to the small-town atmosphere, while still being home to corporate headquarters, such as Panasonic and Goya Foods, major law firms, hotels, industry and TV stations MS/NBC and WWOR-TV. This amount of industry makes the Town a substantial contributor to the job market in the Metropolitan area. Logistically speaking, our

close proximity to New York City, the Meadowlands Sports Complex, Newark International Airport and the New Jersey Turnpike make Secaucus a prime real-estate area for homeowners and industry alike.

The Town of Secaucus will celebrate its 100th birthday on January 23rd, 2000. Secaucus has come a long way from the Lenni-Lenapes, the notable farm-era and the building booms. With wisdom and guidance we will successfully move into the new millennium.

Eleven Mayors, serving the Town over these past 100 years, each brought with him his own specific vision for the Town. Each has propelled the Town further down the road to success. Presently, Mayor Anthony E. Just, Sr, elected to office January 1st, 1992, has created the phrase, "Safe, Clean, Affordable & Honest," and feels personally responsible for implementing those words that describe Secaucus during his Mayoral term.

Secaucus—almost 100 years old and still the "Jewel of Hudson County!" Bravo!

Sources: *Secaucus Home News 50th Anniversary, History of Secaucus Jersey Journal Special Edition,* "Secaucus Looking Back."

THE SOCIETY OF NAVAL ARCHITECTS AND MARINE ENGINEERS

The Society of Naval Architects and Marine Engineers (SNAME) is a professional engineering society dedicated to advancing the art and science of ship and small craft design and construction, ocean engineering, and the design and construction of offshore structures. From SNAME's Headquarters in Jersey City, a Hudson County city with a proud maritime tradition, a 20-person staff ministers to the needs of the Society's 12,000 members. SNAME disseminates research and information through its meetings, symposia, and publications. These publications include the annual *Transactions*, three periodicals: *Marine Technology*, the *Journal of Ship Research* and the *Journal of Production*; text and research materials for both university classes and corporate reference; and its web site: http://www.sname.org.

Early in 1893, a group of visionary engineers from the shipbuilding industry and the United States Navy gathered in New York to discuss the future of the maritime industry. The latter half of the nineteenth century was a period of expansion for the United States, but the nation's attention had long been focused on our westward expansion. Our merchant vessels were almost non-existent, and our navy was in the earliest stages of modernization to match the European fighting fleets. The maritime industries were moribund, and the shipbuilders, faced with the construction of increasingly larger vessels fitted with more complex machinery, found that the ship design and shipbuilding industry in the United States did not have an engineering forum to which it could turn for technical guidance for both commercial and military ships.

It was under these circumstances

that SNAME was founded in 1893. Coincident with that event, a naval construction program of significant size and scope was undertaken, and two large, fast liners: the *St. Louis* and *St. Paul*, were ordered for the American Line. These magnificent vessels, advanced for their time and capable of conversion for military duties (which was carried out during the Spanish-American War and World War I), were the first transatlantic passenger ships built in the United States since the 1870s.

The earliest activities of SNAME centered on the presentation and discussion of technical papers at annual meetings, and through the first century of the Society's existence, this has remained its cornerstone. However, from the World War II period onward, the seventeen local Sections in the United States and Canada have provided an important forum for networking and discussing the technical and ethical issues faced by our shipbuilders, naval architects, and marine engineers in ship design and construction. In addition,

The Steamship St. Louis, *built at Philadelphia in 1895 by Wm. Cramp Ship & Engine Building Co. for the American line. The shipbuilding yard was headed by Charles H. Cramp, one of the founders of The Society of Naval Architects and Marine Engineers. Courtesy, the Steamship Historical Society of America Collection at the University of Baltimore.*

widespread concern about the operation of ships has added significantly to the scope of the Society's activities.

From the 1950s, a structured Technical and Research (T&R) program has channelled the resources of SNAME and the talents of its members toward providing a focal point for maritime research in North America. Among the more than sixty working panels that comprise the T&R program, the subjects range from hull structure and hydrodynamics to ship operation, ship production, and the offshore industry. Ad-hoc panels are also currently addressing such important issues as vehicle ferry safety, tanker stability, and ballast water management. The Society is unique among professional organizations for funding this research.

During two World Wars, the success of the Allied activities was in large measure the result of having sufficient naval and merchant vessels at the disposal of the armed forces. Although American shipbuilders played a major role in the 1914-18 war, it was the vast armada that sailed from American shipyards between 1941 and 1945 that tipped the balance during that conflict. The 2,710-vessel Liberty Ship fleet, led appropriately by one named Patrick Henry, formed a floating bridge to supply the European and Pacific theatres. But these "Ugly Ducklings," (although this name was coined by President Roosevelt, the sentiment was not necessarily shared by those who sailed in them) were only part of the American maritime world's contribution of over 7,000 naval and merchant ships that were delivered in less than four years! That magnificent production effort could not have been accomplished without the skill, dedication, and technical expertise contributed by a legion of SNAME members. In times of peace, the world's mer-

One of 2,710 Liberty Ships built in American shipyards during World War II. This immense fleet of 10,000-ton vessels formed the backbone of our wartime supply lines and many of the Liberties had long careers after the end of hostilities. Courtesy of the American Bureau of Shipping and the War Shipping Administration.

Hvide Marine's double-hulled product tanker, HMI Ambrose Channel, *built by Newport News Shipbuilding, on sea trials in January 1999. The 45,000-dwt tanker combines the latest in ship design and building techniques, and features state-of-the-art electronics for navigation and ship operation. Courtesy, Newport News Shipbuilding/Mike Dillard*

chant fleets perform a vital task that is largely unsung. World trade is the engine that drives civilization, and shipping plays a major role in efforts to globalize the economy. Over 95 percent of international commerce is carried by ship. The cargo liners, bulk carriers, and petroleum tankers that call at our ports are vital to the nation's well-being and prosperity. However, the Society's interest does not stop at the ports; our vast system of inland waterways also receives its attention.

Most of the major new achievements in the field of marine transportation were developed in the United States. These include containerization, liquefied natural gas transport, barge carrying ships, and the application of computers to shipboard systems. The mission of SNAME remains much as it was a century ago; in addition to its traditional tasks of designing and building ships which are efficient and profitable, the Society and its members are constantly striving to ensure that maritime transportation is increasingly safe, reliable, and environmentally friendly. The quest

for cleaner seas and safer ships now drives a major portion of SNAME's technical and research program activities.

Today, the Society's increasingly international membership reflects the globalization of the maritime world. Nearly 25 percent of the men and women who constitute its rolls represent 86 nations outside the United States.

SNAME looks to the new millennium with optimism. A continuing increase in the level of world trade is forecast for the transportation of energy, raw materials and manufactured products to supply the needs of both developed and emerging nations. SNAME is prepared to provide the leadership in assuring that future waterborne commerce will be safe, peaceful, and efficient commerce.

THE SYSTEMS GROUP

In 1993, three consultants in the field of systems engineering and integration who had met while working for a previous employer, decided to join forces and take the broadcast industry by storm. The systems engineering and integration industry plans, engineers, fabricates, and installs advanced audio, video, and multimedia systems for diverse clients such as major broadcast networks; cable channels; corporations; and foundations. Scott G. Griffin, Christopher Mehos, and Alan Rudolph had that magic mix of vision and ability that would propel the company on a growth pattern that continues today.

Hoboken, NJ, a city characterized by reinventing itself regularly, proved the ideal location for the explosive growth of The Systems Group. TSG, entering a boom period for the economy in general and the systems integration market in particular, needed to locate their offices in an area close to Manhattan where they could expand as the business grew. TSG found its ideal location in an old industrial complex, the R. Neumann and Co. leather tannery plant. From 1863 to 1963, this city block-sized complex, employing several hundred workers,

View of smokestack of Neumann Leather Building built in 1863 and staircase leading to TSG's early office space.

The Systems Group's executive management team from left to right: Alan Rudolph, Christopher Mehos, Bud Rigley (lower), and Scott Griffin.

was the largest leather tannery in the Northeast. R. Neumann and Co. provided all the leather materials for the U.S. Military from the Civil War to the Vietnam War. Today, the original complex still stands and is home to a thriving community of local businesses ranging from artists and recording studios, to woodshops and a chocolate manufacturer.

TSG began by renting less than 500 square feet of loft space from R. Neumann and Co. By the mid-nineties, TSG's facilities occupied well over 25,000 square feet of the industrial complex with additional expansion an on-going process. TSG radically renovated the original warehouse spaces to reflect their commitment to providing their employees with a productive and open environment that encourages corporate and personal growth The facilities provide easy access to all points in the tri-state area as well as all three major airports and provided the necessary space, operating systems and technology required of a modern systems integration company. The facility houses all aspects of TSG's operations including administrative offices, fabrication and staging areas, shipping and

receiving loading dock and office area, inventory storage and management areas. The 20,000 square foot fabrication and staging area provides ample room for the most demanding projects, including expandable production trailers which can easily be driven into their staging area. Ample storage space for equipment and materials enable fabrication and staging areas to remain uncluttered and organized and the shipping and receiving area can accommodate large tractor trailers for lift truck loading and unloading of materials and equipment.

The Systems Group quickly outgrew the original loft space as they made the transition from subcontractor to major contractor when they bid on and won their first prominent project, the engineering and integration of NBC's Television Broadcast Center in Rockefeller Center, NYC in 1995. TSG was up against many well established systems integration companies including their former employer but TSG's unique approach and the accessibility of the partners, won them the bid. By the time of the competition for the NBC project, TSG had grown to six staff employees and eight freelance technicians.

During the mid-nineties, TSG won the bid for Microsoft and NBC's joint venture—the MSNBC 24-hour news facility in Secaucus, NJ. This project was the largest undertaking of its kind on the east coast since the three network built their television centers in NYC during the 1950s and 1960s. The project took eleven months and propelled the company into major facility expansion and personnel growth including the addition of Bud Rigley to Senior Management. Bud's extensive broadcast experience provided the final complement to TSG's leadership team. The high visibility and tremendous scope of the project gave TSG the opportunity to design and build some of the most interesting projects in the broadcast industry throughout the nineties:

- Hudson River Studios - *in progress*; Studio Production Complex (NYC)
- CD Radio - *in progress*; Broadcast Origination Center (NYC)
- KABC - *in progress*; Ground-up, Digital Broadcast Facility (CA)
- Ethnic American Broadcasting - *in progress*; Broadcast Operations Facility (Fort Lee, NJ)
- CBS - Sports Coordination Master Control Area - NFL broadcast distribution (NYC)
- VH1 - Multimedia Graphics Suite (NYC)
- Smith Barney, Inc. - Corporate Communications Teleproduction Workshop (NYC)
- Primestar - Network Quality Control Monitoring Facility (Philadelphia, PA)
- Central Florida News (CFN) - 24 Hour Regional News Operation (Orlando, FL)
- MTV Networks - Times Square Concourse Studio (NYC)

- The National Basketball Association; Audio/Video Teleconferencing Facilities (NYC)
- WQCD - CD 101.9 FM - Top 10 Market Radio Station Upgrade and Rebuild (NYC)
- WGNO-TV, Tribune Broadcasting - News Production Facility (New Orleans, LA)

Today, TSG employs nearly 50 full-time staff employees and, on a project-by-project basis, any number of contract and freelance employees. Close proximity to a wide range of public transportation has made it possible for TSG to attract and employ many employees from the local area including Hoboken and Jersey City. TSG's reputation as a growth company with a good work environment coupled with interesting and diverse projects has attracted employees from as far away as Sparta, NJ, Yorktown Heights, NY and Bayshore and West Islip, Long Island!

The Systems Group takes pride in their employees and their community and has begun to define itself as a patron of some of the many cultural events Hoboken has to offer. Many of TSG's employees are musicians

The "Green Room" at MTV Networks, from which many MTV shows are broadcast, overlooks Times Square.

MSNBC's Acquisition Control Room located in Secaucus, NJ—the facility was so large it utilized over two million feet of cable to connect everything together.

involved in regional bands and recording projects. By patronizing the cultural events in Hoboken, TSG is able to encourage and support the outside interests of their employees. Our philosophy is simple, says Alan Rudolph: "We are as good as our people. In five short years TSG emerged from the unknown to enjoy a reputation as one of the best in the business. We attribute this success to our employees. Each one, from technician to engineer, is highly regarded for their integrity and professionalism. Solid leadership and dedicated employees will ensure that The Systems Group will continue to grow and thrive well into the new millennium."

UNIVERSAL FOLDING BOX COMPANY, INC.

Universal Folding Box Company, Inc. was founded in 1910 on Mercer Street in New York City. Hyman Batkin invested his life savings in 1912 and took over complete ownership of the company a few years later.

Batkin came to this country as a little boy of six from Lithuania and later graduated from Dewitt Clinton High School in New York City. He became a self made bookkeeper, accountant and credit man and worked for a number of firms before investing in Universal. He was a great athlete and believed in the preservation of the physical body, once winning a race from 125th street in New York to The Battery. This race was sponsored by the Hearst newspaper of the time.

In approximately 1919 the factory was moved to the Bush Terminal Buildings in Brooklyn where it occupied space in Building 19 on thirty-ninth street. A payroll record book dated April 23, 1921 shows some people working for as little as $.25 per hour. At that time there was a standard 48 hour week. A highly skilled printing pressman was paid $35 for the 48 hour week, the equivalent of $.73 an hour.

Prior to WWII most folding carton companies were established in multi-storied buildings. Printing was done on the fourth floor, cutting and creasing on the third floor, stripping and gluing on the second floor and shipping and receiving out of the first floor. Hyman Batkin was very impressed with the success of Henry Ford in manufacturing cars in a one floor in-line production method. As a result of this, in 1936 the plant moved to its present location in Hoboken, New Jersey where Hyman Batkin bought a series of four buildings totaling 50 thousand square feet, 40 thousand square

feet of which were on one floor. This one floor in-line manufacturing materially lowered his costs and contributed greatly to the future growth and success of the company. In subsequent years he bought additional land alongside the buildings, and in 1947 one of the older original buildings was torn down and 50 thousand square feet was added. Then again, in 1981 another 40 thousand square feet was added, bringing the total to 130 thousand square feet.

Most printing in the industry was done by the letter press method, and in 1970 the company bought its first four color offset lithography press. This materially changed the manufacturing of folding cartons and introduced Universal into highly printed four color process cartons. As the company progressed and grew and acquired new clients of a national nature, it constantly plowed back the profits into the latest state of the art equipment. In the early 1970s new cutting and creasing equipment was acquired and then in the 1980s and 1990s three new high speed six color presses were introduced, making the company one of the most efficient producers on the East Coast.

Hyman Batkin's eldest son Stanley Batkin joined the company in 1936, and in 1946 after 3 1/2 years in the US Air Force, serving in the Pacific, Sanford Batkin also joined the firm. The two brothers worked diligently together until 1986 when Stanley decided to retire and Sanford acquired his half of the business, making him the sole shareholder. Today, Sanford's grandson David Younger is the director of marketing of Universal, representing the fourth generation of the Batkin family in the business.

The basic philosophy of Universal is summed up in its mission statement. "We are a company driven to be a world class folding carton manufacturer, providing superior cost-effective packaging and services through an ongoing commitment to our customers, to our employees, and to our environment. We strive on a daily basis to perform to our highest standards and capabilities and to foster innovation, honesty, and a dedication to excellence."

WEST HUDSON HOSPITAL

West Hudson Hospital has long been dedicated to excellence in the delivery of care, and is today one of New Jersey's finest community hospitals—providing and promoting quality care to its surrounding neighborhoods. Located in the heart of Kearny, New Jersey, West Hudson Hospital is an affiliate of the Saint Barnabas Health Care System and central to the communities of North Arlington, Lyndhurst, Harrison, East Newark and other neighboring towns.

The original Hospital, a converted residential structure, opened its doors on October 1, 1913 with 36 beds, a staff of nine, and a medical staff of 12 physicians and surgeons. Then known as the Jacob Stumpf Memorial Hospital, in honor of a local businessman who donated the property and dwelling, the facility admitted 329 patients during its first year of operation

In 1922, the Hospital was renamed West Hudson Hospital to better reflect its area of service, and in 1926, a new building featuring 58 beds was erected. Additions throughout the years brought the Hospital to its current care complement of 217 beds. In 1997, West Hudson Hospital affiliated with the Saint Barnabas Health Care System.

With more than 200 physicians, 600 employees, and 200 volunteers, West Hudson Hospital today offers the finest medical and diagnostic treatments, and a wide range of health related professional services utilizing new age technological advances, to the people of Hudson, Essex and Bergen counties. West Hudson Hospital is accredited by the Joint Commission on the Accreditation of Healthcare Organizations (JCAHO).

West Hudson Hospital's out-standing medical team is trained in assessing and planning for the daily needs of patients. Its medical surgical divisions administer nursing care around the clock in an acute care setting for all hospitalized patients. Critically ill patients in the multifaceted medical surgical Critical Care Unit receive the latest in intensive care services, while those who have progressed in their recovery and no longer require specialized care benefit from the Hospital's Intermediate Care Unit. Physicians and the nursing team in the state-of-the-art Emergency Services Department utilize all of the Hospital's diagnostic and emergency treatments for their patients with traumatic injuries and medical emergencies.

The newest West Hudson Hospital programs are its Wound Healing and Cardiac Rehabilitative Centers. The Wound Healing Center treats all types of open wounds and ulcers with the very latest technological advancements for quick recovery. The Center uses High Frequency Ultra-Sound Scanner, an innovative technology that makes the invisible visible without the need for painful cutting. The Topical Hyperbaric Oxygen Extremity Chamber at West Hudson Hospital's Wound Healing Center is a simple, safe and effective treatment that saves limbs from amputation.

The Cardiac Rehabilitation Program at West Hudson Hospital provides education, exercise training and psychosocial support for patients and families coping with the consequences of cardiac-related illnesses. This program is medically designed to meet individualized needs to help patients reach and maintain a "heart healthy" lifestyle. Cardiac rehabiliation sessions enable patients and their

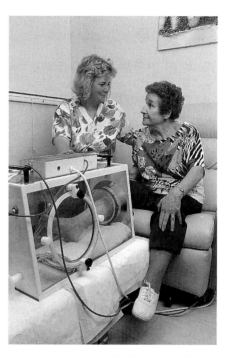

West Hudson Hospital's Wound Healing Center.

families to better understand and take control of their lives.

Also at West Hudson Hospital is the West Hudson Extended Care Facility. Located on the third floor of the Hospital, the West Hudson Facility provides continuous 24-hour nursing care under the direction of registered nurses, and combines medical and nursing care with a structured, multi-disciplinary program of rehabilitative services, and social and recreational activities. The Hospital's Sub-Acute Unit provides continued specialized rehabilitative care and treatment to prepare patients for discharge.

As its community's acute care hospital, West Hudson Hospital's offerings are comprehensive, including: a Pain Management Program; an Oncology Center; Rehabilitative and Respiratory Services; Nutritional Support; a Center for Kids and Family and a Wound Healing Center.

TIMELINE OF
HUDSON COUNTY'S HISTORY

1609 Under contract to the Dutch, Henry Hudson sails the *Half Moon* up the river that will later bear his name. Robert Juet, a ship's officer, describes the surrounding land in his journal "as pleasant with Grasse and Flowers, and goodly Trees, as ever they had seen."

1624 The Dutch send colonists to the Manhattan Island on the east bank of Hudson's river and name the tiny new settlement New Amsterdam. It will soon become the most important part of New Netherlands, the Dutch colony in the mid-Atlantic area. The Dutch encourage patroons to purchase land and send more colonists.

1630 Michael Pauw, a burgomeister of Amsterdam,

CAPITOL THEATRE, UNION CITY, N. J.

buys land on the west bank of the Hudson River and calls the area Pavonia, the land of the peacock. In Dutch, Pauw means peacock.

Pauw never crosses the Atlantic and never sees his New Netherlands holdings. Within three years he hires Cornelius Van Vorst to conduct the fur trade and to make arrangements for new settlers.

1633 To protect its interests in the fur trade the Dutch West India Company hires an agent, Michael Paulusen, who erects a dwelling on the sandy peninsula in Pavonia that juts out into the river. That area, now part of Jersey City, becomes known as Paulus Hook.

1643 & 1655 Pavonia is twice destroyed during

This brochure, issued on the 250ᵗʰ anniversary of the founding of Bergen in 1660, depicts the Columbian Academy on the northeast corner of Bergen Avenue and Academy Street. This site has been occupied by a school longer than any other site in New Jersey. It is now the location of Martin Luther King, Jr., School. Courtesy, JCPL

Good Times in Union City. The old heart of Union City, the Capitol Theater. Courtesy, JCPL

conflicts with the native Americans. The Pavonia farmers flee across the river to the safety of the fort at New Amsterdam.

1660 Peter Stuyvesant, the governor of New Netherlands, approves the first permanent settlement in what will become New Jersey. Situated on the hill at the intersection of present day Bergen Avenue and Academy Street in Jersey City, it is known as Bergen Township. Its boundaries include all the land in present day Hudson County east of the Hackensack River.

1664 The British conquer New Netherlands, change the name of New Amsterdam to New York, and award to Sir George Carteret and Lord John Berkeley all the land of the former New Netherlands that lies west of the Hudson

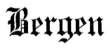

Bergen

1660

Columbian Academy, 1790

Jersey City

1910

River. This land is called New Jersey.

1675 Bergen County is formed consisting of Bergen Township and the "surrounding plantations."

1709 With terrain better suited to farming than Bergen, the town of Hackensack grows rapidly and in 1709 replaces Bergen Township as the county seat of Bergen County.

1765 Jersey's colonial legislature authorizes a road extending from Newark to Paulus Hook, where travelers can catch a sail-powered ferry to New York.

1769 Hoping to lure gamblers from Newark and New York, Cornelius Van Vorst, a descendant of Pavonia's original Van Vorst, lays out a racetrack at Paulus Hook.

1779 During the American Revolution the British occupy New York and erect a fort at Paulus Hook to aid in the defense of the harbor. On August 18 American forces led by "Light Horse Harry" Lee raid the fort and capture a number of British soldiers.

1798 The Hazzard family buys land at Constable Hook (Bayonne) where it builds a gunpowder factory. During the War of 1812 the factory makes ammunition for the harbor's warships and forts.

1804 Thirty-five investors from New York and New Jersey, including two men numbered among the mayors of New York, hire Alexander Hamilton as their attorney to negotiate the purchase of Paulus Hook. The goal of the Associates of the Jersey Company is to establish a new little city, the Town of Jersey, and to attract residents who feel that New York is becoming too crowded.

On July 1, soon after completing his legal work for the Associates, Hamilton suffers a mortal wound inflicted by Aaron Burr during a duel fought on the shore of the Hudson at Weehawken.

The year 1804 also sees land offerings by John Coles in the Hamilton Park area of present day Jersey City and by John Stevens, owner of most of Hoboken.

1808 Using his invention, the twin-screw propeller, John Stevens completes work on his steamboat, the *Phoenix*, but the Fulton-Livingston steamboat monopoly, awarded by the state of New York, bars him from launching ferry service on the Hudson.

The St. Francis Hospital Motorized Ambulance. St. Mary Hospital, opened in Hoboken in 1863, and its sister institution, St. Francis Hospital in Jersey City, opened one year later, were the first private hospitals in New Jersey. Courtesy, JCPL

Old Court House, Jersey City, N.J.

The Original County Court-house. When Hudson County was created in 1840, a site near Five Corners was selected as the site of the new courthouse, because it was situated near the major roads. This was the first Hudson County courthouse. Visible at its top and on the left is the 1910 county courthouse. Courtesy, JCPL

1812 Robert Fulton starts steam ferry service between Paulus Hook and New York City. Crossing time is 14 minutes.

1815 Isaac Edge, founder of a family still active in Jersey City, erects a large windmill at Paulus Hook.

1820 The Town of Jersey is incorporated as "The City of Jersey City" within Bergen Township. The intention had been to name the area the City of Jersey, but a printer makes an error and the redundant "City" remains.

1824 The U.S. Supreme Court, in the case known as Ogden v. Gibbons, declares void the New York steamboat monopoly. This is the first time New Jersey slipped a bit from under the thumb of the Empire State.

1825 Jersey City Porcelain and Earthenware Company opens, employing French and Irish artisans to make products so fine that in the second year of operation the company is awarded a silver medal by the Franklin Institute in Philadelphia.

1826 John Stevens runs the first steam engine locomotive in America around a circular track on his property in Hoboken.

1828 Isaac Edge, Jr., opens a pyrotechnical laboratory on Steuben Street in Jersey City, the first of many fireworks factories in Hudson County. In the same year the area's first newspaper, the *Bergen County Gazette and Advertiser*, begins publication in Jersey City.

1830 Charles F. Durant of Jersey City, rising aloft in a balloon and flying across New York Bay, becomes the first native born American aviator.

1834 A long simmering border dispute between New York and New Jersey is resolved by a treaty between the states that sets their boundary as the middle of the Hudson River and awards the existing islands in the river to New York.

1836 The Morris Canal, constructed to bring coal from Pennsylvania to the New York region, reaches the Hudson River waterfront, terminating in a basin at the southern end of Paulus Hook.

1838 Jersey City, a small area on the waterfront at Paulus Hook, separates from Bergen Township and becomes an independent municipality. Dudley Gregory, who made his fortune in lotteries and later railroad investments, becomes the city's first mayor.

1839 On New Year's Day a steam powered locomotive of the New Jersey Railroad leaves Jersey City for Newark and points south and west; it marks the start of the century-plus domination of the Hudson County waterfront by the railroads. In the same year the Provident, the first savings bank in New Jersey, opens in Jersey City.

1840 Hudson County is formed by splitting from Bergen County; the new county courthouse is located near Five Corners in Bergen Township.

In 1840 Harrison Township, named for the hero of Tippecanoe, President William Henry Harrison, separates from Lodi Township in Bergen County and joins Jersey City and Bergen Township in Hudson County

1841 Van Vorst Township separates from Bergen Township; 10 years later it joins Jersey City.

1843 North Bergen Township splits from Bergen Township.

1845 David LaTourette buys *Bon Sejours*, a DuPont mansion, and starts a first class resort on the shores of the Kill Van Kull in Bayonne.

John Cox Stevens organizes the New York Yacht Club and donates a clubhouse near the Elysian Fields in Hoboken.

1846 The first organized game of baseball is played on June 19 in Hoboken when the Knickerbocker Club defeats the New York Club.

1846-48 The first big waves of Irish and German immigrants arrive.

1849 Hoboken becomes an independent city.

1850s The Weehawken area, dotted with the summer homes of the wealthy from nearby cities, becomes a suburban retreat.

1851 Under the command of John Cox Stevens the yacht *America* defeats the entry of the Royal Yacht Squadron in a race around the Isle of Wight. Stevens returns to the family home in Hoboken with the nation's first international trophy, the America Cup.

1852 Hudson Town separates from North Bergen Township and in 1855 becomes Hudson City.

Ferry service between Weehawken and New York is incorporated.

1855-56 The New Jersey Railroad buys the water and ferry privileges of the Associates of the Jersey Company and builds a new terminal on landfill, thereby creating the area known as Exchange Place.

1859 Weehawken is formed from parts of Hoboken and North Bergen.

1860 The first Erie Railroad locomotive steams through the first tunnel through the Bergen Hill.

PAULUS HOOK MONUMENT, JERSEY CITY, N.J.

Above
This monument celebrates the 1779 Battle of Paulus Hook, when a raiding party led by "Light Horse Harry" Lee captured the British defenders of the fort. Located at the intersection of Washington and Grand streets, it was erected in 1903 and knocked down by a truck in 1936. A new obelisk, more sensibly situated on the sidewalk, was erected in the 1980s, thanks to a campaign led by the Historic Paulus Hook Association. Courtesy, JCPL

Left
The writer of this postcard, postmarked December 1, 1908, bragged that she had traveled under the river to New York in one of these new trains. Originally known as the Hudson and Manhattan Railway, and informally as the Tubes, the line was acquired by the Port Authority of New York and New Jersey in 1962 and is now known as the PATH, Port Authority Trans-Hudson. Courtesy, JCPL

VIEW IN HUDSON & MANHATTAN R.R. COMPANY'S TUNNEL.

1861 West Hoboken Township, Union Township, and Bayonne Township all become independent.

1862 Bergen Town absorbs Bergen Township. The next year Greenville Township separates from Bergen Town.

1863 St. Mary Hospital opens in Hoboken. One year later St. Francis Hospital opens in Jersey City. These sister institutions, run by the Sisters of the Poor of Saint Francis, are the first private hospitals in New Jersey.

1864 Union Town separates from Union Township.

On August 1 of 1864 the Central Railroad of New Jersey opens its new terminal in the Communipaw section of Jersey City and later in the year launches its ferry service

to Liberty Street in New York. The first Jewish synagogue in Hudson County opens in Jersey City.

1861-65 During the Civil War years the national conflict is reflected in the local scene; those who had helped runaway slaves escape through the Underground Railroad stations in Jersey City back Lincoln. The Civil War is good for business, especially for the railroad industry, which increases its traffic transporting troops and supplies to the battle areas. The Secors Company constructs six iron clad Monitor type ships at its Jersey City dry-dock, and the Joseph Dixon Crucible Company in Jersey City begins the manufacture of lead writing sticks for soldiers in the field, a product that

develops into the Ticonderoga line of pencils.

1867 Kearny Township separates from Harrison Township. It is named for General Phillip Kearny of Harrison who died at the Battle of Chantilly, Virginia in 1862. In the 1870s many Scots emigrate to Kearny to work in its thread and linoleum firms.

The first municipal hospital in Hudson County opens on Essex Street in Jersey City.

1868 Bergen Town becomes Bergen City.

Edwin Stevens leaves a bequest of $500,000 to found the Stevens Institute of Technology in Hoboken.

1869 Harrison Township becomes Harrison Town.

The Three Buildings of Harborside in the 1930s. The building on the right is now the home of Bankers Trust of New York. The other two buildings are linked by a new glass atrium, and all are joined by a glass-walled promenade right at the river's edge. In 1999 5,000 people work in Harborside for firms such as Columbus Lines, the American Institute of CPAs, and Dean Witter. Courtesy, JCPL

1869 Bayonne Township becomes Bayonne City.

1869-1870 Jersey City annexes Bergen City and Hudson City.

1871 The Pennsylvania Railroad leases the Exchange Place and Harsimus Cove rail properties, making Jersey City its eastern terminus. The mayor laments, "We might as well be an inland city."

1872 The first public high school in the county opens in Jersey City.

1873 Jersey City annexes Greenville thereby giving the city its current boundaries.

1878 Guttenberg separates from Union Township.

The Jesuits open St. Peter's College in Jersey City with a first year roster of 107 students.

1870s In the late 1870s oil refiners open plants at Bayonne's Constable Hook.

1880 One year after the invention of the light bulb Thomas Edison opens a factory in Harrison to manufacture his new product.

1886 The New York Central Railroad signs a 475 year lease for the West Shore line property in Weehawken.

1888 The State Home for Disabled Soldiers moves to Kearny from Newark.

1892 The federal government opens its immigrant reception center on Ellis Island, just off the shore of Jersey City. In the same year electric trolleys are introduced.

1893 Cornelia Bradford starts Whittier House on Grand Street in Jersey City; named in honor of the poet John Greenleaf Whittier, it is the first settlement house in NJ.

1895 East Newark becomes independent of Kearny.

1898 Union Township changes its name to West New York.

1899 The Pennsylvania Railroad buys land in southern Jersey City, opposite Brooklyn, and constructs the port's largest marine freight terminal, complete with lighters and carfloats. It is known as the Greenville Yards.

1900 Secaucus separates from North Bergen Township, the last breakaway municipality in the county.

Disastrous fires rage at the Constable Hook refineries in Bayonne and on the Hoboken piers.

1908-1911 The Hudson and Manhattan "Tube Trains"

The Margaret Hague Maternity Hospital: This county facility, opened in 1931, was named for the mother of Jersey City's mayor, Frank Hague. Lifelong residents identify one another by asking, "Were you born in the Margaret Hague?" Courtesy, JCPL

Hudson County Executive Robert Janiszewski at the Podium in the Brennan Court House, 1998. This 1910 building was designed by the architect Hugh Roberts and is listed on the National Register of Historic Places. It was saved from demolition in the 1960s and subsequently restored. It is now known as the William J. Brennan, Jr. Courthouse in honor of the late Supreme Court Justice who once served as Assignment Judge in Hudson County. Courtesy, HC Executive's Office

(now PATH) start service between Hoboken, Jersey City, Newark, and New York.

1910 The Pennsylvania Railroad opens its passenger tunnel under the Hudson River. New York's Penn Station replaces Jersey City's Exchange Place as the terminus of the mighty PRR.

1910 In 1910 the new county court house opens. Designed by Hugh Roberts, in 1970 it will become Hudson County's first entry on the National Register of Historic Places.

1916 Barges laden with explosives roar into flame at the Black Tom piers (now the southern part of Liberty State Park in Jersey City.) Wartime saboteurs are blamed.

The Industrialized Workers of the World, the Wobblies, lead the strike of the coopers and the still cleaners at the Bayonne plant of Standard Oil.

1917 Frank Hague becomes mayor of Jersey City and political boss of Hudson County. His tenure as mayor lasts 30 years.

1917 Hoboken is designated the port of embarkation for American soldiers heading for World War I.

1925 West Hoboken and Union Town merge to become Union City.

1927 The Holland Tunnel linking Jersey City to Manhattan opens; it is the world's first large-scale, underwater vehicular tunnel.

1931 The county's Margaret Hague Maternity Hospital opens; for many years it has the nation's lowest mother-child mortality rate.

1937 The first tube of the Lincoln Tunnel, joining Weehawken to New York, opens for traffic.

1941-45 The Port of New York works around the clock to supply the troops in Europe. The Hudson County rail and marine facilities loom large in this effort.

1946 Jackie Robinson breaks the color line in U.S. organized baseball when he comes to bat at Roosevelt Stadium in Jersey City.

1947 Frank Hague resigns as mayor of Jersey City. In

1949 his once invincible organization loses to John V. Kenny.

1951 Mary Teresa Norton retires from Congress after serving 13 terms. She was the first woman of the Democratic Party elected to the House of Representatives.

1967 Railroad ferry service to New York ends as the railroads continue their postwar decline.

1969 The Hackensack Meadowlands Development Commission is established to clean up the Meadowlands and to organize development within its 19,000 acres. Secaucus soon attracts new housing and commercial development in the district.

1975 Hudson County changes to a strong executive form of government.

1976 Liberty State Park opens and soon records more visitors than any other state recreational facility.

1980s New developments on former railroad land promise to turn the Hudson River shore into the Gold Coast. Hoboken and Jersey City capitalize on their historic housing stock.

1986 Arthur Imperatore starts ferry service between Weehawken and New York. His fleet of ferries, to be known as NY Waterway, later expands to cover nine routes.

1987 Newport, a mixed-use development, opens on the site of the old Erie Railroad terminal in Jersey City.

North Bergen Public Library, 1999. The modern quarters of the North Bergen Public Library located on Bergenline Avenue, across the street from James Braddock North Hudson County Park. Although the area on the east side of the park has many apartments that enjoy a great view of New York, most of North Bergen is filled with one and two family homes. The western Meadowlands section is the industrial zone, with numerous warehouses, distribution centers, and an intermodal train-truck terminal. Photo by Michael Lovero

1988   Robert C. Janiszewski begins his first term as Hudson County Executive.

1992   Jersey City elects Bret Schundler as mayor, the first Republican to fill that post since Mark Fagan in 1913. Schundler subsequently is reelected in 1993 and 1997.

101 Hudson Street opens at Exchange Place in Jersey City. At 550 feet it is the state's tallest building.

1993   Liberty Science Center opens to provide hands-on science learning.

1998   The U.S. Supreme Court decides that 90% of Ellis Island lies within the jurisdiction of New Jersey.

2000   The Hudson Bergen Light Rail Transit System is scheduled to begin service.

Ellis Island, July 4th, 1998. Jersey City Mayor Bret Schundler, Senator Robert Torricelli, and Governor Christine Todd Whitman headed an Independence Day visit to Ellis Island to celebrate the U.S. Supreme Court ruling that most of the island is in New Jersey. The case for New Jersey was researched and argued by the New Jersey Attorney General and his staff. The New Jersey argument developed from the 1834 treaty between New York and New Jersey that originally set the boundary between the states. Photo by Alton O'Neill

Bibliography

GENERAL NEW JERSEY HISTORY AND SOCIOLOGY

Craven, Wesley Frank. *New Jersey and the English Colonization of North America.* Princeton: D. Van Nostrand Company, Inc., 1964.

Effross, Harris I. *County Governing Bodies in New Jersey.* New Brunswick: Rutgers University Press, 1975.

Juet, Robert. *Juet's Journal. The Voyage of the Half Moon from 4 April to 7 November 1609.* Edited by Robert M. Lunny. Newark: The New Jersey Historical Society, 1959.

Lee, Francis Bazley. *New Jersey as a Colony and as a State.* 5 vols. New York: The Publishing Society of New Jersey, 1902.

Leiby, Adrian. *The Early Dutch and Swedish Settlers of New Jersey.* Princeton: D. Van Nostrand Company, Inc., 1964.

McCormick, Richard P. *New Jersey from Colony to State.* Princeton: D. Van Nostrand Company, Inc., 1964.

Myers, William Starr, ed. *The Story of New Jersey.* 5 vols. New York: Lewis Historical Publishing Company, Inc., 1945.

Pomfret, John E. *Colonial New Jersey: a History.* New York: Charles Scribner's Sons, 1973.

Schonbach, Morris. *Radicals and Visionaries: a History of Dissent in New Jersey.* Princeton: D. Van Nostrand Company, Inc., 1964.

Schwartz, Joel and Daniel Prosser. *Cities of the Garden State.* Dubuque: Kendall/Hunt Publishing Company, 1977.

Snyder, John P. *The Story of New Jersey's Civil Boundaries, 1606-1968.* Trenton: New Jersey State Bureau of Geology and Topography, 1969.

Stansfield, Charles A., Jr. *New Jersey, a Geography.* Boulder, CO: Westview Press, 1983.

Tanner, Edwin P. *The Province of New Jersey, 1664-1738.* New York: Columbia University Press, 1908.

Wacker, Peter O. *Land and People: a Cultural Geography of Preindustrial New Jersey: Origins and Settlement Patterns.* New Brunswick: Rutgers University Press, 1975.

Whitehead, John. *The Passaic Valley, New Jersey.* 2 vols. New York: The New Jersey Genealogical Company, 1901.

HUDSON COUNTY HISTORY

Feldra, Robert, comp. *History of Hudson County: Genealogies of Prominent Families.* Town of Union, NJ: Michel and Rank, 1917.

Harvey, Cornelius Burnham, ed. *Genealogical History of Hudson and Bergen Counties.* New York: The New Jersey Genealogical Publishing Company, 1900.

Robinson, Walter F. *Old Bergen Township (Now Hudson County) in the American Revolution.* Bayonne: Bayonne Bicentennial Committee, 1978.

Shaw, William H., comp. *History of Essex and Hudson Counties, New Jersey.* 2 vols. Philadelphia: Everts & Peck, 1884.

Stinson, Robert R. *Hudson County To-Day.* Town of Union, NJ: Hudson Dispatch, [1915].

Van Winkle, Daniel, ed. *History of the Municipalities of Hudson County, New Jersey.* 3 vols. New York: Lewis Historical Publishing Company, Inc., 1924.

Winfield, Charles H. *History of the Land Titles in Hudson County, N.J. 1609-1871.* 2 vols. New York: Wynkoop & Hallenbeck, Printers, 1872.

_____. *History of the County of Hudson, New Jersey.* New York: Kennard & Hay Stationery M'fg and Printing Co., 1874.

MUNICIPALITIES WITHIN HUDSON COUNTY

Drescher, William H., Jr. *History of West Hoboken, N.J.* West Hoboken: Lehne & Drescher, 1903.

Eickmann, Walter T. *History of West New York, N.J.* West New York: The Golden Jubilee Committee, 1948.

Fiftieth Anniversary of the Incorporation of the Town of West Hoboken, N.J., Souvenir History. West Hoboken: Town of West Hoboken, 1911.

Foster, Edward Halsey and Geoffrey W. Clark, eds. *Hoboken: a Collection of Essays.* New York: Irvington Publishers, Inc., 1976.

Glaser, Walter G. *Guttenberg, New Jersey: Its Early Days.* Guttenberg: Guttenberg Centennial Committee, 1959.

Grundy, J. Owen. "Weehawken: a Glimpse of Its History, an Address at the Weehawken Historical Society." Typescript, 1969.

_____. *The History of Jersey City.* Jersey City: Jersey City Chamber of Commerce, 1976.

Heaney, John J. *The Bicentennial Comes to Hoboken.* Hoboken: Hoboken American Revolution Bicentennial Committee, 1976.

Littauer, Kalman J., comp. *Brief Early History to Present Day: Union City.* Union City: Free Public Library, 1964.

Lynch, Kevin. *The Image of the City.* Cambridge: The Technology Press & Harvard University Press, 1960.

McLean, Alexander. *History of Jersey City, N.J.* Jersey City: *The Evening Journal, 1895.*

Moller, George Long. *The Hoboken of Yesterday.* 2 vols. Hoboken: George Long Moller, 1964 and 1966.

Mutz, Henry A. *Harrison: the History of a New Jersey Town.* Harrison: Harrison, N.J., American Revolution Bicentennial Commission, 1976.

Procter, Mary and Bill Matuszeski. *Gritty Cities.* Philadelphia: Temple University Press, 1978.

Reed, Gertrude S. and Robert E. Henkel, eds. *History of Secaucus, New Jersey.* Secaucus: Secaucus Home News, 1950.

Robinson, Walter F. "The Historical Heritage of Modern Bayonne," in *Bayonne Centennial Historical Revue, 1861-1961.* Bayonne: Bayonne Centennial Committee, 1961.

Schnitzer, Henry R. *As They Were: Bayonne and Jersey City.* New York:

Vantage Press, 1973.

Shaw, Douglas. "The Making of an Immigrant City: Ethnic and Cultural Conflict in Jersey City, New Jersey, 1850-1877." Dissertation. The University of Rochester, 1973.

Sinclair, Gladys Mellor. *Bayonne Old and New*. New York: Maranatha Publishers, 1940.

Vilardi, Emma May. *Heritage and Legacy: Town of Kearny*. Kearny: The Kearny Centennial Commission, 1967.

Winfield, Charles H. *Hopoghan Hachingh. Hoboken, a Pleasure Resort for Old New York*. New York: The Caxton Press, 1895.

BUSINESS AND ECONOMICS

Cadman, John W., Jr. *The Corporation in New Jersey*. Cambridge: Harvard University Press, 1949.

Cunningham, John T. *Made in New Jersey: the Industrial Story of a State*. New Brunswick: Rutgers University Press, 1954.

Day, Walton. *The History of a Lead Pencil*. Jersey City: Jos. Dixon Crucible Company, 1894.

Hubbard, Elbert. *Joseph Dixon, One of the World-Makers*. East Aurora, NY: Elbert Hubbard, 1912.

Knittle, Rhea Mansfield. *Early American Glass*. New York: D. Appleton-Century Company, 1935.

Levitt, James H. *For Want of Trade: Shipping and the New Jersey Ports, 1680-1783*. Newark: New Jersey Historical Society, 1981.

Newark Museum. *The Pottery and Porcelain of New Jersey 1688-1900: an Exhibition*. Newark: Newark Museum, 1947.

Raciti, Sebastian J. "An Analysis of the Decline of the Jersey City Economy and an Evaluation of Proposals for Its Resurgence." Dissertation. Fordham University, 1968.

Schneider, Coleman. *Embroidery: Schiffli & Multi-Head*. Tenafly, NJ: C. Schneider, 1978.

Turnbull, Archibald Douglas. *John Stevens: an American Record*. New York: The Century Company, 1928.

MILITARY HISTORY

Bill, Alfred Hoyt. *New Jersey and the Revolutionary War*. Princeton: D.

Van Nostrand Company, Inc., 1964.

Depeyster, John Watts. *Personal and Military History of Philip Kearny*. New York: Rice and Gage, Publishers, 1869.

Kemmerer, Donald L. *Path to Freedom*. Princeton: Princeton University Press, 1940.

Lundin, Leonard. *Cockpit of the Revolution*. Princeton: Princeton University Press, 1940.

Miers, Earl Schenck. *New Jersey and the Civil War: an Album of Contemporary Accounts*. Princeton: D. Van Nostrand Company, Inc., 1964.

Shanks, David C. *As They Passed Through the Port*. Washington, DC: The Cary Publishing Company, 1927.

Snell, King W. *With the Army at Hoboken*. New York: Elbert E. Wonderly, 1919.

PEOPLE, RELIGION, SOCIAL AND HEALTH SERVICES

Cooley, Henry Scofield. "A Study of Slavery in New Jersey." From *Johns Hopkins University Studies in Historical and Political Science*. Fourteenth series. September and October, 1896. New York: Johnson Reprint Corporation, 1973.

Cross, Dorothy. *The Indians of New Jersey*. Trenton: The Archeological Society of New Jersey, 1953. Reprinted from *Proceedings of the New Jersey Historical Society*, January 1952.

Flynn, Joseph M. *The Catholic Church in New Jersey*. Morristown: Joseph M. Flynn, 1904.

Handen, Ella. "In Liberty's Shadow: Cornelia Bradford and Whittier House." *New Jersey History*, 100, #3-4. Fall/Winter, 1982.

Leiby, James. *Charity and Correction in New Jersey*. New Brunswick: Rutgers University Press, 1967.

Petrick, Barbara. *Mary Philbrook: the Radical Feminist in New Jersey*. Trenton: New Jersey Historical Commission, 1981.

Pitkin, Thomas M. *Keepers of the Gate: a History of Ellis Island*. New York: New York University Press, 1975.

Price, Clement A. *Freedom Not Far Distant: a Documentary History of*

Afro-Americans in New Jersey. Newark: New Jersey Historical Society, 1980.

Rogg, Eleanor Meyer. *The Assimilation of Cuban Exiles*. New York: Aberdeen Press, 1974.

Sharkey, (Sister) Mary Agnes. *The New Jersey Sisters of Charity*. 3 vols. New York: Longmans, Green and Co., 1933.

Stanton, Martin W. *History of Public Poor Relief in New Jersey, 1609-1934*. New York: Fordham University, 1934.

Taube, Josephine A., ed. *The Center Story*. Jersey City: The Jewish Community Center of Jersey City, [1958].

Taylor, Benjamin C. *Annals of the Classis of Bergen*. New York: Board of Publication of the Reformed Protestant Dutch Church, 1857.

Vecoli, Rudolph J. *The People of New Jersey*. Princeton: D. Van Nostrand Company, Inc., 1965.

PLANNING AND REGIONALISM

Bard, Erwin Wilkie. *The Port of New York Authority*. New York: Columbia University Press, 1942.

Bird, Frederick L. *A Study of the Port of New York Authority*. New York: Dun & Bradstreet, Inc., 1949.

Danielson, Michael N. and Jameson W. Doig. *New York, the Politics of Urban Regional Development*. Berkeley: University of California Press, 1982.

Goldman, Clifford A. "The Hackensack Meadowlands: the Politics of Regional Planning and Development in the Metropolis." Dissertation. Princeton University, 1975.

Lim, Gill C., ed. *Regional Planning*. Totowa, NJ: Allanheld, Osmun, 1983.

Miri, Joseph A. "The Politics of Water Supply in Northern New Jersey: Regional and Institutional Cleavages in a Metropolitan Area." Dissertation. Rutgers University, 1971.

Simko, Robert A. "Political Regionalism in New Jersey, 1916-1964." Dissertation. Indiana University, 1968.

Stein, Abraham. "The Port Authority of New York and New Jersey and the 1962 Path-World Trade Center Project." Dissertation. New York

University, Graduate School of Business Administration, 1980.

POLITICS

Amato, Matthew, Jr. *Jersey City: a City in Socio-Economic and Political Change.* Hicksville, NY: Exposition Press, 1980.

Bloodgood, Fred L. *The Quiet Hour.* Trenton: MacCrellish & Quigley Company, 1940.

Connors, Richard J. *A Cycle of Power: the Career of Jersey City Mayor Frank Hague.* Metuchen, NJ: The Scarecrow Press, Inc., 1971.

Kincaid, John. "Political Success and Policy Failure: the Persistence of Machine Politics in Jersey City." Dissertation. Temple University, 1980.

Lemmey, William. "Bossism in Jersey City: the Kenny Years, 1949-1972." Dissertation. City University of New York, 1978.

McKean, Dayton David. *The Boss: the Hague Machine in Action.* New York: Russell & Russell, 1967. Reissue of 1940 publication.

Norton, Mary. "Autobiography." Typescript.

Orkin, Saul. "New Jersey Democratic Party Politics, 1949-1953: the Downfall of State Boss Frank Hague." Dissertation. Columbia University, 1971.

Sackett, William E. *Modern Battles of Trenton.* 2 vols. Volume 1, Trenton: John L. Murphy, Printer, 1895. Volume 2, New York: The Neale Publishing Company, 1914.

Smith, Thomas F.X. *The Powerticians.* Secaucus: Lyle Stuart, Inc., 1982.

Steffans, Lincoln. *Upbuilders.* Seattle: University of Washington Press, 1968.

Tobin, Eugene M. "Mark Fagan and the Politics of Urban Reform: Jersey City 1900-1917." Dissertation. Brandeis University, 1972.

Varacalli, Joseph A. *Ethnic Politics in Jersey City: The Changing Nature of Irish-Italian Relations, 1917-1983.* Unpublished typescript of paper read at the 16th Annual Conference of the American Italian Historical Association, State University of New York at Albany, November 1983.

THE RIVER AND THE PORT

Adams, Arthur G. *The Hudson Through the Years.* Westwood, NJ: Lind Publications, 1983.

Albion, Robert Greenhalgh. *The Rise of New York Port, 1815-1860.* New York: Charles Scribner's Sons, 1939.

Axelrod, Donald. "Government Covers the Waterfront." Dissertation. Syracuse University, 1967.

Bunker, John G. *Harbor & Haven: an Illustrated History of the Port of New York.* Woodland Hills, CA: Windsor Publications, Inc., 1979.

Morris, James. *The Great Port: a Passage through New York.* New York: Harcourt, Brace & World, Inc., 1969.

Rattray, Jeannette Edwards. *Perils of the Port of New York.* New York: Dodd, Mead & Company, 1973.

Smith, Harry J., Jr. *Romance of the Hoboken Ferry.* New York: Prentice-Hall, Inc., 1931.

Trachtenberg, Marvin. *The Statue of Liberty.* New York: The Viking Press, 1976.

TRANSPORTATION AND SHIPPING

Anderson, Elaine. *The Central Railroad of New Jersey's First 100 Years: a Historical Survey.* Easton, PA: Center for Canal History and Technology, 1984.

Archer, Robert F. *The History of the Lehigh Valley Railroad.* Berkeley: Howell-North Books, 1977.

Baxter, Maurice G. *The Steamboat Monopoly: Gibbons v. Ogden, 1824.* New York: Alfred A. Knopf, 1972.

Burgess, George H. and Miles C. Kennedy. *Centennial History of the Pennsylvania Railroad Company.* Philadelphia: The Pennsylvania Railroad Company, 1949.

Carlton, Paul. *The Jersey Central Story.* River Vale, NJ: D. Carlton Rail Books, 1976.

_____. *The Erie Lackawanna Story,* revised 2nd edition. River Vale, NJ: D. Carlton Rail Books, 1978.

Casey, Robert J. and W.A.S. Douglas. *The Lackawanna Story.* New York: McGraw-Hill Book Company, Inc., 1951.

Condit, Carl W. *The Port of New York.* 2 vols. Chicago: The University of Chicago Press, 1980 and 1981.

Cranmer, Horace Jerome. "The New Jersey Canals: State Policy and Private Enterprise 1820-1832." Dissertation. Columbia University, 1955.

Cudahy, Brian. *Rails Under the Mighty Hudson.* Brattleboro, Vermont: The Stephen Greene Press, 1975.

Doig, Jameson Wallace. "The Politics of Metropolitan Transportation: a Study of the New York-New Jersey Metropolitan Rapid Transit Commission." Dissertation. Princeton University, 1961.

Gilbert, Gilbert H. and others. *The Subways and Tunnels of New York.* New York: John Wiley & Sons, 1912.

Gregg, Dorothy. "The Exploitation of the Steamboat: the Case of Colonel John Stevens." Dissertation. Columbia University, 1951.

Kalata, Barbara N. *A Hundred Years: a Hundred Miles: New Jersey's Morris Canal.* Morristown: Morris County Historical Society, 1983.

Lane, Wheaton J. *From Indian Trail to Iron Horse.* Princeton: Princeton University Press, 1939.

Lucas, Walter Arndt. *From the Hills to the Hudson: a History of the Paterson and Hudson River Rail Road.* [New York]: Railroadians of America, 1944.

Reilly, George L.A. "The Camden and Amboy Railroad in New Jersey Politics, 1830-1871." Dissertation. Columbia University, [n.d.].

Saunders, Richard Leroy, Jr. "Railroad Consolidation in the Eastern United States, 1940-1964." Dissertation. University of Illinois at Urbana-Champaign, 1971.

Taber, Thomas Townsend. *The Delaware, Lackawanna & Western Railroad in the Nineteenth Century, 1828-1899.* Muncy, PA: Thomas T. Taber III, 1977.

_____. *The Delaware, Lackawanna & Western Railroad in the Twentieth Century, 1899-1960.* Muncy, PA: Thomas T. Taber III, 1981.

AGRICULTURE

Woodward, Carl Raymond. *The Development of Agriculture in New Jersey 1640-1880.* New Brunswick: New Jersey Agricultural Experiment Station, Bulletin 451, 1927.

Index